JOURNAL FOR THE STUDY OF THE PSEUDEPIGRAPHA SUPPLEMENT SERIES

19

Sheffield Academic Press

JOURNAL FOR THE STUDY OF THE PSEUDEPIGRAPHA
SUPPLEMENT SERIES

19

'Time and Times and Half a Time'

Historical Consciousness in the Jewish Literature of the Persian and Hellenistic Eras

Ida Fröhlich

Journal for the Study of the Pseudepigrapha
Supplement Series 19

Published by Sheffield Academic Press Ltd
Mansion House
19 Kingfield Road
Sheffield S11 9AS
England

Printed on acid-free paper in Great Britain
by Bookcraft Ltd
Midsomer Norton, Bath

British Library Cataloguing in Publication Data

A catalogue record for this book is available
from the British Library

ISBN 1-85075-566-3

CONTENTS

PREFACE

Ancient Judaism had a very special attitude to history. 'Historiography', in the Greek sense of the word is not known from biblical literature; even the apocryphal books of the Maccabees are a special mixture of 'Jewish' and 'Greek' historiography. 'Greek' historiography tries to embelish, giving as much detail as possible about events and persons. Contrary to this, Jewish works on history are extremely taciturn on details of events; still they show astonishing familiarity with historical tradition, referring to events regarded to be important. The reason for this taciturnity is that the aim of the authors of Jewish historiographic works is not to report events, but to show a special system in the sequence and order of the events.

But history is present not only in chronicles. Ideas about the past, and the aim to schematize tradition about the past appear also in apparently non-historiographic genres as visions and prophecies, aetiological myths (stories about the origin of special notions in human history), 'rewritten Bibles'—that is, reformulations of Biblical historical traditions—and in exegetical works on prophetic tradition. Literary narratives placed in a historical milieu by their authors represent a further group of works expressing the author's attitude to history. Patterns of earlier narrative traditions of legendary history (mostly the Exodus-pattern) are used in these works, transforming them into later parallels of old events.

The first version of this book was my PhD dissertation written more than ten years ago (Leningrad/St Petersburg 1984); a few years later, owing to a grant from the Soros Foundation I reworked the manuscript for publication. Here I would like to express my gratitude to all those who contributed to the writing of this book, especially to the late Professor I.D. Amussin who was my helper and teacher. All the merits of this book should be attributed to him—all its faults are mine.

ABBREVIATIONS

AB	Anchor Bible
ABD	*The Anchor Bible Dictionary*
AfO	*Archiv für Orientforschung*
AGJU	Arbeiten zur Geschichte des antiken Judentums und des Urchristentums
ANET	J.B. Pritchard (ed.), *Ancient Near Eastern Texts*
AOS	American Oriental Series
ArOr	*Archiv orientálni*
ARW	*Archiv für Religionswissenschaft*
ATD	Das Alte Testament Deutsch
AUSS	*Andrews University Seminary Studies*
BA	*Biblical Archaeologist*
BARev	*Biblical Archaeology Review*
BASOR	*Bulletin of the American Schools of Oriental Research*
BeO	*Bibbia e oriente*
BETL	Bibliotheca ephemeridum theologicarum lovaniensium
Bib	*Biblica*
BibLeb	*Bibel und Leben*
BN	*Biblische Notizen*
BOH	Bibliotheca Orientalia Hungarica
BSO(A)S	*Bulletin of the School of Oriental (and African) Studies*
BSt	Biblische Studien
BV	*Biblical Viewpoint*
BZAW	Beihefte zur *ZAW*
CBC	Cambridge Bible Commentary
CBQ	*Catholic Biblical Quarterly*
CBQMS	*Catholic Biblical Quarterly*, Monograph Series
ConBNT	Coniectanea biblica, New Testament
CRINT	Compendia rerum iudaicarum ad Novum Testamentum
CTM	*Concordia Theological Monthly*
DB	*Dictionnaire de la Bible*
DBSup	*Dictionnaire de la Bible, Supplément*
DD	Dor le-Dor
DJD	Discoveries in the Judaean Desert
EBib	Etudes bibliques
EncJud	*Encyclopaedia Judaica*
EvQ	*Evangelical Quarterly*
ExpTim	*Expository Times*
FO	*Folia Orientalia*

GCS	Griechische christliche Schriftsteller
HAR	*Hebrew Annual Review*
HDR	Harvard Dissertations in Religion
HNT	Handbuch zum Neuen Testament
HS	Hebrew Studies (University of Wisconsin)
HSM	Harvard Semitic Monographs
HSS	Harvard Semitic Studies
HTR	*Harvard Theological Review*
HUCA	*Hebrew Union College Annual*
HZ	*Historische Zeitschrift*
ICC	International Critical Commentary
IDB	G.A. Buttrick (ed.), *Interpreter's Dictionary of the Bible*
IEJ	*Israel Exploration Journal*
ITQ	*Irish Theological Quarterly*
JAOS	*Journal of the American Oriental Society*
JBL	*Journal of Biblical Literature*
JBQ	*Jewish Biblical Quarterly*
JCS	*Journal of Cuneiform Studies*
JEOL	*Jaarbericht... ex oriente lux*
JETS	*Journal of the Evangelical Theological Society*
JJP	*Journal for the Study of Judaism in the Persian, Hellenistic and Roman Periods*
JJS	*Journal of Jewish Studies*
JNES	*Journal of Near Eastern Studies*
JQR	*Jewish Quarterly Review*
JRAS	*Journal of the Royal Asiatic Society*
JSHRZ	Jüdische Schriften aus hellenistisch-römischer Zeit
JSHRZ	Jüdische Schriften aus hellenistisch-römischer Zeit
JSJ	*Journal for the Study of Judaism*
JSOT	*Journal for the Study of the Old Testament*
JSOTSup	*Journal for the Study of the Old Testament*, Supplement Series
JSP	*Journal for the Study of the Pseudepigrapha*
JSPSup	*Journal for the Study of the Pseudepigrapha*, Supplement Series
JTC	*Journal for Theology and the Church*
JTS	*Journal of Theological Studies*
KAT	Kommentar zum Alten Testament
LD	Lectio divina
MGWJ	*Monatsschrift für Geschichte und Wissenschaft des Judentums*
NovTSup	*Novum Testamentum* Supplements
NTS	*New Testament Studies*
OLZ	*Orientalistische Literaturzeitung*
OS	*Oudtestamentische Studiën*
OTG	Old Testament Guides
OTL	Old Testament Library
PAAJR	*Proceedings of the American Academy of Jewish Research*
PEQ	*Palestine Exploration Quarterly*
PSBA	*Proceedings of the Society of Biblical Archaeology*
PVTG	Pseudepigrapha Veteris Testamenti graece

RB	*Revue biblique*
RE	Pauly–Wissowa, *Real-Encyclopädie der classischen Altertumswissenschaft*
REJ	*Revue des études juives*
RevQ	*Revue de Qumran*
RGG	*Religion in Geschichte und Gegenwart*
RSR	*Recherches de science religieuse*
RV	Religionsgeschichtliche Volksbücher
SBLSBS	SBL Sources for Biblical Study
SBLDS	SBL Dissertation Series
SBLMS	SBL Monograph Series
SBLTT	SBL Texts and Translations
SC	Sources chrétiennes
ScrHier	Scripta hierosolymitana
SEÅ	*Svensk exegetisk årsbok*
Sem	*Semitica*
SJLA	Studies in Judaism in Late Antiquity
SJOT	*Scandinavian Journal of the Old Testament*
SPB	Studia postbiblica
SSAW.PH	Sitzungsberichte der Sachgischen Akademie des Wissenschaften. Philologische-historische klasse
SSS	Semitic Study Series
ST	*Studia theologica*
Str–B	[H. Strack and] P. Billerbeck, *Kommentar zum Neuen Testament aus Talmud und Midrasch*
ST	Studies in Theology
SUNT	Studien zur Umwelt des Neuen Testaments
SVTP	Studia in Veteris Testamenti pseudepigrapha
SwJT	*Southwestern Journal of Theology*
ThStKr	*Theologische Studien und Kritiken*
TBT	*The Bible Today*
TBü	Theologische Bücherei
TK	*Texte und Kontexte*
TLZ	*Theologische Literaturzeitung*
TRu	*Theologische Rundschau*
TSK	*Theologische Studien und Kritiken*
TynBul	*Tyndale Bulletin*
TZ	*Theologische Zeitschrift*
VAB	Vorderasiatische Bibliothek
VT	*Vetus Testamentum*
VTSup	*Vetus Testamentum*, Supplements
WUNT	Wissenschaftliche Untersuchungen zum Neuen Testament
WZKM	*Wiener Zeitschrift für die Kunde des Morgenlandes*
ZA	*Zeitschrift für Assyriologie*
ZAW	*Zeitschrift für die alttestamentliche Wissenschaft*
ZDMG	*Zeitschrift der deutschen morgenländischen Gesellschaft*
ZDPV	*Zeitschrift des deutschen Palästina-Vereins*
ZNW	*Zeitschrift für die neutestamentliche Wissenschaft*

Chapter 1

THE BABYLONIAN EXILE AND THE BEGINNINGS OF THE DANIELIC TRADITION: DANIEL 2–6 AND DEUTERO-ISAIAH

The present form of the book of Daniel shows an overall literary unity. The stories constituting the book—visions and legends—are arranged concentrically in the Aramaic section (2–7, 3–6, 4–5)[1] and a chronological series can be found in the dating of the stories.[2] The dating and the prefatory words introducing the visions are also of the same type. The same names—Nebuchadnezzar, the king, and Daniel-Belteshazzar, the dream interpreter, appear in almost all the chapters of the book. Finally, the intention of all the chapters of the book is the same: Daniel is a book *about* history in which several historical elements are repeated: thus the fourfold succession-pattern[3] (generally as three units and a broken unit);[4] the element of the king's *hybris* and the consistent use of calculations are repeated in several visions throughout the whole work.[5]

Based on the similarities and common features there have been—and are—those who think that the visions and legends constituting the book were written in their present form at the same time and in the same place.[6]

1. Hartman and DiLella 1985: 15; Lacocque 1976.

2. Dan. 1.1 begins in the third year of the rule of Joiakim, king of Judah; 2.1 takes place in the twelfth year of the rule of Nebuchadnezzar; 7.1 in the first year of Belshazzar; 8.1 in the third year of Belshazzar; 9.1 in the first year of Darius; 10.1 in the 3rd year of Cyrus. However, the chronological framework of Dan. 1–6 is between the fall of Jerusalem and the beginning of the reign of Cyrus; see Kratz 1991: 17.

3. Daniel 2, 5, 7, 8.22, 11.2.

4. Z. Stefanovic, 'Numeric Structures in the Book of Daniel', paper read at the SBL International Meeting, Münster 25–28 July, 1993.

5. For example, there are literary parallelisms between Dan. 4 and 5; on this see Shea 1985b.

6. See Koch 1980: 59, 61, 74; von Gall 1895; Marti 1901: 18; *idem*, in Kautzsch 1923: 459; Bennet, apud Charles 1973: I, 625-37; Rowley 1950–51; Frost 1962: 764-67; Eissfeldt 1964: 527; as well as Driver 1913: 497-514; 1912: lxv-lxvii.

The date of the final compilation of the book as a whole is the middle of the 160s BCE, more precisely the period between 167 and April 163 BCE.[7] This, however, does not mean that the visions and legends constituting the work, which had been created at different points in time and in different places, were at that time simply collected and edited. The book of Daniel—like all works containing prophecies—has a 'dynamic structure': over time the oracles were used, read and reinterpreted, adapted to new situations, and may even have been supplemented.[8] The individual pieces are the result of the growth of a tradition; in addition the visions and legends created at a later date could have consciously used (and did use) the older ones, replying as it were to them, applying to a new era the schemas known from the old one (the most apt example is the relationship between Daniel 2 and 7, where Daniel 7 uses the schema of Daniel 2 providing a different set of symbols and enriching it by new motifs). In the stories of mixed origin, created at different times and in different places, not only do the questions and answers change, but the figure of Nebuchadnezzar is also transformed into Antiochus, and Daniel into the 'wise' of ch. 12.[9] If, however, we look at the details the differences between the stories become striking—from the point of view of possible place of origin, background, genre and language—and they all indicate that they had been written separately, not at the same time, and possibly not at the same place. The seeming unity and structured nature of the work does not mean a unity with respect to all characteristics; there are differences in several respects. Thus for example chs. 2–7, and 1 and 8–12 differ from a linguistic point of view: the language of the former is Aramaic, the common language which had become widespread in the ancient Near East from the Persian period on, while the language of the latter is Hebrew, the language of the biblical tradition.[10] With regard to themes and style, however, chs.

7. It is a generally accepted view that the book came into being after the second Egyptian campaign of Antiochus IV Epiphanes (175–163 BCE) but before his death (April 163 BC); Dan. 11.40-45 contains a genuine prophecy about the death of Antiochus. See Eissfeldt 1964: 705; Schürer-Vermes 1973–79: III.1, 247.

8. According to Grelot (1992), the book was intended for a continuous reading.

9. Davies 1985a: 96-97; 109-11.

10. Naturally, this does not mean that the parts in Aramaic are of the same genre or that they would have been created at the same time and in the same milieu. Several theories have been formulated about the relationship of Aramaic and Hebrew in the work: Ginsberg 1948: 38-39, 41-61 provides detailed arguments for the theory that the Hebrew parts were translated from an often imperfectly understood Aramaic

1–6 constitute a unit; these tell their stories in the third person singular. The locale is the Babylonian court, the stories therefore are 'court tales', and they are told by an 'omniscient narrator', while the author of chs. 7–12 gives an account of his visions or the events befalling him ('Ich-Bericht') in the first person singular.[11] As for the historical milieu and details appearing in the stories, chs. 1–6 take place in the Neo-Babylonian and the Persian royal courts, and the authors characterize the locale with several minute details, whereas chs. 7–12 unfold in locales only designated symbolically: at Elam, 'beside the Ulai canal' (8.2), or 'on the bank of the river Tigris' (10.4). Chapters 1–6 mention the name of the protagonist in dual form (Daniel, who is called Belteshazzar), while chs. 7–12 use Daniel alone (the only exception is 10.1, where the above-mentioned dual form appears).

It is generally accepted today that the stories of different types and origins were unified in several steps, and that two or more authors from the third and second centuries BCE and probably a final redactor had a hand in the production of the book.[12] Naturally, the fact that redactions begin from the third century BCE does not exclude the possibility that certain parts of the book of Daniel are of an earlier origin than the third century BCE—rather it forces us to suppose this. However, scholars divide the work into two parts in different ways, based on the above outlined differences. It is noticeable that the subject of ch. 7 of the collection (the fate of the four empires) coincides with the subject of ch. 2. This is definitely not a chance coincidence, but either the result of the use of shared sources or of conscious revision.[13] It seems likely that Daniel 7 made use of ch. 2 and therefore it is of a later date. The question is how much later? In both cases the language is Aramaic, without significant differences, and thus the language does not provide a clear guideline.[14]

original. According to others—and this is the more convincing theory—the original language of the Hebrew sections is Hebrew.

11. On the literary division see Hartman and DiLella 1985: 9-10.

12. So, for instance, Montgomery 1927: 88-89; Ginsberg 1948: 27-40; Bentzen 1952: 5-10; Delcor 1971: 10-13.

13. Noth 1926: 143-63; Eerdmans 1947: 22-277.

14. As for the possible date and linguistic place of the Aramaic of Daniel, Rowley (1929: 98) was sceptical about dating the text; the traditional proposition of dating it in the sixth century was excluded by him. Recently, both Kitchen (1965) and Stefanovic (1992) consider it to be of an early date; the first pieces of the Aramaic sections of Daniel could have been written at the beginning of the Persian era (fourth century BCE). Kitchen (1965: 79) dates the composition of the Aramaic part between

The answer can only be found with the help of the hermeneutics of the text—based on a detailed analysis of its symbolism and meaning. I consider the entire vision of Daniel 7 and its interpretation and the section supplementing the vision—based on arguments to be fleshed out below—to belong to the second layer of the collection which was created at a later date (in the second-century BCE). That is, we are not dealing with a revised and adapted earlier vision but with a second-century literary product. In addition, Daniel 7 which serves as the introduction of the Hebrew visions of chs. 8–12[15] is just as crucial as the vision of ch. 2 in the first part; in a certain sense it repeats it with some changes. By invoking the older prophecy about the downfall of the 'fourth kingdom' its goal is to relate it to a new era, to new events. This point of view has precedents in the literature.[16] The two collections[17] of the book of Daniel (2–7, 8–12)[18] are connected by internal links: the visions of the section constituted by chs. 7–12 refer back to the narratives of the first section (chs. 2, 4 and 5). This is what gives rise to the supposition that not only does ch. 7 mirror ch. 2, but that the entire second part was created as a reaction to the first one. It is a conscious revision and reinterpretation of the prophecies of the first part.

The first part, however, is not homogeneous either. It is not a collection of narratives created at the same time even though their themes, form and style show a certain degree of unity. The narrative of ch. 1—in contrast to the Aramaic of the other narratives—is in Hebrew,

the sixth and second centuries BCE; similarly Beyer (1984: 33) (in general, Biblical Aramaic comes from the Achaemenid period—the text itself has suffered intrusions of elements that come from a later period). See also Montgomery 1990: 280-82 ('not earlier than within the 5th century'). According to Fitzmyer (1970: 50, n. 4) the final redaction of Daniel is from about 165 BCE, but 'it may be that parts of the Aramaic portions derived from an earlier period'. See also Koch 1980: 45-46.

15. The oracles of chs. 7, 8–12 clearly call up events of the second century BCE.

16. Hölscher 1919: 113-38; Montgomery 1927; Ginsberg 1948; 1954b: 246-75. Sellin (1910; 1933: 153), Haller (1925: 273) and Noth (1926: 143-63) give a different classification; they divide the Danielic collection into the cycles of chs. 1–7 and 8–12.

17. The present book probably resulted from the merging of two collections, an Aramaic one (chs. 2–7), and a Hebrew one (chs. 8–12). The latest Aramaic piece (ch. 7) is contemporaneous with the Hebrew oracles; see also Miller 1991.

18. Chapter 1 in Hebrew most likely did not belong to the earliest core of the collection—most probably it is the result of the latest redaction; the story written after the pattern of chs. 3 and 6 serves as an introduction to the entire collection written subsequently; on this question see below.

and although it contains motifs referring to the period of the exile, on the whole it represents a subsequent perspective. It is a narrative frame created at a later point using the other narratives as models. Its only aim is to prove after the fact that a righteous Jew who always abides by the religious laws (dietary laws) will always be helped by his God. This idea, which is typically of later origin (from the Maccabean period), unequivocally indicates that the story was placed at the beginning of the collection at the time of the final compilation of the text.

In chs. 2–6, however, numerous elements appear which with great probability originate from the Mesopotamian and the Persian tradition. In some instances even words of Greek origin appear.[19] The book of Daniel is first mentioned in the Jewish tradition in 1 Maccabees (2.59-60).[20] According to Josephus (*Ant.* 11.8.5.337) Alexander the Great, on his way to Egypt via Jerusalem, had been shown the book of Daniel, in which it is said that 'one of the Greeks would destroy the empire of the Persians'.[21] Although the story itself is legendary since even the possibility of Alexander the Great's stay in Jerusalem is extremely remote, the fact that Josephus mentions 'Daniel's prophecies' in connection with Alexander indicates that already at the time of the Macedonian conquest some kind of historical oracles, linked to Daniel's name, may have existed, the texts of which—above all most probably the narrative of ch. 2—may have been referring to recent events, such as the Macedonian conquest.[22] This actualization may have meant more than just attaching

19. Words of Greek origin only appear in the narratives of chs. 3 and 6, most probably as a result of later revisions. It is likely that the history of the legends prior to their finding their way into the collection may have been different to that of the prophecies of chs. 2, 4, and 5. On the names of the musical instruments in ch. 3 cf. Mitchell and Joyce 1965.

20. Mattatiah's speech before his death is an overview of the 'deeds of the fathers' to be remembered and emulated. He mentions by name the three youths appearing in the narrative of Dan. 3 and he recalls their story and the tradition of Dan. 6.

21. The statement most likely represents one phase of the reinterpretation of Dan. 2: at that time the fourth מלכו was regarded as referring to the Persian empire, or rather to the rule of Darius III (cf. Dan. 11.1-4, which interprets the four מלכו-s as the four consecutive reigns of the four Persian rulers, clearly referring to the prophecy of Dan. 2). Thus according to this interpretation, Alexander the Great could have been the stone which shatters the statue and establishes the fifth kingdom. From among the early pieces of the Danielic cycle, Dan. 2 is the one which seems to lend itself to reinterpretations the most conveniently—and as Josephus's reference indicates this possibility was made ample use of on the occasion of various historical turning points.

22. The tradition of Alexander the Great's trip to Jerusalem only appears in

a new interpretation to the text. It may also have led to certain changes in the narrative itself. The final text of Daniel 2–6 in the Masoretic tradition also came into being at this time, in the Hellenistic era, most likely in the course of the second half of the third century BCE.

In chs. 2–6 of Daniel there are three narratives which are not only placed in a Babylonian milieu, but in which there are other characteristics of a Mesopotamian origin. The first among them is the narrative of ch. 2, Nebuchadnezzar's dream about a great image, the four parts of which are constituted of five different kinds of materials. The parts of the statue symbolize successive kingdoms. The second narrative can be found in ch. 4. This is Nebuchadnezzar's dream about the hewing of the tree: 'its top reached to the sky, and it was visible to earth's farthest bounds...' (4.11), which predicts the downfall of the king, though not permanently. The third piece is the narrative of ch. 5 about Belshazzar's feast, where a mysterious hand appearing on the wall conveys a prophecy about the downfall of the Neo-Babylonian monarchy. In addition there are two other narratives to be found in chs. 2–6. These describe ordeals where innocently accused pious Jews are saved by their God. The narrative of ch. 3 is about the three young men, the companions of Daniel (Daniel himself does not appear in this narrative), who as a punishment—they refused to obey the decree of the king that they should bow before the colossus which he had had built—had been cast into the fiery furnace. The fire, however, does not harm the youths, but rather lashing out of the furnace it annihilates their accusers. The narrative of ch. 6 tells us how—again despite the royal edict forbidding it—Daniel prays to the God of his ancestors. As a punishment he is cast into the den of lions, but the animals do not harm him. Finally, the introduction, the narrative of ch. 1, had also been created following the pattern of the two narratives discussed above. This story is about four youths, Daniel and his companions, who had been captured and taken to the Babylonian royal court. The physical and intellectual development of the youths outstrips that of their coevals who eat at the table of the king; the four youths only consume such foods as the prescriptions of their religion allow.

The prefatory narrative of ch. 1 about the four Jewish youths who lived in Babylonian captivity may have been created following the

Josephus. According to Arrianos (Arr. 2.25.4) after the conquest of Tyrus the Palestinian cities surrendered themselves to the Macedonians; cf. Curtius Rufus 4.2.24; Plutarch, *Alexandros* 24. For an analysis of the sources see Hengel 1980: 6-12.

pattern of these narratives.[23] All tell of an ordeal, and the protagonist of each of them is a Jew living in a foreign court in a position of high rank.

The narratives depicting ordeals in chs. 3 and 6 are structured according to the same scheme. The author places the narrative of Daniel 3 in the court of Nebuchadnezzar, even though the text contains words of Persian and Greek origin and therefore the time of the final compilation can only have been the third century BCE.[24]

The situation depicted by the narrative of ch. 3 does not quite fit in with the religio-political practices of either the Neo-Babylonian or the Persian empires: there is no evidence of similar practices in the history of either state. The worshipping of idols is a Babylonian historical feature, prostration (*proskunesis*) is a Persian religious practice. The obligation to participate in the cult does have some historical basis: in the Neo-Babylonian empire high-ranking officials were expected to participate in the state cult. The narrative of Daniel 3, however, was not inspired primarily by the historical tradition, but rather by a literary example: the Ahiqar novel. The narrative was based on a tradition, which is traceable to this novel, which by the fifth century BCE had become very popular.[25]

The narrative told in ch. 6 of the book of Daniel also follows the pattern of the story of the innocently accused official. Here it is Daniel who is accused of following the religion of his fathers despite a royal edict forbidding it. The king has forbidden, on pain of death, that his subjects should supplicate any gods in the course of the month. Only the king is entitled to do this (Dan. 6.8-9; LXX 6.7). According to Bickerman, the situation outlined in the narrative is a misunderstanding, a mistaken explanation of a religious prescription known from Mesopotamian

23. As I have already mentioned the language of Dan. 1 is Hebrew, chs. 2–7 are in Aramaic, then from ch. 8 on the language is again Hebrew. Dan. 8–12 contains several references to the historical events of the second century BCE, and it is the more recently created part of the collection. The narrative of ch. 1 corresponds to the material of chs. 2–6 and constitutes the main motif of the story. Based on the perspective and language of the narrative, however, it is highly probable that this section also forms part of the section which had been created in the second century BCE and was only inserted as an introductory story to the beginning of the collection at a later date.

24. Bickerman 1967: 91.

25. For the Aramaic text found in Egypt, at the Jewish military colony of Elephantine, see Cowley 1923: 204-48; English translation: Charles 1973: II, 715-84. The name Ahiqar is mentioned in a Mesopotamian text listing post-diluvian sages ('Aba-Enlil-dari, whom the Ahlamu [= Arameans] call Ahuqar'); see van Dijk 1962: 45, 51-52; 1963: 217.

religious customs.[26] In any case, in the narrative a prohibition and its violation give rise to the conflict: the question is decided through an ordeal, and Daniel is thrown into the den of lions (6.16).

The theme of the Ahiqar novel is modified in Daniel 3 and 6: as much as possible the authors place the emphasis on the motif of the ordeal. In the narrative about Ahiqar—the wrongly accused vizier—Ahiqar's innocence comes to light only accidentally. In the Jewish narratives of the Persian era, which essentially use the same material, the motif of chance is replaced by the motif of divine providence. Both narratives serve to prove that the Lord, who protects those who are falsely accused, is more powerful than the gods of the accusers. Thus the ordeal also constitutes a rivalry between the gods worshipped by the characters of the narrative.

In connection with these narratives the apocryphal *Daniel, Bel and the Dragon* (*βὴλ καὶ Δράκων*) should also be mentioned. The tale survived in Greek in the supplemental part of the book of Daniel. The scheme of this narration is similar to the two mentioned above, despite the fact that *Daniel, Bel and the Dragon* is not about an ordeal but rather about the unmasking of a crude deception by the priests of Bel and the Snake. It is Daniel who ingeniously finds him out. This narrative belongs to the same tradition as those of Daniel 2–6. A whole series of similar motifs prove this: for example the mention of the impotence of the idols, which had been made of different metals, or the mention of historical names and the name of the god Bel.[27]

Finally, there is the narrative of ch. 1, in which the four youths—Daniel, Hananiah, Mishael, and Azariah (whom the author of Dan. 1 identifies with Shadrach, Meschach and Abed-nego of ch. 3)—scrupulously observe the dietary prohibitions even in royal captivity, refusing the foods sent from the royal table, and only feeding themselves with fruits and water. Despite this they outstrip their fellows who eat at the table of the king. Most likely the text is of later origin than the stories of Daniel 3 and 6 which are of the same type. We can deduce this from the emphasis laid on the necessity of observing dietary rules—this is a typical characteristic of the literature of the Hasmonean period of the second century BCE. The names indicate a Mesopotamian milieu, as do the names of Daniel 3 (with which, however, they are not identical).

26. Bickerman 1967: 83.

27. On the apocryphal narratives attached to the book of Daniel see Baumgartner 1926: 259-80; Heller 1936: 281-87; Zimmermann 1958: 438-44.

References to a daily food and wine allowance indicate familiarity with court custom, though this does not go beyond generalities.

As I have already mentioned, most probably this narrative is of later origin than the previous two, and had been written with them in mind, making use of certain motifs from them. All the narratives aim to prove that the God of the Jews who had been carried to Mesopotamia is mightier than the local gods. Yahweh's help is more effective than that of the others.

Let us return to the historical prophecies of Daniel 2–6. One of the striking characteristics of the three narratives (Dan. 2, 4, 5) is the *identity of names* found in them. It is not only the double name of the protagonist, Daniel-Belteshazzar that is common to them, but also the name Nebuchadnezzar. The oracle of ch. 2 predicts the downfall of the fourth kingdom (מלכו) following the reign of Nebuchadnezzar. The great fall which took place after the reign of Nabû-kudurri-uṣur II—with whose name the name Nebuchadnezzar (נבוכדנאצר) may be identified—was the collapse of the Neo-Babylonian empire in 539 BCE. This, however, took place at the time of the rule of the fourth successor after Nabuna'id (556–539). The oracle of ch. 4 also relates to a period of Nebuchadnezzar's rule. Although the oracle of ch. 5 of Daniel refers to Belshazzar, the author of the text states that Belshazzar is the son of Nebuchadnezzar (5.2). This, as is well known, is not borne out by the facts: Nebuchadnezzar had no son of that name. The son of Nabuna'id, whom the king at one point in his reign appointed governor of Babylonia, however, was called Bēl-šarra-uṣur.[28] Thus the narratives of Daniel 2–6 extend the period of the rule of Nebuchadnezzar II, to the reign of the last Neo-Babylonian ruler, Nabuna'id, and to the time of the governorship of his son, Bel-sharra-usur. The fact that, instead of Nabuna'id, the author of Daniel 2–6 mentions Nebuchadnezzar is most likely not accidental but rather the result of conscious consideration; for the Jewish reader the name had a special significance. The name was a reference to events which were well known to the readers of these stories. No further explanation was necessary for them. It was Nabû-kudurri-usur II who conquered Jerusalem in 586 BCE and formally put an end to the independent Judean kingdom (Jer. 39; 1 Kgs 25). For the population of Judea this meant not only the end of the independent state, the resettlement, and the beginning of the Babylonian exile, but also the pillaging

28. For extant documents relating to him see Dougherty 1929; Beaulieu 1989: 185-203.

and destruction of the Temple of Jerusalem. Until that time the Temple was the symbol of independence and religious unity. A little later this date became pivotal in Jewish tradition, denoting an event which became a determining factor in the history of the nation. Just as the date of the destruction of the Temple was the landmark between two eras, the figure of the conquering Nebuchadnezzar also gained symbolic significance, and in all probability this is why the redactor of Daniel 2–6 connected his person to the text of each and every oracle.

The double name of the protagonist, Daniel-Belteshazzar, indicates that the material of the stories had been revised and one of the names was the result of renaming. As the double name appears in the dream descriptions of the first parts of the book, which may be regarded as older, it is likely that the original protagonist of the stories was called Belteshazzar (Hebrew בלטשאצר, probably from the Akkadian *balatsu-uṣur*).[29]

In the case of the book of Daniel, the name Belteshazzar was probably first complemented by the name Daniel at the time of the compiling of the pieces and the unification of the Aramaic collection.[30] This name can be grammatically related to the name of one of the characters of the Ugaritic epic entitled Danel and Aqhat. There is, however, an enormous gap between the traditions attached to the two names, Danel and Daniel, with respect to their era and milieu. In any case, it is noteworthy that in the Jewish tradition the name appears during the Babylonian exile and in the following era. Ezekiel, the prophet living during the Babylonian exile mentions Noah, Daniel and Job as 'righteous' ones, those who had been saved thanks to their righteousness (בצדקתם) (Ezek. 14.14, 20). In addition, Ezekiel also mentions Daniel as a wise (חכם) one (28.3). According to ch. 6 of the *Ethiopian Book of Enoch* (*1 Enoch*)—a Jewish tradition whose origins probably go back to a Mesopotamian milieu and the beginnings of the Persian era—one of the 'fallen angels' who appeared

29. Cf. the Joseph story of Genesis, in which Joseph's other name, Zaphenath-paneah (Gen. 41.45), is of Egyptian origin, just as one part of the literary motives of the narrative is also of Egyptian origin. See Janssen 1955–56: 63-72; Montet 1959: 15-23; Vergote 1959; Redford 1970.

30. Daniel 7, which is also Aramaic in language, does not use the double form of the name. In this same chapter Daniel's role also changes; he is no longer a dream interpreter, but a seer, and it is not he who provides the interpretation of his vision, but 'one of those who were standing there' (7.16). All these considerations indicate, that the background and origin of Dan. 7 differs from that of the other oracles in Aramaic.

prior to the Flood also bears the Daniel name.[31] In the Chronicles David's son Kileab (2 Sam. 3.3) is renamed Daniel (1 Chron. 3.1). The Daniel name as an ordinary personal name is also known from Jewish sources of the Persian period, thus Ezra 8.2; Neh. 10.7. In the Jewish tradition of the sixth–third centuries BCE two characteristics were attached to the name: one was the 'righteousness' of Daniel, that is his god-fearing behaviour (this is what the Ezekiel tradition mentions), and the other his extraordinary knowledge and wisdom (Ezek. 28.3 and 1 *En.* 6) which, however, is meant pejoratively, because according to this same tradition theangels teach wickedness—sorcery, magic—to the 'daughters of men'.[32]

Mesopotamian Elements in Daniel 2–6

Chapter 2 of the book of Daniel recounts that 'Nebuchadnezzar was troubled by dreams', so much so that 'he could not sleep' (2.1).[33] The king commanded that 'the magicians, and the astrologers, and the sorcerers, and the Chaldeans' (חרטמים, אשפים, מכשפים, כשדים) be called together to interpret his dream, but he does not tell them the dream itself. The dream interpreters cannot fulfil the command of the king, and therefore one by one he kills the 'wise men of Babylon' (2.12-13). At this point, Daniel-Belteshazzar appears on the scene and with the help of his God finds out the king's dream and interprets it. According to Heller this element of the story, the motif of the 'untold dream', is the invention of the author of Daniel 2. In his view the motif spread to world literature following the Daniel tradition.[34] Undoubtedly, the Daniel tradition influenced this narrative type. However, this unusual story is not merely the creation of the literary imagination. Most probably it originates from an actual practice, that is, from the practice of a 'science' with which, at least indirectly, the Jewish author of Daniel 2 who had lived in Mesopotamia could have been familiar. This is the science of oneirocriticism, which in Mesopotamia had a millennia-long tradition.

31. *1 En.* 6.7 = 4Q En^{a} 1.3; Milik 1976: 150.

32. Sorcery, magic, and in the later tradition the preparation of cosmetics and weapons and the art of seduction are among the teachings of the 'fallen angels', see *1 En.* 6–11. About the tradition see Dimant 1974; Fröhlich 1988.

33. Cf. the introductory sections of Nabuna'id's dream descriptions, which usually mention that the content of the dream disturbed the king; see Langdon 1912: 219-29.

34. Heller 1925: 243-46; cf. Baumgartner 1927: 17-19.

The Mesopotamian handbooks of oneirocriticism, which systematize the dreams and provide their interpretations based on groupings of the main motifs, are well known.[35] The text of the Old Testament, however, even when it writes about oneirocriticism and is familiar with its practice, always mentions it disparagingly and considers it an illegitimate practice. The story of Joseph constitutes an exception. The dreams in this story—just as the majority of the literary material of the narrative—can be proved to be of Egyptian origin: identical or similar motifs can be found in dream interpretation texts from there, and the interpretations are also similar in nature to those of the Egyptian dream books.[36] Aside from the dreams of the Joseph narrative, one other dream description and interpretation can be found in the Old Testament, in the book of Judges (7.13), about Gideon's dream, which predicts his victory in the battle against the Midianites.

The dreams recorded in the book of Daniel have nothing to do with those just discussed and with the dream-interpreting tradition. They can, however, be well interpreted on the basis of the Egyptian tradition of oneirocriticism. Those expressions of the description which describe the circumstances of Nebuchadnezzar's dream vision are almost identical word-for-word to the introductory words of certain inscriptions of the last Neo-Babylonian ruler, Nabuna'id, which describe the dream visions of the ruler.[37]

In the beliefs connected to dream visions, the dream—which is a manifestation of the divine revelation—always appears as objective truth. Therefore, like all revelations, it is valid even if it does not become public, that is, even if the dreamer cannot retell his dream, or does not recall it.[38] A similar case is known from the Assyrian dream book in which the dreamer supplicates the God Nusku: 'this dream...was brought to me and which you know but I do not know—if [its content predicts something] pleasant, may its pleasantness not escape me—if [it predicts something] evil, may its evil not catch me—[but] verily [this dream] be

35. Their best summary, with texts, translation, and accompanying essay is Oppenheim 1956.

36. See Vergote 1959: 43-94. On Egyptian dream interpretation cf. Foucault, in Hastings 1908–19: 34-37. On the dreams of the Old Testament see Ehrlich 1953; Zeitlin 1975.

37. Not only is the dating of the dreams according to regnal years reminiscent of the description of Nabuna'id's dreams, but so are the circumstances of the dream visions. For the texts see Langdon 1912: 219-29.

38. Oppenheim 1956: 232.

not mine!'[39] According to an Ancient Babylonian text 'if a man cannot remember his dream that he saw, [it means] that his [personal] god is angry with him'.[40] Consequently, the forgotten dream potentially contains a bad omen. Nebuchadnezzar's dream also prophesies something negative, that is, it predicts failure. For the meaning of the forgotten, and then re-dreamed, dream to become known it is not enough to know the contents, but it is also necessary to provide the interpretation (Ar. פשר), as is also mentioned by Nebuchadnezzar. The dream in Daniel 2 is a 'symbolic dream', that is, it does not contain a direct prophecy. In a symbolic dream the dreamer is informed of events in visual form, and these visual symbols have to be translated to the language of reality according to a code.

In Daniel 2 a great image appears in the vision: 'the head of the image was of fine gold, its chest and arms of silver, its belly and thighs of bronze, its legs of iron, its feet part iron and part clay' (2.32-33). The statue is hit by a stone (according to the version of the LXX: 'from a mountain'), which is 'hewn...by no human hand, and shatters the image' (2.34). It must be noted that in the extant Mesopotamian dream descriptions and dream interpretations symbolic dreams are known most often from the Assyrian and Neo-Babylonian periods, and are associated with the names of two rulers—Ashurbanipal (668–627) and Nabuna'id (555–539).[41] The Mesopotamian symbolic dreams always relate to future events, containing oracles. Their dream interpretations are never based on the individual inspiration of the dreamer, but with the help of an oneirocritic, are 'scientific'. The Mesopotamian dream books isolate the main motifs of dreams, arrange them in groups and provide the permanently valid interpretations of individual motifs. The thus obtained interpretation is called *puššuru* in the Mesopotamian dream-interpreting terminology (cf. Dan. 2.4 *et passim*).[42]

In the book of Daniel, however, the interpreter of the dream does not interpret on the basis of a special code, but—since he was not told of the

39. Oppenheim 1956: 298.

40. Oppenheim 1956: 229. The Babylonian Talmud also knows the case of 'the forgotten dream'; see *Ber.* 55b (quoted by Oppenheim 1956: 299).

41. Oppenheim 1956: 249ff.; Gadd 1958: 35-92, tables i-xvi; Langdon 1912: 218-97.

42. In the Mesopotamian texts the interpretation of the dream is introduced by the formula *kī anni piširšu* ('this is the [relevant] interpretation'); cf. Oppenheim 1956: 220.

content of the dream—communicates the dream and its interpretation as a revelation, which he himself had seen at night, in a dream. Similar cases of the practice of re-dreaming the dream are known in the Mesopotamian literature of oneirocriticism. The goal of re-dreaming is not to find out the interpretation (for that purpose well-compiled handbooks are available), but to verify its content, to prove that the dream had truly contained divine revelation. Therefore the dream interpreter turns directly to god, the source of the dream. According to the text of a Middle Assyrian political letter, the priest who functions as dream interpreter (*bārû*)[43] also acts similarly; as oneirocritic he establishes indirect contact with the god with the help of an incubational dream.[44] According to Oppenheim, the Sumerian name for the dream interpreter priest—(*lú.sag.sè.ná.a*) 'the man, who sleeps beside' (lit. at the head of another person)—also refers to this practice in the Mesopotamian tradition. The corresponding Akkadian expression—*mupašir* [*šunāte*]—does not refer to the method, only to the circle of activities of the priest: 'he who does the *puššuru* [of dreams].'[45]

The basis for the story relating to Daniel—or rather to his literary forerunner, Belteshazzar—may have been this characteristic of the Mesopotamian dream-interpreting tradition. In the biblical text, which is related to the Mesopotamian one, the term for the dream interpretation is also פשר (cf. Akkadian *puššuru*). Daniel-Belteshazzar appears in the story not as a Mesopotamian oneirocritic, but as a Jew taken into captivity. The most important change is that the author of Daniel 2 makes it appear that the common method used in the Mesopotamian dream-interpreting tradition is unique and absolute. In the book of Daniel the 'wise men of Babylon' state that it is impossible to interpret an unknown dream (2.4, 10-11). In the book of Daniel the interpretation of the untold dream is presented as an extraordinary event, and not as the common method of the Mesopotamian practice of oneirocriticism. Therefore Daniel's dream and the interpretation of Nebuchadnezzar's dream in the course of a 'night vision' (בחזוא די־ליליא) (2.19) serves as

43. Oppenheim 1956: 205.

44. In the Old Testament incubational dreams are those of Solomon at the shrine of Gibeon (see 1 Kgs 3.5-6; 1 Chron. 1.7-12) and of Samuel in the temple of Silo (see 1 Sam. 3.2-15). Both dreams contain direct divine revelation, they are not symbolic dreams. Jacob's dream in Bethel is, in effect, also an incubational dream (Gen. 28.12-15).

45. Oppenheim 1956: 224

proof of the dedication of the interpreter and proves his superiority over rival dream interpreters.[46]

The Mesopotamian written tradition mostly retains dreams that had been dreamt by kings or referred to kings. We know especially many dreams referring to the ruler from the age of the reign of Nabuna'id.[47] In a dream dated to the reign of Nabuna'id a certain Shumukin sees the Great Star, Venus, Sirius, the moon and the sun and he interprets their constellation as an oracle relating to Nabuna'id and his successors.[48] The dream, similarly to the narrative of Daniel 2, begins with the dating of the vision, identifying it by the king's regnal year (seventeenth day Tebetu month, Nabuna'id's seventh year). According to a dream recounted on one of Nabuna'id's inscriptions, a young man appears in front of the king and assures him that the present constellation of stars and planets does not portend any evil. Thereupon Nabuna'id beholds his royal predecessor Nebuchadnezzar standing upon a chariot and receives an interpretation of his astrological dream from him.[49] Both of Nabuna'id's symbolic dreams which concern historical events contain astral omens; the omens have to be interpreted by a dream interpreter. No dream with motifs similar to the dream in ch. 2 of Daniel can be found in any of the dream descriptions: not in the dream descriptions relating to the Neo-Babylonian rulers, nor in the previous ages, and not even in the catalogues listing the omina. Nor can we find dreams of a similar content in the dream books. In the Mesopotamian dream descriptions the one who makes the revelation is one of the gods, as for example in one of Nabuna'id's dreams[50] where the gods Marduk and Sin appear prior to the vision. Marduk encourages Nabuna'id to rebuild the temple of Sin of

46. One of Nabuna'id's dream descriptions depicts a similar scene, where a young man appears and calms the king's troubled mind. He, however, provides a favourable interpretation of a dream about a constellation of stars. The youth probably is a scholar, specialized in astrological lore; see Beaulieu 1989: 112.

47. Nabuna'id's dream descriptions begin with precise dating, according to the king's regnal years. In the dreams—not only in those of the king, but in other dream descriptions from the same period as well—the constellations of heavenly bodies appear as omens, or deities announce oracle-like revelations. See Langdon 1912: Nabuna'id's inscriptions; Oppenheim 1956: 224, 250. On one occasion the omen appears on the statue of the god Sin; see Oppenheim 1956: 25.

48. Oppenheim 1956: 205. For other Mesopotamian reports of stars and planets, but always 'in a dream', see Oppenheim 1956: 203-205.

49. Oppenheim 1956: 203-205.

50. Oppenheim 1956: 250.

Harran and informs the king, who is afraid of an attack by the *ummān-manda* (the Medes[51]), that he 'made rise against them Cyrus, king of Anshan, his young servant, and he (Cyrus) scattered the numerous *ummān-manda* with his small army...'[52] In another text, in the description of the dream of Gyges in a letter by Ashurbanipal, the god making the revelation is Ashur. In Hittite texts it is usually Ishtar who communicates the oracle, and in the description of the dream of a Babylonian man the oracle appears on the pedestal of the statue of the god Sin. This oracle—which is a typical *vaticinium ex eventu*, that is to say, the projection of a past event into the future—informs us of a revolt and its suppression at the time of Ashurbanipal.

The vision of the image cannot be derived from the motifs of the Mesopotamian literature of oneirocriticism, and therefore we have to suppose a different origin. The key to the dream vision is provided by the Jewish literature of the Persian era, or rather, by the preceding oracular tradition. Deutero-Isaiah, who lived and worked at the time of the downfall of the Neo-Babylonian empire and at the beginning of Persian rule, sharply contrasts Yahweh, the creator of the world, with the 'idols', statues of gods, made by human hands, in several prophecies—including the one where he calls Cyrus משיח; that is, 'anointed' (Isa. 45.1-7).[53] In prophecies of the downfall of the Neo-Babylonian empire these statues appear as impotent objects, unable to help. 'Bel has crouched down, Nebo stooped low'—it is with these words that Deutero-Isaiah summarizes the fall of Babylon and of the city's tutelary deities (Isa. 46.1).[54] The concept of the impotent, disintegrating statues of deities

51. The Mesopotamian sources denote various foreign peoples by the name *ummān manda*; when the Medes appeared they applied the name to them as well; see Komoróczy 1977.

52. Oppenheim 1956: 250.

53. E.g. Isa. 46.5-10: 'To whom will you liken me? Who is my equal? With whom can you compare me? Where is my like? Those who squander their bags of gold and weigh out their silver with a balance, hire a goldsmith to fashion it into a god; then they prostrate themselves before it in worship; they hoist it shoulder-high and carry it and set it down on its place; there it must stand, it cannot stir from the spot. Let a man cry to it as he will, it does not answer; it cannot deliver him from his troubles. Remember this...Remember all that happened long ago, for I am God, and there is none other...From the beginning I reveal the end...' Similarly Isa. 44.6-17.

54. The poetic image of the impotence of idols appears in the early Israelite prophecies; cf. Hos. 8.6: 'the workman (חרש) made it; therefore it is not God: but the

may originate from two sources. One is the idea, used in the earlier prophetic literature, according to which the statues of deities, in the protective power of which the inhabitants of the Aramaic cities trusted at the time of the Assyrian attacks, were impotent, since they were unable to provide protection to their faithful against the enemy (Hos. 8.5-6; Hab. 2.18-20); this concept is especially common in the sixth and fifth centuries BCE, in the works created at the time of the Babylonian exile and at the beginning of the Persian period (see Isa. 44.9-20; 46.5-9; 4QPr Nab; *Daniel; Bel and the Dragon*). The other source of the concept, which may have come from the personal experience of the authors living at the time of the Persian conquest, was that prior to the Persian attack, during the summer of 539, Nabuna'id, fearing the devastation of the enemy, ordered all statues of deities in the region to be transported to Babylon (his precaution proved to be unnecessary, as the Persians did not harm the statues).[55] For the Jews familiar with the events, the transportation of the statues of deities to Babylon may have been unequivocal proof of the impotence of the gods protecting the Babylonian state. Consequently, they considered the fall of Babylon—which its impotent idols were unable to protect—to be the just deserts for the destruction of the Temple of Jerusalem and the carrying off into captivity of the population of Judea. Deutero-Isaiah considers Cyrus, the victor, to be the executor of Yahweh's will, his anointed (משיח) (Isa. 45.1-4). The special interest of Babylonian Jewish literature in the statues of idols may have been stimulated by other local events as well: such an event may have been the erection of the unusually shaped enormous statue of Sin by Nabuna'id, which is also mentioned in the Verse Account mocking the king compiled by the Marduk priests of Babylon.[56] In any case, the political views of the Marduk priests and their pro-Cyrus stance agree with the views of the Jewish Deutero-Isaiah, and it is not impossible that these two traditions coalesce at several points.

calf of Samaria shall be broken in pieces'; Hab. 2.18-19: 'What use is an idol after its maker has shaped it? It is only an image, a source of lies! What use is it when the maker trusts what he has made? He is only making dumb idols!...Overlaid with gold and silver it may be, but there is no breath in it'; cf. the text of 4Q 242 = 4QPr Nab; see Milik 1956: 407-15; Jongeling *et al.* 1976: 121-31; furthermore the apocryphal narrative entitled Βὴλ καὶ Δράκων.

55. Chronicle of Nabuna'id III.9-11, published in Smith 1924: 110-18, tablets xi-xiv; its translations in *ANET*, p. 306-309.

56. Published in Smith 1924: 27-97, tablets ix-xiv; its translation Pritchard, ANET, pp. 312-15.

The colossus in Daniel 2, however, is a more complex symbol than the idols representing the rise and fall of states in the Jewish oracular literature of the eighth century BCE and of Deutero-Isaiah who lived at the time of the exile. The four metals and the clay constituting the statue, according to the interpretation of the vision, each represent a kingdom (מלכו). The motif of statues made of different materials can also be found in the Jewish literature of the Persian period. It is mentioned in the text of Deutero-Isaiah (44.9-20; 46.6), and also in the Prayer of Nabonidus 4Q 242 = (4QPr Nab) which is known from the Qumran tradition, but reaches back to the Mesopotamian Jewish tradition. In the latter text the enumeration of the metals constituting the idols are supplemented by further materials (stone, wood, clay).[57] The literature considers metals representing eras to be of Persian origin. At the same time, however, based on the text of Habakkuk (2.18-19), it seems that the metal symbolism itself is of a more ancient origin, and its roots have to be sought in Jewish tradition.

In the interpretation following the vision in Daniel 2 four consecutive kingdoms are mentioned. The kingdoms may be identified in different ways. According to the interpretation provided by Daniel in 2.36-39, the first kingdom (מלכו) is identical with the *person* of Nebucchadnezzar—and not with the entirety of the Neo-Babylonian empire—'you yourself are that head of gold' (2.38). This characteristic has to be kept in mind in the course of the entire system of identification. This is so not only because the first segment of the interpretation referred to the rule of one person, but also because the word מלכו has several meanings already in the Old Testament: in addition to 'organized (world-) kingdom' it can also mean 'royalty, kingship, kingly authority'; 'realm (territorial)'; and 'reign', 'period of reigning'.[58] According to Bickerman the prophecy

57. 4Q 242 = 4QPr Nab 1.7 'silver, gold [bronze, iron], wood, stone'. *Bel and the Dragon* talks of such a god statue to which they take food daily for it to consume; however, the idol is incapable of doing this because 'inside it is only clay, and outside it is bronze'—incidentally, the comment also reflects knowledge of the technology of casting ancient metal statues. See also Bickerman 1967: 68.

58. Gesenius and Robinson 1978: 1100. Ezra 4.24, 6.15 uses the word to mean 'time of reigning' and Gammie (1976) explains the word with this meaning in mind, although his entire system of identification is different, since he identifies the מלכו-s which are represented by the elements of the image with the first four Ptolemaic kings of Egypt.

originally may have referred to four kings.[59] Bickerman identifies the first ruler—on the basis of the above consideration—with the historical Nebuchadnezzar II. The other three rulers in his opinion are most likely to have been three other members of the ruling dynasty in question: Amel-Marduk (562–560), the son of Nebuchadnezzar; his brother-in-law, Neriglissar (560–556); and Labashi-Marduk, the latter's son who, after reigning for a few months, fell victim to a palace plot. His successor was not one of the members of the dynasty, but the candidate of the conspirators, Nabuna'id (556–539), a member of an aristocratic family of Harran.

The end of Nabuna'id's reign coincided with the fall of the Neo-Babylonian empire.[60] Nabuna'id had no family ties whatsoever with the previous ruling house, and therefore the original dynastic prophecy could not have referred to him.[61]

Based on the foregoing, the following may be concluded about Daniel 2:

1. The story of the interpretation of the untold dream reflects familiarity with the Mesopotamian practice of dream interpretation, and the Jewish author of the story immediately reinterpreted and re-evaluated this tradition.
2. The poetic image of the statue made of several different kinds of materials originates in the poetic apparatus of the Jewish oracular tradition. The concept, in various forms, is especially popular in the Jewish literature of the Neo-Babylonian and Persian periods.

59. The four *malku* were identified with the reign of four kings (Nebuchadnezzar, Belshazzar, Cyrus and Darius) by P. Riessler (who identified the Nebuchadnezzar of chs. 2–4 with Nabuna'id); see Riessler, quoted by Rowley 1935: 161. Similarly Eerdmans 1932 and 1947, pp. 49-55 (Nebuchadnezzar, Awel-Marduk, Nergal-sharezer, Nabuna'id); furthermore Harenberg, quoted by Rowley (1935: 166) and more recently Bickerman (1967: 65). The dynastic prophecy about Nebuchadnezzar was most likely the 'Uruk prophecy', published by Hunger 1976; see also Beaulieu 1989: 20.

60. Nabuna'id-stele iv-v. Its text in Langdon 1912: 270-89; translation in *ANET*, p. 309. Berossus in Josephus, *Apion* 1.20; Herodotus 1.188, 191. See also Burn 1968: 33.

61. Bickerman, 1967, pp. 62-63. Cf. Jer. 27.6-7, which also only mentions Nebuchadnezzar, his son and grandson, as members of the dynasty.

3. The basis for the prophecy in Daniel 2 may have been a Neo-Babylonian fourfold dynastic oracle.[62] Since all elements of the narrative originate from the Neo-Babylonian and Persian circle of tradition, it is likely that the oracle itself was formulated for the first time in this circle.

This final supposition is contradicted in one instance in the present text. This concerns the description of the foot of the statue and the interpretation of the fourth kingdom. According to the text the foot is constituted of two kinds of material ('its feet part iron and part clay', 2.33). According to the interpretation the two materials mingle but do not mix with each other: 'iron does not mix with clay' (2.43), and this is the characteristic which causes the disintegration of the fourth kingdom. On the basis of the allusions in the interpretation ('there will be a mixing of families by intermarriage, but such alliances will not be stable', 2.43) it is not hard to determine that the text refers to the dynastic peacemaking attempts of the Seleucid and Ptolemaic empires, and to the failure of these attempts and the ensuing bitter struggle between the two kingdoms. This is how Jerome, the most significant ancient commentator of the text, identified the fourth kingdom as well.[63]

The historical events to which the prophecy refers are the following: in 252 BCE Antiochus II, the Seleucid king, married Berenice, the daughter of Ptolemy II, the Egyptian ruler. The dynastic relationship between the two ruling houses, however, proved to be shortlived. In 246, after the death of Antiochus, Laodice, the king's first wife, seized power and she had Berenice and her son killed. Ptolemy III, the Lagide king, Berenice's brother, in order to revenge his sister's death set out with an army against the Seleucid kingdom, and entered Syria, Mesopotamia and occupied almost all of Asia Minor as well. He was

62. Bickerman 1967: 62-63; the four-monarchy theory originates in the Persian period according to Flusser (1972) as well. Ginsberg (1948: 5) also supposes a Persian-period origin; however, in his opinion every four-monarchy theory is based on a three-monarchy theory of Achaemenid Persia (Assyria–Medea–Persia). To this sequence of monarchies was added a fourth, Macedonian one, when Alexander absorbed the dominions of Darius. These views are not widely held; the usual point of reference is Swain's earlier article (1940) which demonstrates that the theory of four successive world-empires was current at Rome at least as early as the first quarter of the second century BCE—this, however, could have been the transformation of an earlier theory.

63. Jerome, *Commentar libri Danielis*, *ad loci*.

only obliged to turn back due to a rebellion which broke out at this time. Thus the two countries made peace in 242 BC These events appear in the later tradition of the book of Daniel, in the *vaticinium ex eventu* of ch. 11 (11.5-9). The events and the conclusions to be drawn from them captured the imagination of the Jewish authors of the historically inclined oracles.[64]

The fourth kingdom of Daniel 2 then can be identified with the Hellenistic states, inheritors of the empire of Alexander the Great. There are obvious discrepancies between the entire text of the oracle and this part of the interpretation which we can only explain by suggesting that it (2.40-45) may have been an insertion into the text of the oracle which had not appeared in the original Persian period variant. The original text of Daniel 2 mentions the consecutive reigns of four kings (in any case, the Aramaic word מלכו does not mean empire or dynasty, but rather is used in the sense of 'rule', 'rule of a king'). The choice of words in the text then makes it not only possible but probable that in the Jewish prophecy of the Persian period the rules of four rulers are meant.

Who could have been the four rulers of the Jewish oracle of the Persian period? Nabû-kudurri-usur II was followed on the throne by three successors from his own family, and thus his dynasty had four members. The ruler following the dynasty was Nabuna'id, an aristocrat of Harran. The Jewish author of Daniel 2 living in Mesopotamia could not have deemed this change to be the coming of a new, 'benevolent' eternal rule, and therefore he could not have identified Nabuna'id with the stone, which, smiting 'the image upon his feet', leads to its collapse (cf. 2.34-35). It is much more likely that he may have identified the collapse caused by the stone with the next change in dominion, when Nabuna'id's reign was overthrown—not unexpectedly but with surprising swiftness—by the attack of Cyrus's army, thereby causing the collapse of the Neo-Babylonian empire. We have three documents on how this event was assessed by various groups in Babylon or Mesopotamia, and on what kind of propaganda the conqueror himself was disseminating in Mesopotamia. One of these is the so-called Verse Account[65] expressing the opinion of theMarduk priests, which portrays Nabuna'id as a weak figure of eccentric religious views, who because of the mistakes of his religious and social policies incurred the hostility of his protective deity. In contrast, the author of the text presents Cyrus as a ruler ordained by the

64. Bickerman 1967: 70; Hengel 1980: 29 and 147, n. 46.

65. Published in Smith 1924: 82-91; pls. v-x; 89-90. Translation in *ANET*, pp. 312-15.

gods and especially supported by Marduk, who will rectify everything that Nabuna'id had spoilt. Another text is Cyrus's Akkadian cylinder-inscription,[66] which is based on earlier Mesopotamian literary models.[67] The inscription calls Nabuna'id a 'weakling' and accuses him of faults similar to those mentioned in the previous text, while referring to Cyrus as a legitimate king and a 'friend'. The third one expresses the opinion of its Jewish author, Deutero-Isaiah, living in Babylonian exile, who greets Cyrus as the anointed one (משיח), that is as the ruler ordained and supported by Yahweh 'whom he [i.e. the Lord] has taken by the right hand,[68] subduing nations before him' (Isa. 45.1). The assessment of Deutero-Isaiah then agrees with that of the Marduk priests and with the announcements of the Persian royal propaganda.[69] We have no reason to doubt that the opinion of the Persian period author of the Daniel oracle would have been similar to Deutero-Isaiah's. In the original oracle the downfall of the fourth kingdom meant the collapse of the kingdom of Nabuna'id and of the Neo-Babylonian empire. This is supported by the poetic image that could signify the collapse itself. The statue collapses as a result of being struck by a stone hewn 'from a mountain'.[70] The stone was hewn 'by no human hand' (2.34). After the collapse of the statue 'the stone which struck the image...became a huge mountain

66. Its editions: Weissbach 1911: 2-4; Eilers 1971: 156-66. Translation in *ANET*, pp. 315-16.

67. Harmatta 1971; Kuhrt 1983.

68. The text of Deutero-Isaiah reflects not only the contemporary Mesopotamian view of the legitimacy of the kingdom here, but also the literary influence of the first part of the Cyrus-cylinder. In Babylon, holding the hand of a god (Marduk) signified the legitimacy of the king symbolically. Nabupolassar, in one of his inscriptions, according to Langdon (1912: 66) refers to himself as 'who seizes the hands of the gods Nabu and Marduk'. In the annually repeated ceremony of the *akîtu*-feast, the Babylonian New Year celebration, the king touched the hand of Marduk's statue in the course of a procession. The Neo-Babylonian Chronicle also mentions that from the seventh year of his rule, Nabuna'id did not perform this ceremony; see Smith 1924: 110-118, pls. xi-xiv; translation in *ANET*, pp. 305-307. On the literary influence of the Cyrus-cylinder see Smith 1963: 417; Barstad 1987.

69. Cyrus had already appeared earlier, in a stele text dated to the third year of Nabuna'id's rule, as the tool of divine justice. The positive evaluation is due to the fact that at that time Cyrus was probably Nabuna'id's ally (Nabuna'id was able to travel to Arabia for a protracted period most likely in part because of this alliance); for the text, see Langdon 1912: 270-89; a discussion of the historical problems of the inscription appears in Beaulieu 1989: 108-109.

70. Supplement to the text of LXX Dan. 2.34.

which filled the whole earth' (2.35). To readers of the Persian period, the stone rolling rapidly from a mountain may have evoked the image of the Persians who appeared swiftly from the direction of the Iranian mountains, and who only a little while earlier played no part in the life of the region. The stone hewn 'by no human hand' expresses the role of the conqueror—Cyrus—as a tool in the service of the divine will.[71] In Daniel, Cyrus is the means of salvation, the destroyer of the idol representing the Neo-Babylonian empire,[72] and the tiny stone which becomes a huge mountain[73] alludes to the world rule following the conquest.

There remains one contradiction requiring explanation in connection with the thus reconstructed Jewish political oracle of the Persian period: how can the five rulers of the period from Nebuchadnezzar II to Nabuna'id be reconciled with the the fourfold scheme of the oracle? The rulers of the first and last kingdoms cannot be identified with anyone else but Nebuchadnezzar and Nabuna'id. None of the reigns of the three rulers between theirs was long-lasting and none of them were significant personages either politically or in the historical tradition. It is likely that it was Labashi-Marduk, who ruled last among them, whom the author of Daniel 2 dropped either in order to retain the fourfold schema, or

71. The idea of the changing of rulers as retaliation appears earlier in Mesopotamian historical thought; see the document published by Gerardi (1986), and cited in Beaulieu 1989: 115. Cf. the above-cited inscription of Nabuna'id, where the destruction of Assyria in the seventh century is seen as a retaliation for the destruction of Babylon by Sennacherib (Langdon 1912: 270ff.); cf. also the Cyrus-cylinder where the change of the reigns of Nabuna'id and Cyrus appears as a retaliation by Marduk for the sins of Nabuna'id, and Cyrus is referred to as the 'tool of a divine plan in history'; Weissbach 1911: 2-4; *ANET*, pp. 315-16.

72. Similarly, Eerdmans 1947: 51; Beek 1935: 48 (quoted in Koch 1980: 102) also identifies the stone which annihilates Babylon with Cyrus, and connects this perspective to Deutero-Isaiah.

73. Similarly to the meaning of the image used in Daniel 2—where the powerful and the insignificant are contrasted and where the latter destroys and replaces the former due to divine will—the Mesopotamian royal inscriptions also describe the fact of *translatio imperii* in similar terms. The inscription of Nabupolarrar, the first ruler of the Neo-Babylonian dynasty who overthrew the power of Assyria (see Langdon 1912: 66-69), mentions Assur as the master of humankind, and refers to himself as the 'weak and powerless' one, who defeats the enemy with [the help of] the troops of Marduk and Nabu. Cyrus, the conqueror of the Neo-Babylonian empire, talks of himself in his cylinder-inscription as the chosen one of Marduk, whom the god has made the ruler of Babylon, because he had become angry at Nabuna'id who had transgressed against his cult. See Weissbach 1911: 2-8; *ANET*, pp. 315-16.

because he did not consider him to be a legitimate ruler. Labashi-Marduk ruled only for nine months and in the course of his reign there was no ceremony of enthronement which was traditionally held at the time of the spring New Year festival.[74] It is likely then that the reign of Labashi-Marduk was simply not taken into account. In any case the fourfold schema of the dynastic oracle proved to be stronger than his short-lived rule; this is how the author of Daniel 2 could create the picture of the Neo-Babylonian kingdom consisting of four 'reigns' which was supplanted by Persian rule through divine will.

This then is how the text and interpretation of the original oracle can be reconstructed, which, in agreement with the view of Deutero-Isaiah, assessed the oncoming Persian rule as a new, positive and everlasting era. This is in harmony with the poetic image of the vision itself, that four parts of the same statue represent the parts of the same monarchy, beginning with Nebuchadnezzar, who deposing Zedekiah, the member of the Davidic dynasty, put an end to the independence of the Judean state. The fate of the kingdom is sealed during the divided monarchy of Nabuna'id in whose reign the Persians conquer Babylon. The message of the vision and the oracle originally is about power and downfall—it is reporting on the power of the oppressors of Judea and on their subsequent downfall, and it bears witness to the righteousness of divine justice manifest in history, which punishes by failure those who have taken the chosen people into exile, after first bringing them to power; the conquerors are now ruled over by a new ruler. The vision of Daniel 2 originally is not a world historical overview but rather the evaluation of an era—of the historical turning points of the sixth century BCE, the Babylonian exile and the downfall of the Neo-Babylonian empire. Earlier, Jeremiah saw Nebuchadnezzar as the means of Yahweh's punishment. In Daniel 2 we witness the downfall of his descendants, the annihilation of those means (Jer. 27). Both Jeremiah and Daniel 2 present Yahweh as the one who determines history—in the words of Daniel 2 'He changes seasons and times; He deposes kings and sets up kings...' (2.21). In Daniel 2 he deposed the descendants of Nebuchadnezzar and ordered a new rule in their stead.

The insertion of the third century BCE[75] is also a reinterpretation. If

74. Dougherty 1929: 7. Harenberg (quoted by Rowley 1935: 167) identifies the four מלכו with the reign of the four kings from Nebuchadnezzar to Nabuna'id, and the stone with Cyrus. He also omits Labashi-Marduk based on similar considerations.

75. Several authors have suggested that chs. 2 and 7 'were glossed during the

the divided 'fourth מלכו' refers to the strife and division within the Seleucid and Ptolemaic empires, then the Hellenistic period, naturally, brings about a change in the entire historical perspective. The מלכו-s of the oracle no longer refer to the reign of successive rulers, but to larger eras— from the beginning of the Neo-Babylonian empire hallmarked by the name of Nebuchadnezzar until the middle of the third century BCE. Maybe it was at that time that the four מלכו-s began to be interpreted as the *translatio imperii* of the Babylonian, Medean, Persian and Hellenistic reigns, and that the oracle gained a world historical perspective. It is due to this insertion that Jerome interpreted the succession of the four kingdoms as the history of succession of the Neo-Babylonian, Medean, and Persian empires and the Hellenistic successor states. All later re-interpretations, following Jerome, identified the 'rules' with world empires, larger historical eras.[76] Each reinterpretation was prompted by some significant historical event. The causes of the third century BCE addition and reinterpretation were the already outlined events, when foreign powers fought on the territories of the one-time states of Israel and Judea; the soldiers of two empires were devastating the land and the people experienced directly the dire effects of dividedness and the subsequent power struggles. It was under such historical circumstances that the unknown Jewish—or at thi time most likely Palestinian—redactor revised the historical oracle about the four reigns and supplemented the interpretation of the fourth one.[77]

In the next interpretation the text of the oracle no longer changed, the transmitters merely providing a new key to the interpretation. Several works of the Jewish tradition of the first century CE mention the four empires, highlighting the fourth one and detailing its imminent downfall. (In the New Testament Mk 13.14 mentions it. The most famous instances in the apocryphal literature are the fourth and fifth visions of *4 Ezra*.) These texts identify the fourth rule with the Roman empire, the downfall of which signifies the coming of the messiah. That the text of Daniel 2 could have been interpreted similarly in the first century CE may be surmised from one of Josephus's references: 'In the same manner Daniel

Maccabean age' which is the origin of the last chapter; see Rowley 1935: 65; Hölscher 1919: 120-21; 122-23; Sellin 1933: 153-54; Noth 1926: 155; Montgomery 1927: 176-77; and others. More recently see Kratz 1991: 70-76.

76. For overviews of the 'four empires' and the idea of *translatio imperii* see Swain 1940; Goez 1958.

77. Bickerman 1967: 70.

also wrote about the empire of the Romans and that Jerusalem would be taken by them and the temple laid waste' (*Ant.* 10.11.7.276).

It seems then that the theory of *translatio imperii*[78] is not a schema with a constant meaning in the Jewish tradition; in the book of Daniel the first appearance of the four מלכו is the adaptation of a Mesopotamian dynastic oracle by a Mesopotamian Jewish author, in the vision of ch. 2. The oracle refers to the changeover from the Neo-Babylonian empire to the Persian one. It was in the third century BCE that the idea gained the meaning which later became the accepted one and which was continued to be applied, and it was after this time that the oracle was seen as a world historical overview.[79]

The Other Pieces of Daniel 2–6: Further Traditions of Jewish Historicism of the Persian Period

The second historical oracle is contained in the text of Daniel 4. The text shows many formal similarities to the narratives of Daniel 2: here too we read about a dream vision and its interpretation, and again the author most probably was inspired by the Mesopotamian tradition and practice of dream interpretation. The person of the dream interpreter—Daniel-Belteshazzar—is also identical and the seer of the dream is also Nebuchadnezzar. The narrative consists of two larger parts: the description of the dream and its interpretation (4.1-25) and the description of the fulfilment of the dream (4.26-34). In the dream Nebuchadnezzar sees a 'very lofty tree', 'at the centre of the earth', its top reaching to the

78. In the classical literature of the first years of the second century BCE the 'four empires' and the *translatio imperii* already functioned as a political ideology; see Swain 1940. For the idea in the book of Daniel see Noth 1954. Flusser (1972) considers the meaning of the vision of Dan. 2 and the idea of the 'four empires' to be very early and originates them in a Persian source; similarly Koch (1991) traces back an Iranian origin for the succession theory.

79. Herodotus, however, talks about the changing of 'Assyrian, Medean, Persian' reigns already in the fifth century BCE; this idea dates back to very early in the Mesopotamian historiographic tradition. The idea, according to which the monarchy descended from the heavens at the beginning of historical times, and then after being wrenched away from one city state it was given to the other (or rather to their rulers), appears already in the Sumerian king list of the third millennium BCE. The idea that in the eyes of contemporaries the rise of the Neo-Babylonian and the Persian empires was considered to be a 'changing' is clearly expressed in the above-quoted historical sources of the Neo-Babylonian period.

sky, 'and it was visible to the earth's farthest bounds'; its fruit was abundant, and 'it yielded food for all'; 'beneath it the wild beasts found shelter, the birds lodged in the branches' (4.10-12 [4.7-9]). At the order of a 'watcher, a holy one' (עיר וקדיש) they hew down the tree (4.14-15; it is not clear from the text who destroys the tree). According to the words of the watcher, however, a stump remains rooted in the ground 'bound with iron and bronze among the lush grass, let him be drenched with the dew of heaven, and share the lot of the beasts in their pasture...' (4.15 [4.12]). According to the dream all this happens in order to demonstrate that 'the living will know that the Most High (עליא) is sovereign in the kingdom of men (במלכות אנשא)' (4.22). The explanation given by Daniel-Belteshazzar is similar to the method of interpretation familiar from Daniel 2. Daniel interprets the vision motif by motif, identifying each motif with its historical equivalents. The omina of the oracle—similarly to the omina of the oracle of Daniel 2—cannot be originated from the motifs of the omina known from the Mesopotamian dream-interpreting literature. Many authors consider the tree of life of the oracle of Daniel 4 to be of Iranian origin.[80] However, the Iranian texts used to prove the origins are of later provenance and, although it is not impossible that they retain earlier traditions, they are inconclusive proof.[81] At the same time the motif of the tree of life also appears in another Jewish author, Ezekiel, who lived at the time of the Babylonian exile (Ezek. 17.22-24). Here too the tree represents royal power, the kingdom of Israel. In another part of the book of Ezekiel (Ezek. 31.1-13) the cedar reaching to the sky symbolizes Egypt, and the felling of the cedar means the downfall of the kingdom. The imagery of Ezekiel—tree, tree of life as the symbol of the kingdom, and the destruction of the

80. Duchesne-Guillemin 1962: 212; Hengel 1969: 332. Recently see Coxon 1986.

81. The Iranian source which seems to prove this hypothesis, the familiar form of the Bahman Yasht apocalypse, however, is from the ninth–tenth century CE. Although it does contain earlier material, it cannot be used as proof in evaluating a motif which appears in a Jewish text of the second century BCE; the motif could easily have been of Jewish origin and been lifted from there into the Persian, or both traditions could have adapted it from a third one. In the above-mentioned Iranian apocalypse Zarathustra sees a four-branched (or according to another version seven-branched) tree. The branches are constituted of different metals, which symbolize the eras of the first millennium. For the text see Ringgren 1957. In a fragment found in Cave IV at Qumran (4Q 520; 4Q 552; 4Q 553; see Beyer 1994: 108-109) and defined as Danielic, however, we can also find the motif of the tree symbolizing 'reigns'; see Milik 1956.

tree as the downfall of the kingdom—belong to the same system as the imagery in Daniel 4, and the two traditions may originate in the same period. The symbol may have been inspired by the frequent tree of life motifs in the artistic representations of Mesopotamian culture. This is how the tree originally symbolizing fertility and flourishing may have become a symbol of the king who ensures the well-being of the country.[82]

In the interpretation of the vision about the tree the remaining roots, following the logic of the imagery, can only mean what Daniel-Belteshazzar's explanation also refers to: the downfall is not final, the stump refers to the possibility of a new beginning. The symbolism of the remaining root refers us back once again to the Jewish oracular tradition. Isaiah's messianic prophecies (11.1, 10) also talk of a root, about the shoot springing from it: 'Then a branch will grow from the stock of Jesse, and a shoot will spring from his roots'; 'On that day a scion from the root (שרש) of Jesse will arise like a standard to rally the peoples.'

In the prophecy of Daniel 4 the author treats the motif of the remaining stump as a central element. The individual elements of the imagery ('let him be drenched with the dew of heaven', 4.15) do not receive individual attention in the interpretation. However, the part of the oracle according to which the stump will 'share the lot of the beasts in their pasture' (4.23) and which is taken by the interpretation to refer to the king (4.25), is amplified in the description of the fulfilment of the vision by elements which do not appear in either the text of the oracle or of the interpretation; the king becomes externally similar to animals: he grows a lion's mane and eagle's talons (4.33).[83] According to the oracle of Daniel 4 Nebuchadnezzar's downfall is not final; after 'seven

82. In addition to the frequently occurring visionary elements in Ezekiel we also find novel poetic imagery by comparison with the earlier prophetic tradition. It is unlikely that these can be explained by the merely personal characteristics of the prophet. (Ezekiel's visionary personality has been the subject of several analyses; see Smend 1984: 167.) The influence of the Mesopotamian literature and tradition on Ezekiel and his oeuvre is for the most part unexplored.

83. The story about the human who assumes animal characteristics out of necessity (usually as a result of magic) and who sinks into an animal existence is a widespread motif of folklore. In one type of Hellenistic Greek novel, the picaresque (e.g. Apuleius, *Metamorphoses*), it is a basic motif for the expression of the philosophical message and *Weltanschauung*. In Dan. 4—without supposing any kind of connection between the Jewish oracle and the Hellenistic novel—the motif expresses the same idea: it symbolizes the omnipotence of the God of the Jews and the fallibility of the rulers of world powers.

times' (שבעה עדנין) pass the king's mind will be restored and his kingdom will become even greater (4.34).

One of the keys to the interpretation of this unusual text is given by another, the narrative fragment called the Prayer of Nabonidus, which was found at Qumran (4Q 242 = 4QPr Nab).[84] The Aramaic text of Qumran describes a similar case to that of the oracle fulfilled in Daniel 4, and its content is essentially the same as the Danielic text describing Nebuchadnezzar's madness (4.22-34). Although the person of the protagonist is different,[85] the two texts nevertheless show close connections. In the text of Qumran the last Babylonian ruler, Nabuna'id, tells the story of his illness, which lasted seven years. During his illness—his condition was similar to the condition of Nebuchadnezzar described in Daniel 4—he supplicated 'the silver, gold, [bronze, iron], wooden, stone and clay gods in vain' (4Q 242 = 4QPr Nab 1.2-3, 7-8). To recover, he finally turns to a Jewish ([גבר] יהודי מ]ן בני גלותא]) dream interpreter (גדר) (4Q 242 = 4QPr Nab 1.4.), whose name is not given in the text, and who is one of the Judeans who had been taken into exile.

The Aramaictext had been written with an awareness of the Mesopotamian historical folk tradition and adapts its material from a Jewish point of view,[86] according to the same principle as that used by Daniel 2 for its own folk tradition. The deviation from the Mesopotamian folk tradition in the Prayer of Nabonidus is probably only that the dream interpreter who cures the king is Jewish. The text of Qumran reflects an earlier state of the tradition than the narrative of Daniel 4. In connection with Nabuna'id, a whole series of legends came into being already in his lifetime. The peculiar behaviour of the king, his idiosyncratic religious ideas and their forceful popularization gave rise to the legends. The propagation of the cult of the god Sin and the erection of the statue of Sin in Babylon were the main provocations to the resistance of the Marduk priests; Nabuna'id became the object of the priests' ridicule. (The Verse Account mentions the strange statue of Sin in Babylon which

84. Editions of the text: Milik 1956: 407-415; Vogt 1956: 532-34; Freedman 1957: 31-32; Amussin 1958: 104-117; Meyer 1960: 831-34; 1962; Jongeling *et al.*, 1976: 121-31.

85. W. von Soden (1935) had shown long before the finding and publication of the Prayer of Nabonidus that the Nebuchadnezzar figure of chs. 3 and 4 of the book of Daniel refers to the historical Nabuna'id or to legends about him; see also McNamara 1970.

86. On the Jewish Nabuna'id legend see Amussin 1958; 1971: 326-35; Dommershausen 1964; Meyer 1962.

does not correspond to the canon of Mesopotamian representations.) The other point of conflict was that the king had moved for a while to the Arabian city of Teman, where he had another Sin temple built. He was here in the years 7–17 of his reign while he entrusted the government to his son, Bel-sharra-usur, who had stayed behind in Babylon.[87] During this time, according to the Neo-Babylonian Chronicle, Nabuna'id did not even appear in Babylon for the New Year festival, and did not perform the annual enthronement ceremony either. Although his acts may have had certain political-economical motives (by developing the cities of Haran and Teman he might have intended to bring about the control of trade routes going through the outlying areas), in the eyes of the contemporary public, most likely due to the propaganda of the Marduk priests, he became an eccentric. In the text of the Cyrus-cylinder the Marduk priests dub Nabuna'id a 'weakling' (maybe mentally as well as physically).[88] It is probable that already in the Neo-Babylonian period a considerable Jewish community lived in Teman, which was well informed about the king and the legends surrounding him. The Prayer of Nabonidus considers the king to be ill. His illness is not madness but some kind of skin disease (שחנא באישא).[89] The only goal of the document is to prove that the god of the Jewish dream interpreter is more powerful and effective than the 'idols' made of silver, gold and other materials, whom the king had earlier supplicated for a cure. Daniel 4 represents a later tradition than the Prayer of Nabonidus; in the text of Dan. 4.20b-34 we can read an adapted and modified version of this legend, or one very similar in content. The author of the text most likely was familiar with

87. Nabuna'id goes to Arabia in the third year second month. He returns in the thirteenth year seventh month. During this time his son, Belshazzar rules as regent in Babylon; see Beaulieu 1989: 12; Nabuna'id left everything completely to Belshazzar, who otherwise had no official title; see Dougherty 1929: 107-37. Belshazzar—who in archival documents most often appears as 'the king's son'—was otherwise a 'wealthy businessman'; see Beaulieu 1989: 90; Gadd 1958: 35-92; 1959: 132-34; Burn 1968: 34-35.

88. Col. 1.4, GAL ma-ṭu-ú; its translations: 'a weakling' (Oppenheim, in *ANET*, p. 315); 'weak old one/man'. Text in Weissbach 1911: 2-8. Nabuna'id's assessment in the Dynastic Prophecy: 'a *rebel* prince will arise'; see Grayson 1975.

89. 4QPr Nab 1.2, 6. The expression probably means malignant skin disease; see Amussin 1958: 100. The Neo-Babylonian Chronicle (1.14) mentions Nabuna'id's illness and his recovery, in the third year of his reign, without, however, referring to the nature of the illness. For the text see Smith 1924; translations in *ANET*, pp. 306-11.

the folk tradition surrounding Nabuna'id: from this he adopted the motif of the king's madness and made Nebuchadnezzar into the protagonist of the narrative. The choice of Nebuchadnezzar is not accidental: he represents the Neo-Babylonian kingdom, which at all times appcared in extremely unfavourable light in the Jewish tradition. Originally Nebuchadnezzar had nothing to do with the story: thus he could have nothing to do with the first half of the narrative, the vision about the large tree. In the vision the felling of the tree unequivocally symbolizes downfall, the cessation of the monarchy. The remaining root, however, according to the internal logic of the imagery, refers to a person who had lost his kingdom, but who has not died, and nor has his family died out. The vision predicts the termination of a kingdom, while at the same time predicting the survival of the dynasty. In the light of the events this cannot refer to Nebuchadnezzar: once again it is the person of Nabuna'id with whom the oracle may be brought into connection. The interruption either means that during his sojourn at Teman the king did not participate in political life or that in 539, as a result of the Persian attack, he lost his throne. At this time, however, he was not executed, but rather, at least according to one of the historiographical traditions, he became the governor of Karmania,[90] a high position in the Persian administration.

Daniel 4 then is a conflation of narratives and oracles. The material that serves as its basis is provided by events that happened during the reign of Nabuna'id, or more exactly the folk legends associated with it, which tell of the illness and recovery of the king during his retreat at Teman. The author of Daniel 4 modifies the story somewhat; here the narrative is no longer about the voluntary seclusion and illness of the king, but about his being cast away from among people and his animal-like existence (4.30), which lasts for 'seven times'. The modified story is preceded by a dream containing an oracle (the vision about the tree), which refers to the fate of the king. The oracle is fulfilled when the king feels himself to be at the apex of his power (4.26-34). Thus, the entire narrative serves to prove that history, including the fate of kings, is directed by divine power. The author of Daniel 4 links both of the traditions he makes use of to the person of Nebuchadnezzar. The content of the two conflated stories is further enriched thereby: Nebuchadnezzar's expulsion and his animal existence is no longer an accident, as was the illness of Nabuna'id in the Prayer of Nabonidus, nor is it arbitrary divine punishment, but it is just punishment for the destruction of the Temple

90. Bickerman 1967: 73.

of Jerusalem. The text of Daniel 4 of course does not mention the precedents, just as Daniel 2 does not mention them—the interpretation is left to the reader familiar with the biblical historical tradition.

The third historical narrative can be found in ch. 5 of the book of Daniel. The narrative begins with the description of the feast of Belshazzar. Belshazzar here is the ruler of Babel, that is to say Babylon, who in the course of the feast orders the vessels which his father, Nebuchadnezzar, had pillaged from the Temple of Jerusalem, to be brought forth. The participants of the feast drink wine from the vessels of the Temple, and praise the golden, silver, bronze, iron, wooden and clay gods. Suddenly a human hand appears and writes something on the wall of the hall (5.1-5). The king orders that 'the wise men of Babel' should be called together to read the writing and to tell him its contents (5.7).[91] No one is able to satisfy the royal order (cf. Dan. 2.25) except Daniel, who is led in front of the king on the advice of the queen (5.10). Daniel refuses gifts and honours, and begins his interpretation of the inscription. Unlike the two narratives analysed previously, here the interpretation of the oracle is preceded by a short introduction in which Daniel talks of the cause of the appearance of the omen, that is the writing (5.18-23). He briefly recounts the story of the arrogance and punishment of Nebuchadnezzar (the narrative of Dan. 4). Unlike Daniel 4, the justification of events gains much more emphasis here: the illness of the king is the consequence of his arrogance (רם לבבה, 5.20) and he has to live under punishment 'until he came to acknowledge that the Most High is sovereign over the realm of humanity and appoints over it whom he will' (5.21; cf. 4.22, 30). Daniel 5 presents Belshazzar and Nebuchadnezzar as analogous characters: 'but although you knew all this, you, his son Belshazzar, did not humble your heart' (5.22).

This is why Belshazzar receives the oracle written on the wall. The meaning of this enigmatic text and its interpretation are greatly debated in the literature.[92] The inscription of the oracle in the text is the following: MENE MENE TEKEL UPARSIN (מנא מנא תקל ופרסין) (5.25). The interpretation, however, only explains the word MENE once (5.26-28). Is the repetition of the word MENE accidental in the text of the

91. Cf. Dan. 2.3-5 where the king does not know the meaning of the dream either and calls for specialists. Nabuna'id also 'does not understand' what the writing means. See Beaulieu 1989: 128-29.

92. Bauer 1925; Rowley 1930–31; Kraeling 1944; Eissfeldt 1951; Alt 1954; Grelot 1985.

inscription, or on the contrary was the interpretation of one of the elements omitted from the text of the interpretation accidentally? It is possible that for the author the explanation of the identical element seemed unnecessary. The interpretation of the short text written on the wall, in any case, is more complex and longer than one would expect based on the text itself.

The interpretation of the inscription is the following: 'mene, God has numbered the days of your kingdom and brought it to an end; tekel, you have been weighed in the balance and found wanting; uparsin, your kingdom has been divided and given to the Medes and Persians' (5.26-28).

This interpretation seems to be the result of later revision and it is probable that the interpretation of the oracle had an original, shorter variant. Unlike the earlier ones, the oracle of Daniel 5 is immediately fulfilled: Belshazzar is killed that very night 'and Darius the Mede took the kingdom, being then about sixty-two years old' (6.1; Eng. 5.30-31).

The narrative about the inscription appearing on the wall and its interpretation is most likely of Mesopotamian origin. Oppenheim quotes an inscription of Ashurbanipel according to which an oracle appears to the king in his dream, on the pedestal of the Sin statue.[93] The names appearing in the narrative also go back to the Neo-Babylonian tradition. Belshazzar, the protagonist of the narrative, is identified with Nabuna'id's son, called Bēl-šarra-uṣur, who from 553 to the spring of 539 governed the empire from Babylon as a regent in his father's stead. For this reason the folk tradition of Babylon considered him to be the ruler: most likely this is why he appears in the book of Daniel as 'king of Babel'. Nebuchadnezzar is mentioned as Belshazzar's father (5.2), even though the two people had no blood relationship at all. It may be supposed that the folk historical tradition would have considered the last Neo-Babylonian ruler to be the son of Nebuchadnezzar,[94] but definitely not Belshazzar; it is quite certain that Nebuchadnezzar and Belshazzar became connected only through the intention of the author of Daniel 5.

93. According to a letter quoted in Oppenheim (1956: 249) the 'pronunciation' (*nibittu*) of the name of Assurbanapli appeared to Gyges in his dream, and then he heard a revelation from the god Assur.

94. According to Herodotus 1.77.188, the last Neo-Babylonian king Labynetos (= Nabuna'id) was the son of a ruler also called Labynetos. This latter, based on other parts of Herodotus, may be identified with Nebuchadnezzar; cf. Bickerman 1967: 78.

The narrative mentions the carrying away of the vessels from the Temple of Jerusalem—this is based on historical fact: after capturing the city, in 586 BCE the army of Nebuchadnezzar looted the Temple and the vessels used for ceremonial purposes were transported to Babylon.

The narrative of Daniel 5, however, contains details which refer to Persian customs. Such is the description of the feast (cf. Est. 1). The participants in the feast are the king and his invited dignitaries.[95] According to the narrative the king offers Daniel, who reads and interprets the inscription, a garment of scarlet, a gold chain and the position of the third highest ranking official in the country as a reward (Dan. 5.16).[96] Knowledge of Persian circumstances is reflected in the explanation for the last word of the vision (ופרסין), according to which the kingdom of Belshazzar is to be divided and will be given to the Medes and the Persians (למדי ופרס).[97]

Thus, separating the Mesopotamian historical legends and the later elements in the narrative of Daniel 5 we can distinguish between two layers; the text was compiled by a Jewish redactor who lived in the Persian period, from Mesopotamian elements, but already viewing and representing the earlier tradition from the milieu of the Persian empire. This redactor used an oracle which he explained, putting the interpretation into Daniel's mouth, with the Persian conquest in mind. What could have been the original interpretation of this fourfold oracle (מנא מנא תקל ופרסין) (Dan. 5.25)? The words refer to units of weight, in order of decreasing value (mina, seqel, half seqel).[98] It may be supposed that the original *pesher*, that is interpretation of the oracle, similarly to the *pesher* of the vision of Daniel 2, refers to the succession of Neo-Babylonian rulers. The last element, the half seqel, may have meant the last ruler, most likely Nabuna'id.

In my opinion the oracle was also fourfold originally and the appearance of the element מנא (mina) in the text could not have been accidental. As

95. However, unlike the feast of the book of Esther, here the wives and concubines of the king participate with the men.

96. Cf. Est. 6.8-11, where a royal garment, horse and crown is the reward, and furthermore Est. 10.3, where the office of the second highest ranking official constitutes the reward.

97. Based on the use of the divine name אל עליון and the assumption that the text refers to another piece of the Danielic cycle, Dan. 4, Bickerman had supposed a later, final revision which, however, did not alter the content of the text. This last revision may have been made in the third century BCE. See Bickerman 1967: 80.

98. Clermont-Ganneau 1886; Alt 1954; Bauer 1925.

the text of the narrative, with its Persian elements, seems to be of later origin than the narrative of Daniel 2 with purely Mesopotamian elements, it seems highly likely that the narrative of Daniel 2, its fourfold historical schema and the Nebuchadnezzar figure are older than the narrative of Daniel 5 and may have influenced its formulation. In connection with the fourfold schema we are faced with the same problem as in the case of Daniel 2; how can the five Neo-Babylonian rulers from Nebuchadnezzar to Nabuna'id be identified with the four elements of the historical oracle? The narrative of Daniel 5 suggests that the transgression committed by the sinner (Nebuchadnezzar) brings about the punishment, the downfall of the Neo-Babylonian kingdom and the coming into power of 'the Medes and the Persians'. In reality, between the transgression (Nebuchadnezzar) and the downfall (Nabuna'id, or Belshazzar) three other rulers followed each other. It is certain, however, that the author of Daniel 5 used the fourfold schema of Daniel 2 mechanically. The influence of Daniel 2 is also shown by the fact that the elements following each other are of decreasing value in this oracle too, just like the value of the metals of Daniel 2.

The report of conquest by the enemy which happened unnoticed on the night following the feast in Daniel 5 coincides with a tradition mentioned by Xenophon,[99] according to which the Persians captured Babylon at night, unnoticed, and killed the ruler. According to the other Hellenistic historiographer, Berossus, however, the Persians did not kill Nabuna'id after the conquest of Babylon; the king, having lost a battle, was captured, and then he lived in Karmania until the end of his life, as the governor of the area.[100]

The Jewish redactor generalized and extended the interpretation of the fourfold oracle: in his case it no longer appears as a dynastic oracle, but refers to the entirety of the Neo-Babylonian empire, to its downfall. He combines the oracle and the narrative elements in such a way that in the narrative of Daniel 5 together they constitute a consistent account of crime and punishment: the transgression of the predecessor, Nebuchadnezzar (the pillaging and destruction of the Temple of Jerusalem) is compounded by the descendant, Belshazzar, by a similar new transgression (the use of these same vessels of the Temple at the feast), and he is the one who is punished for these with merciless swiftness. This is why

99. Xenophon, *Cyropaedia* 7.5.26-33

100. Josephus, *Apion* 1.20-21; Eusebius, *Praep. Evang.* 9.4; cf. Burstein 1978: 28.

Belshazzar appears as the son of Nebuchadnezzar at the beginning of the story—the son of the ruler, who in the Jewish tradition was the personification of the Temple-destroying Neo-Babylonian empire. The figures of the two rulers are linked by a common feature, which Daniel recalls in his historical overview prior to providing the interpretation of the oracle (5.18-24). In the overview recalling the tradition of Daniel 4, he singles out arrogance, overconfidence towards Yahweh, as the transgression of the two rulers and the cause of their downfall; Nebuchadnezzar, after a warning oracle still regained his kingdom (cf. Dan. 4) but his 'son' who did not learn from the precedent, and even compounded it by a further transgression, is punished by lasting failure.[101]

The statement about 'the 62-year-old Darius, the Mede'[102]—in all probability the result of a later editorial insertion—signals the *end of an era*, and at the same time serves to foreshadow the story of ch. 6 which takes place in the Persian period, during the reign of Darius. It seems likely that as a result of later editorial intervention the entirety of the visions and narratives of the book of Daniel do not merely present a chronological sequence, but also a pattern of world historical periods. The first chapter which takes place in the third year of the reign of Joiakim (1.1) is followed by chs. 2–5 which take place during the reign of Nebuchadnezzar, that is to say at the time of the Neo-Babylonian empire. These are followed by ch. 6 taking place in the Persian period, during the reign of Darius, together with the well-known preface. Although the prefaces to chs. 7–12 date the visions according to the regnal years of Belshazzar (7.1; 8.1), Darius (9.1), or Cyrus, nonetheless in all cases very clearly they refer to the downfall of Antiochus IV Epiphanes, that is to say to the Seleucid period, which followed the

101. Burrows 1966: 99-131.

102. He is a problematic figure. Opinions differ about him. On Darius see Waterman 1940: 53-61; Torrey 1946: 1-15; Galling 1954: 152; 19. For an overview of the various opinions and attempts at interpretation from the Middle Ages until today see Koch 1980: 191-93. In the more recent literature, Rowley (1935: 54) considers him to be a 'a fictitious creation' which confused and distorted the traditions relating to Darius Hystaspis and Cyrus; Delcor (1971: 133) also considers him to be fictitious. Koch (1986) considers it likely that the figure of 'Darius the Mede' is prefigured by Gubaru, whom we know from the end of the reign of Nabuna'id, and who was later appointed governor of Gutium by Cyrus. Gutium was identified with the territory of the Medes. Kratz (1991: 17), based on the chronological system of Dan. 1–6, sees him as the figure representing the Medean period, a ruler between Nebuchadnezzar and Cyrus (Dan. 6.29). For an opposite view see Grabbe 1988.

Persian era. The mention of the number 62 in Dan. 6.1 also refers to the Jewish timetable of world historical periods known from the later Danielic tradition (originating in chs. 7–12). Daniel 9 interprets the oracle of Jeremiah about the 70 years of the Babylonian exile as 70 year-weeks: 'Seventy weeks are determined upon thy people and thy holy city' (9.24). The division of the year-weeks is: 7 + 62 + 1. 'From the going forth of the commandment to restore and to build Jerusalem unto the Messiah the Prince shall be seven weeks, and threescore and two weeks: the street shall be built again, and the wall, even in troublous times' (9.25). The period of seven year-weeks is probably concluded by the governorship of Zerubbabel; the 62 year-weeks refer to the Persian period, at the time of which, during the governorship of Nehemiah, they rebuilt the walls of Jerusalem. The mention of the 62-year-old Darius, then, invokes the Persian rule. However, it is not possible to define more exactly with what event the redactor of the book of Daniel associated it. This much is certain, that the strange insertion does not belong to the narrative of Daniel 5, but has a structural function from the point of view of the entire book. It provides a bridge to the 'Persian' section, Daniel 6, and at the same time the number evokes the timetable of the contemporary world historical system. In Daniel 9 the year-week following the 62 year-weeks is the era of a 'messiah'—Antiochus Epiphanes—whose downfall in the course of that year-week the author of Daniel 9 predicts. The prophecies about Antiochus Epiphanes of chs. 7–12 follow the narrative of Daniel 6 according to the same system.

In summary we can state of Daniel 2–6 that the kernel of the collection may have come into being in Mesopotamia among Jews living there, immediately after the Persian conquest. Its earliest piece is the narrative of ch. 2, which, in its world-view and its motifs, shows close similarity to those pieces of Deutero-Isaiah which were created at the same time and in the same place. The author of Daniel 2 is clearly preoccupied with the same problems as Deutero-Isaiah, and he assesses the great historical turning point that just passed similarly: he greets the reign of Cyrus as the beginning of a new, positive era. The first form of the vision of Daniel 2 does not yet express a world historical schema, but merely presents the retaliation against the Babylonian empire as punishment for the destruction of the Temple of Jerusalem. The fourfold schema only becomes world historical later, after the reinterpretation and the expansion of the text of the interpretation has occurred. The other two oracles of the collection (Dan. 4, 5) are of somewhat later origin than Daniel 2. Both make ample use of the latter. Not only are the description of the circumstances of the vision and the method of interpretation in the later oracles similar, but the circle of literary sources (the historical legends connected to Nabuna'id), the protagonists and their functions (Daniel-Belteshazzar as dream interpreter, and Nebuchadnezzar as the destroyer of the Temple of Jerusalem) are also the same; furthermore the narrative of ch. 5 also uses the fourfold historical schema, known from ch. 2 and representing the last group of Neo-Babylonian rulers.

It is also in this collection, in those pieces of the book of Daniel (Dan. 3, 6) which came into being in Mesopotamia at the time of the Persian rule, that a narrative type placed into a historical milieu appeared which may be regarded as the beginning of a genre, that of the martyrological narratives, which later became very popular.[103]

103. It is Dan. 1–6 where the prototype of the wise men appears for the first time. Daniel along with his friends represents the ideal and perfect type of absolute piety of the period of persecution; see Efron 1987; Willi-Plein 1991.

Chapter 2

THE THEOLOGY OF THE 'ORIGIN OF EVIL' AND HISTORICAL ATTITUDES IN THE POST-EXILIC JEWISH LITERATURE: THE BEGINNINGS OF THE ENOCH-CIRCLE

The part of the so-called *Ethiopic Book of Enoch* (*1 Enoch*) which exemplifies 'historical attitudes' is the part called the *Book of Watchers* (*1 En.* 1–36). The frame of the *Book of Watchers* is a blessing told by Enoch with which he blessed the 'righteous elect' (בחירי קשיטין), 'who will be present on the day of tribulation to remove all the enemies, and the righteous will be delivered' (*1 En.* 1.1).[1] Subsequently Enoch tells a parable (מטל) whose content he has received from God in a vision (*1 En.* 1.2). The narrative which follows—the story of the Watchers—is a parable which addresses the future, the generation of the author. The actors and events of the *Book of Watchers* apply to the people and events of the era of the author of the text—and it is this characteristic of the text which justifies classifying this story which takes place in the mythical past with works expressing historical attitudes. The story of the *Book of Watchers* begins with the story of creation, then continues with the story of the Watchers (עירין), whose sin—the relationship with the daughters of men, or rather the deeds of the giants born from these relationships—provokes the punishment of the Flood. We are dealing with mythical history, the beginnings of the history of humankind and the origins of the appearance of evil in human history—and according to

1. In the following I quote the text based on the Aramaic fragments, according to Milik's reconstruction and translation; see Milik 1976. In connection with the prefatory words many have noted that they were formulated on the pattern of the introduction of the blessing of Moses, Deut. 33.1, and that in the text Num. 22–24 (the Balaam story) the formulation can also be recognized; see Charles 1893: 4-5; Hartman 1966: 112-14; 1979: 22-23; VanderKam 1984a: 115. Both the Deuteronomy and the Balaam tradition have had special significance in the traditions of the Qumran community; the text of Num. 22–24 was explicitly considered to be revelatory and interpreted as such, for example in the Damascus Document or in the Pesher Genesis.

the intentions of the author this story is a 'parable' for the history of his own age. In later historical overviews this tradition plays a very important role.

Earlier the *Book of Enoch* was only known as a part of the pseudepigraphic tradition, in Greek or Ethiopian translation. It had been supposed that its original language may have been Hebrew or Aramaic, and that the Greek translation[2] was prepared from this, only a part of which has survived; luckily the *ge'ez* (Ethiopian) translation[3] has preserved a much longer text. The work known only in translations earlier was uniformly dated to the middle of the second century BCE. Some parts of it (chs. 37–70) were dated to a somewhat later time.[4]

The finding of fragments of the Aramaic original of the work among the Qumran texts[5] was a turning point in research. The manuscript fragments found at Qumran—despite the fact that we are dealing with very minute fragments[6]—not only answered certain questions about the history of the origin of the text, but also provided an insight into the kind of role the work played in the literary tradition of the group which left behind the library safeguarded in the caves.[7] Based on the number of fragments found[8] we may suppose that the work was not merely known at Qumran, but that it must have been an important work in the tradition of the community. This is also indicated by the fact that

2. Flemming and Radermacher 1901; Black 1970. On the Greek manuscripts see also Denis 1970.

3. The Ethiopian manuscript tradition can be traced back to the fifteenth century. The first edition of the Ethiopian text was Charles 1906; the new, critical edition of the Ethiopian text, which takes into consideration the Aramaic fragments, with translation and annotation is Knibb 1982.

4. For the earlier/prior dating of *1 Enoch* see Schürer 1973–79: III.1, 256.

5. Milik: 1976; the new edition of the Ethiopian text was prepared in the light of the Aramaic fragments, with translation and commentary by Knibb (1982).

6. In the text edition Milik mentions that 50 per cent of the text of the *Book of Watchers* was preserved; in the case of the other parts of the work the percentage is less than this; more precisely; however, these numbers only mean that this is the proportion of the Aramaic text that can be reconstructed on the basis of the fragments; see Milik 1976: 5; also see VanderKam 1984a: 111.

7. On the significance of the Aramaic fragments, see García-Martínez 1992: 45-96.

8. In his edition Milik identified seven manuscript copies on the basis of the fragments found in Cave IV, four manuscripts from the *Astronomical Book*; on the basis of the fragments of the *Book of Giants* we may also suppose the existence of several copies from this part as well; see Milik 1976: 139-317.

numerous other works found at Qumran, some already known from the pseudepigraphic literature and some not, contain a similar tradition to that known from *1 Enoch*, or mention or use *1 Enoch*.[9] No fragments of chs. 37–70 of the work appear among the Qumran fragments—it had already been suggested that these chapters are of later origin that the other parts of *1 Enoch*, and that at the least they show traces of a Christian revision;[10] this lack proved these suppositions right. The Qumran manuscripts, however, also contain texts—fragments of the parts called *Astrological Book* and *Book of Giants* by their editor[11]—which were earlier not known from any of the translations.[12] The oldest Qumran manuscript of *1 Enoch* (4Q En. ara) may be dated to the beginning of the second century BCE, and this manuscript contains the text of chs. 1–12[13] (but most likely the entire *Book of Watchers*, the material of chs. 1–36, belongs to this layer).[14] The later manuscripts contain further parts of the work; this indicates that the work was continually transmitted until the first century BCE, and that in the course of this transmission the

9. To mention just a few important examples: the *Book of Jubilees* (whose Hebrew fragments were also found at Qumran), known earlier from the pseudepigraphic literature, uses and explicitly quotes the book (see Charles 1973: II, 18-19), and elements originating from *1 Enoch* play an important role in its entire narrative; see below in greater detail. The Damascus Document, fragments of which were also found at Qumran, also alludes to the Enochic tradition in its historical overview; similarly the historical schema outlined in 4Q180-81 is also based on the story of the Watchers of the Enochic tradition. On the relationship of the *Book of Watchers* and the Aramaic Levi, and the interconnections and the origins of the sect see Stone 1988.

10. Milik (1976) supposed a Christian origin; Milik's theory was sharply criticized. On the question see Schürer 1973–79: III.1, 257-59.

11. Milik 1976: 273-317.

12. The *Astrological Book* contains fragments of the 364-day calendar known at Qumran and fragments of other calendars. The *Book of Giants* contains the rich tradition concerning the giants, the children of the Watchers, unfortunately in a very fragmentary form. The order of the fragments is very problematic. On this see García-Martínez 1992: 97-115.

13. Earlier works (such as Beer, in Kautzsch 1900: II, 224; Martin 1906: lxxviii; Charles 1893: 2-3) considered the material of chs. 1–5 to be a subsequently written introduction to the whole work—in view of the Aramaic manuscript tradition, however, it seems certain that this part is contemporaneous with the narrative parts that follow, and that it represents a tradition predating the second century BCE.

14. Milik 1976: 140. Milik also supposes that the writer of the text followed the northern Syrian or Mesopotamian scribal customs—and this may also indicate the origin of the tradition. The fragments also prove that chs. 1–5 already belonged to the so far earliest known Enoch tradition.

collection was enriched by further pieces.[15] The manuscript tradition can be traced to the turn of the third and second centuries BCE—this means that the *Book of Watchers* was written at least as early as the third century BCE, but it may have been written even earlier. A few years before the finding of the Qumran manuscripts Jansen examined the figure of Enoch in the light of the Mesopotamian tradition.[16] Grelot's works demonstrating the Mesopotamian origin of the Enoch tradition were also written before the publication of the Aramaic fragments.[17] VanderKam's book[18] re-examines the origin of the tradition associated with Enoch in the light of the already published Aramaic fragments, and affirms the earlier findings relating to a Mesopotamian origin. In all likelihood then the tradition connected to Enoch originates from authors living in a Mesopotamian diaspora community during the Babylonian exile or during the Persian rule following it. The figure of Enoch and the elements of the revelation tradition associated with him originate in the figures of the Mesopotamian *apkallu*-s, that is wise ones,[19] more exactly in the figure of the 'Mesopotamian diviner-king Enmeduranki' and in the tradition about divine revelation given to him.[20] In addition to these in the text of the *Book of Watchers*, numerous other Mesopotamian elements have already been shown to exist.[21] The kernel of the Enochic tradition then—similarly to the early pieces of the Danielic collection—may have come into being in Mesopotamia, most probably in a local Jewish diaspora community. The book of *1 Enoch*, however, contains more than these early pieces. The entire book is constituted of a collection of pieces that came into being at different times, and even if the basis of the early pieces of the collection was the Mesopotamian Jewish tradition, certain later pieces may have been written much later in Palestine.

The contents of the *Book of Watchers* may be summarized as follows:

15. Milik (1976: 164) dates 4Q En/b to the mid-second century (this manuscript also only contains the *Book of Watchers*; the later manuscripts, designated by c, d, and e which can be dated to the first century BCE–first century CE, also contain parts of the *Book of Dreams* (*1 En.* 83–90) and of the *Epistle of Enoch* (*1 En.* 91–107); see Milik 1976: 178, 12, 217, 22, 225.

16. Jansen 1939.

17. Grelot 1958a; 1958b; 1958-59; 1976.

18. VanderKam 1984a.

19. Sir. 44.16 also mentions Enoch as 'a wise one'.

20. VanderKam 1984a: 116.

21. On the geographical description of the part following the Watchers narrative see Grelot 1958a.

chs. 1–5 the prefatory words of Enoch; 6–11 the Watchers and the daughters of men, the story of the teachings of the Watchers and the punishment of the Watchers; 12–16 Enoch's intercession for the Watchers; 17–19 and 21–36 Enoch's first and second journeys. The text of chs. 6–11 clearly contains at least two narratives. Based on the names of the characters the texts of 6.1–7.6 (the narrative about Shemihazah) and of 8.1-4 (the Asa'el tradition) may be separated.

The Shemihazah Tradition

The narrative of the 'Shemihazah-tradition' can be read in *1 En.* 6.1–7.62.[22] The story is the parallel of the narrative of Gen. 6.1-4 about the angels and the daughters of men, but with a different message than the narrative of the Masoretic text. According to the Shemihazah story sons of heaven (6.2), whom the text similarly to the terminology of Daniel 5 calls 'watchers' (עירין), glimpse the daughters of men, desire them, and decide to descend to them. Their leader Shemihazah (שמיחזה) considers the plan to be sinful, and not want to bear the responsibility alone (6.3); therefore the Watchers, in order to fulfil their plan, swear to unite on the Hermon-mountain (*1 En.* 6.6).[23] Then the Watchers 'began [to go in to them, and to defile themselves with them and (they began) to teach them] sorcery and spellbinding [and the cutting of roots; and to show them plants...' (7.1). The women become pregnant from them and bear children, who grow up to become giants. The giants 'were devouring [the labour of all the children of men and men were unable to supply them' (7.4). After this the giants begin to devour men, then 'they began to sin against all birds and beasts of the earth and reptiles...and the fish of the sea, and to devour the flesh of another; and they were]

22. Wedged into the narrative about Shemihazah and his companions there is another story, which is called the Asa'el story after its protagonist. The separateness of the two stories has long been recognized; see Beer, in Kautzsch 1900: II, 225; Charles 1893: 13-14; more recently Hanson 1977; Nickelsburg 1977. On the precise delineation of the parts of the texts and with regard to the origin and role of the stories there are different opinions; on these see VanderKam 1984a: 123-24. Dimant (1974: 23-72) supposes three versions of one story in the narrative of *1 En.* 6–11: 1) the angels defile themselves with earthly women, who bear them giants, and these are the source of evil and aggression; 2) the teachings of the angels betray secrets to humans; 3) Asa'el's teachings corrupt people.

23. Pun based on the similarity of the Aramaic word חרם, meaning root, and the place name חרמון.

drinking blood. [Then the earth made the accusation against the wicked concerning everything] which was done upon it' (7.5-6).[24] These transgressions finally bring about the punishment of the Flood (*1 En.* 9.1-10.22);[25] thus the story serves as a justification for the catastrophic punishment.

How the author of the story evaluated the relationship of the Watchers and the daughters of men may be seen from two comments. One of them is heard before the deed of the Watchers, from the mouth of Shemihazah: 'I fear that you will not wish to do this deed; and I alone shall be guilty of a great sin (חטא רבא)'(6.3). The writer of the Shemihazah tradition thus considers the relationship to be a sin, which contravenes some prescription, from the outset but he does not identify the nature of the transgression.[26] According to the second comment the Watchers defiled themselves[27] with the daughters of men (7.1c)—that is they offended against some prohibition relating to sexual relations.[28]

24. Translated by Milik, based on the Aramaic text reconstructed by him; see Milik 1976: 166-67.

25. In the Ethiopian text of the *Book of Enoch* the narrative about Asa'el is wedged between the narratives of the sins and the punishment. The same is true for the Aramaic fragments. Based on the text of the first copy (Milik 1976: 150, pl. III) it is probable, and based on the second copy (Milik 1976: 166, pl. VI) it is certain, that the Aramaic texts also followed the same order. According to *1 En.* 9.1-11, however, the punishment is clearly connected to the sins (bloodshed upon the earth) described in the Shemihazah story.

26. Most interpretations see the deed of the Watchers, based on the analogy of the *theomachia* stories of Greek and Mesopotamian mythologies, as a rebellion against God; based on the text of *1 Enoch* it is not necessarily so, just as the other comment ('defiled themselves') does not refer to such a kind of sin either. It is self-evident that the mixing of men of heaven and daughters of men violates unwritten laws concerning the relation of divine and human beings, and trespass against the Mosaic laws forbidding the mixing of different kinds.

27. The part containing the expression is missing from the Aramaic manuscript fragments containing the story of the Watchers. In the Ethiopian translations it reads 'they began to go in to them and were promiscuous with them', while the Greek ones have 'they began...to defile themselves with them'. The basis for the difference is most probably the Aramaic טמע 'to be mixed up' and טמא 'to be defiled'; see Knibb 1982: 77; VanderKam 1984a: 123.

28. The cases of the sin of טמא as sexual impurity are enumerated in Lev. 18.19-25. According to this whoever lies with the wife of another, or lies with an animal, or with a menstruating woman will become defiled (although the verb טמא does not appear in this prohibition, logically it results in it); Lev. 15 which also deals with defilements expounds in detail that the bedstead and seat of a menstruating woman are

The protagonists of the story are called עירין, 'Watchers' and 'sons of heaven' (בני שמיא) (6.2). The text also enumerates the names of their leaders.[29] Most of the names contain an element of the name of a deity (אל), and the names of celestial bodies and natural phenomena (Ramt'el, 'Burning heat of God'; Kokab'el, 'Star of God'; Ra'm'el, 'Thunder of God'; Zeq(i)'el, 'Lightning-flash of God'; Baraq'el, 'Lightning of God'; Matar'el, 'Rain of God'; 'Anan'el, 'Cloud of God'; Sataw'el 'Winter of God'; Shamshi'el, 'Sun of God'; Sahri'el, 'Moon of God'; Turi'el, 'Mountain of God'; Yomi'el, 'Day of God'). In other names the 'el element is not linked to natural phenomena (Dani'el, 'Judge of God'; 'Asa'el, 'God had made'; Tummi'el, 'Perfection of God'; Yehaddi'el, 'God will guide'). In two names a natural phenomenon and a geographical name appear but without the אל name element ('Ar'taqoph, 'The earth is power'; Hermoni, 'of Hermon'). Finally the meaning of the name of the leader, Shemihazah, 'My name has seen', probably also refers to the name of a deity. After their descent to the daughters of men the Watchers teach them sorcery, spellbinding and 'the cutting of roots', and 'show them plants' (7.1). The first two terms (כשפה, חרשה) determine the negative nature of the teachings. Thus the seemingly innocuous 'cutting of roots' and 'knowledge of herbs' in the view of the author of the Watchers story are also considered to be negative, that is to say, forbidden things.[30] After the interjection of the Asa'el story we

also unclean and are defiling objects, and sexual relations with such a woman make the man unclean for seven days. Dimant (1974: 43-44) suggests that the sin of Shemihazah and his companions was transgression against the latter prohibition, intercourse with women during their menstrual period.

29. According to the Greek and the Ethiopian texts there are two hundred Watchers, and each group of ten Watchers has a leader; thus the number of names is twenty, of which, with the help of the names appearing in the Aramaic text, nineteen can be identified; see Milik 1976: 152-54.

30. Knowledge and use of medicinal herbs in most cultures is considered natural and applied alongside with magical practices it belongs to the traditional practice of healing. Naturally the use of herbs for malefactory purposes is also known. The severe disapproval of the knowledge of herbs in the text of *1 Enoch* may be related to a view that is also known from other non-canonical texts found at Qumran; according to this the only method of healing considered to be efficacious was the laying on of hands (סמיכת ידים). The healer (גזר) cured the patient with divine help, and exorcised the demon causing the illness through releasing the patient's sins; 4QPr Nab, (Jongeling *et al.* 1976: 121-31); Genesis Apocryphon (Fitzmyer 1971). On this method, which is not only know from Qumran, but also from the New Testament, see Fitzmyer 1971: 140-41. Such a division of methods of healing, incidentally,

once again read about the teachings of Shemihazah and his companions (8.3); Shemihazah 'taught spellbinding and cutting of roots', and Hermoni the 'taught the loosing of spells, magic, sorcery and skill' (8.3a). This section enumerates the teachings of the other Watchers as well, which are always related to those phenomena which appear in the name of the given Watcher: 'Baraq'el taught the signs of thunders. Kokab'el taught the signs of the stars' etc. (8.3). The teachings of Shemihazah and Hermoni then are related to magic in general (in addition, those of Shemihazah also relate more particularly to the knowledge of herbs), and those of the Watchers to natural phenomena, and most probably to the interpretation of astrological and natural omens.[31]

The third element of the narrative, the motif of the giants devouring everything, seems to be without precedent.[32] In the narrative, however,

corresponds to the two methods known from Mesopotamia which are carefully differentiated from each other, that of the activities of the *āšipu*, and the *asû*-doctors. On the one hand, the *asû*-doctors identified the symptoms of the patient with the help of prognostic omina, and also suggested medication for the patient on the basis of texts of omina—usually herbs and potions prepared from them. On the other hand, the *āšipu*-doctor after observing and noting the patient's symptoms cured by magical methods deemed to fit the particular case; see Oppenheim 1956: 359-61.

31. Others (e.g. VanderKam 1984a: 55) have already noted the possible connection of these elements of the Watchers story to the Mesopotamian Enūma Anu Enlil ('When Anu and Enlil') collection, which was the 'canonical' series of the interpretation of the omina of the moon, sun and meteorological phenomena. Naturally, in the *Book of Enoch* this science appears as a synonym of magic and sorcery. The Mesopotamian tradition may have become known to the Jewish author or authors of the Aramaic-language Enochic tradition in the Babylonian exile through Aramaic intermediaries. On the Mesopotamian texts see Weidner 1941–44.

32. The motif of non-human creatures who devour everything is familiar from the Mesopotamian literary tradition, namely in connection with the Anukka deities (see below). It seems that it is not only the figure of Enoch that can be traced back to the *apkallu*-s, wise men, of the Mesopotamian tradition, but also elements of the Shemihazah story, although Enoch does not appear in this part at all, and thus the two traditions could be independent of each other. One of the motifs of the Shemihazah story which suggests a Mesopotamian background is that of omen-interpretation relating to stars and natural phenomena; the omen-interpretation collection of the series entitled Enuma Anu Enlil contains the interpretations of the omina of the moon, sun, meteorological phenomena and the stars—the same items that the Watchers teach the daughters of men.

One of the title characters of the series is the god Anu, the mythological motifs relating to whom merit a thorough examination; all the more so as in the second part of the rule of the Achaemenid dynasty in Uruk Anu appeared as a Sky God and the it is an important element, since this is the origin of the cannibalism of the giants, of their sins against the creatures of the air, earth and the water, of the drinking of blood, and these sins lead eventually so far that the earth accuses against the sinners.

The Asa'el Tradition

The Shemihazah narrative is directly followed by another, the protagonist of which is Asa'el (*1 En.* 8.1-4), and which tells of the kind of teachings Asa'el (עסאל) imparted to the people. According to the narrative it was he who taught the men the making of swords of iron and breastplates of brass; he showed them how they could make jewels out of gold and silver; he informed women of the use of antimon, eye shadow, precious gems and dyes. In the narrative of the Asa'el tradition the teacher is that same Asa'el whose name had been also mentioned in the Shemihazah story.[33]

protector of the town, and according to Diakonoff he was worshipped as 'the god of the sky'—by the same name which becomes the adjective of Yahweh in the same period. Based on Anu's popularity during the Persian period and the similarities that can be demonstrated at this time between the figures of Anu and Yahweh, it is not unimaginable that the Watchers story preserves a certain tradition relating to Anu and the gods connected to him and to demons.

A discussion of the possible origin and relations of the literary material of the story of the Watchers would require much more space, and I will therefore merely refer to a few possible points of connection with Mesopotamian mythological ideas. According to the Mesopotamian tradition Anu, the god and creator of the sky, orders the birth of the Anukka deities on 'the mountain of the sky and the earth'. The Anukka eat cereals and drink milk—which is provided for them by a divine couple, Lahar and Asnan—however, their hunger and thirst is not quenched (*Lahar and Asnan*). In the Mesopotamian mythology the evil demons also appear as the progeny of Anu; he created them with the Earth (*Erṣetu*), and then, determining their fate, he gave them to be the helpers of Erra, the god of pestilence (*Epic Erra*, *Epic Lugalbanda*, and the collection of incantations entitled 'The evil utukku-demons'). The mention of the name of Gilgamesh elsewhere in the Enochic collection is also of Mesopotamian origin. In the Shemihazah story the children of the Watchers are giants; later mentions of the Watchers stories within the Enochic collection, however, always clearly refer to demons; on this question see below.

33. His name is the same as that of the tenth leader of the Shemihazah story. The Aramaic text uses the same form of the name in both places, therefore it may be supposed that we are dealing with the same figure. The manuscripts of the Greek translations, however, provide two different names; it is likely that these forms are the result of corruption of text. Dimant (1974: 52-59) supposes a different figure for the protagonist of the Asa'el story.

Asa'el's teachings differ from those we read about in the Shemihazah story. The story says nothing about who Asa'el is; it does not mention the motif of the oath or the rebellion or the nature of the relationship of Asa'el and the people. The fact that Asa'el does not teach only women, but men also, is different; and the motif of the consequence of the sin is also missing. The section about Asa'el is followed once again by a section belonging to the Shemihazah story (the teachings of the Watchers), which is followed by the description of the punishment in which elements of the Asa'el and Shemihazah traditions mingle. It seems that the punishment of Asa'el belongs to a separate Asa'el tradition. Asa'el is punished for his sin by the angel Raphael: he is cast into darkness, where he will stay until 'the great day of judgment' (10.4-8). On the other hand, the punishment belonging to the Shemihazah story is the devastation of the Flood (10.1-3, 9-22). Based on these Dimant has suggested that the Asa'el part has a narrative tradition of a different origin than the Shemihazah story, and it has nothing to do with the story of the Flood.[34] Nickelsburg has a different theory according to which the figure of Asa'el is a kind of culture hero, *prōtos heuretēs*, like Prometheus, and the story came into being under the influence of the Prometheus myth.[35] Indeed, the possibility of Greek literary influence cannot be excluded, even in the case of a Jewish author of the Persian period; however, there are discrepancies between the contents of the teachings and the functions of the characters which make the borrowing unlikely. The protagonist of the Prometheus myth brings fire from the sky and gives it to the people in order to help them. This motif—the aim of helping humankind—cannot be discovered in the Asa'el tradition. Prometheus teaches people the use of fire; although tradition about metallurgy may be connected with the motif of fire, this motif does not appear in the Asa'el tradition. The comparison with the Prometheus myth does not account for the motif of jewellery-making and the motifs of the teachings imparted to women, the knowledge of eye shadows, of precious gems and dyes of mineral origins. In the light of the Prometheus myth it does not become clear why Asa'el gives separate teachings to men and women. If, however, one consider the general meaning of the Asa'el narrative then one will find that a common feature of Asa'el's teachings to men is the destructive power of arms, and of those given to women is the seductive power of the cosmetics; violence and seduction are basic motifs of the

34. Dimant 1974: 23-72.
35. Nickelsburg 1977.

Shemihazah narrative (the motivation for the deed of the Watchers is that they desired the daughters of men, and in the latter parts the violence and bloodshed begun by the giants becomes the reason for the punishment of the Flood). The fact that the author of thc Asa'el story puts metallurgy, weapon- and jewellery-making into the centre of the forbidden teachings may also have been caused by a homophony: the similarity of the Aramaic word חרש ('magical method') and the Hebrew word חרש ('cut in', 'engrave', plough', 'devise') which may have led the author of the Asa'el story to expand the tradition of magical methods to include teachings on metallurgy. That metallurgy and smithing are very closely related to the notion of magic cannot be left out of consideration; according to the belief system of the Near East, ironsmiths are considered to be sorcerers.[36]

Shemihazah, Asa'el and the Enochic Collection

The two stories—the story of Shemihazah and that on the teachings of Asa'el, added later to the first one—serve as justification for the punishment of the Flood. The text of chs. 1–5, which constitutes the preface to the narrative, is considered to have been a later addition but it appears together with the narrative of 6–11 in the oldest extant manuscript tradition.[37] The first sentences of *1 Enoch* 1–5 are an admonition followed by teachings on the creation of the world and the precedents of the Flood. The preface of *1 Enoch* mentions the fact of the creation, and talks of the ordered nature of the world. It does not narrate the process of the creation, but only mentions the fact and provides a detailed description of everything being defined, and states that the perpetual functioning and annual changes are directed by unchanging eternal laws (2.1–5.3). The *Book of Enoch* does not mention the story of the Fall, the transgression of the divine prohibition by the first human couple, Adam and Eve; similarly, it does not refer to the tradition of Genesis 4–5. The

36. On the beliefs about the relationship of ironsmiths and magical art, see Eliade 1985. In Ethiopian, ironsmith and magician are denoted by the same word (dubanansa); see Leslau 1989: 181; similarly the descendants of Cain, who are ironsmiths in the Bible (Gen. 4.16-24), are associated with magical motifs in the later tradition related to them (Syriac 'Cave of Treasures'; Bezold 1883; German translation in Riessler 1928: 955). In the Ethiopian tradition the belief that ironsmiths have magic capabilities and knowledge is alive to this day; they are considered to be sorcerers and therefore members of other groups do not marry their daughters to them.

37. Milik 1976: 25.

absence of references to this tradition of Genesis cannot be an accident; that story tells how the violation of a rule puts an end to the golden age following creation, and that this is what brings upon humanity the burdens of toil, giving birth and death (Gen. 2–3).[38] In *1 Enoch*, however, the first event after creation is the tradition also known from Gen. 6.1-4, the story of the 'sons of God' and the 'daughters of men', which in the text of Enoch appears as the story of the 'Watchers' and the daughters of men. This system compared to the *Urgeschichte* of Genesis—which originates in different traditions, though its final form was given by P and P determined its theological message—carries a significantly different message. In the narratives of Genesis the origin of evil is associated with the disobedience of the first human couple, and its cause is the violation of a rule. In *1 Enoch*, on the contrary, evil is of 'historical' origin;[39] it is associated with a particular era of the history of humankind, since in the generations prior to Enoch and the period of the Flood, in the generations preceding the contemporaries of the giants there is no evil (although *1 Enoch* does not talk of the period between the creation and the deluge, it may be supposed that it imagines the *Urgeschichte* of humanity similarly to the biblical tradition, beginning with the creation). In addition, according to the Enochic tradition the appearance of evil is not preceded by a prohibition. Shemihazah and his companions are aware that their act, the descent to the women, is a sin—however, we do not know if the women are aware of this. In the Shemihazah story the origin of evil lies in the relationship between the Watchers and the women, the giants born of this relationship, and the teachings given to the women—the receivers of evil and its earthly transmitters are exclusively the women.

38. This part of Genesis, or its paraphrase, incidentally, does not appear in the text tradition of the covenanters, neither among the texts created within the community, nor in the apocryphal texts transmitted by them—however, the Haggadic narratives relating to Gen. 6.1-4 and to the history of the events of the Flood play an emphatic role.

39. On the differing role of the story from that of Genesis see Delcor 1976. The story about 'the origin of evil' is the starting point of Sacchi's apocalypse interpretation. Sacchi considers the story to be the starting point of an apocalyptic tradition and to be the definition of apocalypse as a genre; see Sacchi 1990: 79-98. Sacchi's conclusions about the genre and about the 'apocalyptical point of view' may be debatable; in any case the appearance of a new viewpoint expressed in the *Book of Watchers* is very important from the point of view of the later Jewish tradition. In the later tradition both versions of the origin of evil appear, emphasizing different messages—Eve's responsibility, or the role of the 'sons of God', or the theory of two human inclinations—see Baudry 1992.

The Asa'el story only relates to the teachings, complementing the Shemihazah story in such a way that it talks about two kinds of receivers of the teachings, men and women; thus here the transmitter of evil is the whole of humankind, and not just the women—the author of the Asa'el story attempts to change the point of view according to which the origin of evil among humans would only be associated with women. The women mentioned in the Shemihazah story, and the men and women mentioned in the Asa'el story are only receivers and transmitters, not instigators of evil; according to the *Book of Enoch* evil essentially springs from outside of humankind.

Differences in the Stories

Apart from the significant differences of the textual context—that is the series of narratives in which the stories of the Watchers, or of the 'sons of gods' appear—the story itself in Gen. 6.1-4 differs in important instances from the narrative of *1 Enoch* 6–11. First of all, Gen. 6.1-4 is not a continuous narrative. Earlier it was defined as a myth fragment,[40] which made its way into the text of Genesis in a historical reinterpretation. Gen. 6.1-4, however is a continuous enumeration of events rather than a continuous narrative[41]—and this characteristic requires an explanation. The text of Gen. 6.1-4 tells of how people multiplied on earth 'and daughters were born to them'. Seeing this the 'sons of gods' (בני אלהים) took those women who attracted them. At the time when this happened, the נפילים lived on earth; they were heroes (גברים), they were the 'heroes of old, people of renown' of that era.[42] The comment following the story—that 'when the Lord saw how great was the wickedness of human beings on earth and how their every thought and

40. Supporters of this thesis bring examples of works that deal with demi-gods, heroes or gods who were born of the relationships of gods and human women from the Greek, Ugaritic, and Phoenician mythologies, with which the Israelite author of Gen. 6.1-4 may also have been familiar; see Westermann 1985: II, 512-13.

41. On the problems of the interconnections see Westermann 1985: II, 494-96.

42. Skinner (1930) considers the identification of the two terms to be an after the fact explanation. Cassuto (1943), based on certain verses of Ezek. 32, identifies the נפילים with beings defeated in battle and returned to Sheol, that is the nether world; similarly Zimmerli (1979: 789-90) sees a connection between the texts of Genesis and Ezekiel; he sees an allusion in Ezek. 32.27 to the events narrated in Gen. 6.1-4. In connection with the נפילים he refers to the Greek and Mesopotamian figures of demigods as a general basis.

inclination were always wicked' (6.5)—serves as the justification for the punishment of the Flood, the description of which follows the story about the sons of gods.

Genesis 6 and Enoch

Gen. 6.1-4 is like a series of glosses, which can be interpreted with the help of the text of *1 Enoch* 6–7, or in the light of a tradition similar to it in content, as it seems to be debating with it.[43] In connection with this narrative two factors have to be kept in mind: the first, that according to the narrative the נפילים—whom the text calls 'men of renown' (אנשי השם)[44] (Gen. 6.1-4) are merely the contemporaries, witnesses of the stories; between them and the daughters of men there is no relationship whatsoever—therefore their appearance has no continuation or consequence in human history. In the tradition of the *Book of Enoch*, however, it is the very appearance and activities of the giants that brings about events of decisive importance from the point of view of human history. With this comment the text of Genesis simply cuts off the flow of the narrative, and excludes the consequences of the relationship of 'sons of gods' and the daughters of men from the history of humankind.

The other factor is that in the tradition of Genesis the sins of the antediluvian era have no concrete definition—whereas the promises made in the covenant with God following the deluge are concrete indeed: 'nor shall I ever again kill all living creatures, as I have just done. "As long as the earth lasts, seedtime and harvest, cold and heat, summer

43. According to Milik (1976: 30-32) the tradition of the Enochic *Book of Watchers* may be older than that of Genesis, and he bases this supposition on the 'abridged and allusive formulation' of the text of Gen. 6.1-4, which he considers to be a short summary of the Enochic tradition. Similarly Black (1987) thinks that Enoch may be the source for the episode of Gen. 6.1-4, and not its consequence. Milik also hypothesized that at Qumran *1 Enoch* was transmitted as a work consisting of five books, a kind of 'Enochic Pentateuch'; his hypothesis was strongly and with justice criticized by his reviewers; see Knibb and Ullendorf 1977; Greenfield and Stone 1979. Nevertheless questions pertaining to Gen. 6.1-4 and the *Book of Watchers* are not all answered.

44. The interpretation of the expression is problematic, as in compounds which mean 'reputation' the noun שם always appears without an article; Gen. 6.1-4 and Num. 16.2 constitute exceptions. Professor A. Malamat was kind enough to call my attention to this problem. It is possible that the pronominal form is related to the name of a deity. In any case the problem requires further study.

and winter, day and night, they will never cease"' (Gen. 8.21-22). 'I am now establishing my covenant with you...and with every living creature that is with you...' (Gen. 9.9-10). All the author of the narrative of the Enoch tradition did when he created his narrative was to 'conform' the sins preceding the Flood to these promises and to stress that the sins were transgressions against the order of nature (here, most likely consciously he uses the categories of Genesis 1, the Priestly creation story). This point of view is also reflected in those elements which appear in the prefatory text (*1 En.* 1–5). The latter primarily stresses the perfection and order prevailing prior to the Flood: 'Observe ye the earth and consider its works,...that nothing at all changes...' (*1 En.* 2.2); then it illustrates the constancy apparent in nature from the changing of the seasons through the regularity of the orbit of planets and contrasts this constancy with the characteristics of the era of the giants descending from the Watchers: 'But ye, ye changed your works [and do not do His Word]'; with this it regards them the ancestors of sinners and the wicked (*1 En.* 5.4).

Sins Causing the Flood: The Meaning and Origin of the Watchers

Does the origin of the story of the Watchers lie in historical or social models? There are several suggestions according to which the background and origin of the story of the Watchers and of Asa'el constitute a criticism of the practices of the Temple and of the priesthood in general in the post-exilic period;[45] others suppose that it may have been occasioned by the reforms of Ezra, the prohibition of mixed marriages,[46] or possibly by the *diadochoi* wars.[47] Talmon raises the question that Israel's errors mentioned in the Damascus Document ('those in which all Israel were in error', CD 3.14), which began with the downfall of the Watchers, would in fact have been the use of a calendar system which was considered to be erroneous[48]—thus the isolated group which created

45. Suter 1979.
46. Rubinkiewicz 1988.
47. Nickelsburg 1977.
48. Talmon 1958. The close connection between the collection of Enoch and the calendrical tradition is shown by a part of the collection, the *Book of Luminaries*, which is dated as contemporaneous with the Watchers tradition. Milik considers the *Astrological Book*, found among the Aramaic fragments, also to belong to the *1 Enoch* collection; see Milik 1976: 7-22. In the Qumran library it is not only *1 Enoch* that shows a special interest in calendars; the calendars surviving in the Temple Scroll, 4Q

1 Enoch and also the Damascus Document, and which used its own calendar at variance with the official one, would have tried to justify its separateness and the correctness of its calendar by tracing back the differences in calendric systems to a cosmic upheaval in the mythical past. Although further instances of the errors mentioned in the Damascus Document have nothing to do with chronology and calendars, the Watchers story itself might have been related to ideas concerning the calendrical system (see the names of the Watchers and the partially astral nature of their teachings).

In the story of the Watchers, however, with regard to the message of the story and maybe even its origin the key words are provided by the sins; the טמא, 'becoming defiled', which resulted from the relationship of the Watchers with daughters of men,[49] and furthermore the sins of the giants descending from them: cannibalism, the sins committed against the animals of the land, water and air, as well as the drinking of blood (*1 En.* 7.4-5)—this is why the earth 'made the accusation against the wicked, concerning everything which was done upon it' (*1 En.* 7.6). The origin of evil then is found in the sins defiling the land. The relationship between the Watchers and the daughters of men—whether they transgressed against a specific sexual prohibition in their relationship or not—in and of itself is considered to be unclean, to be the violation of the boundaries raised between different groups.[50] The relationship of the Watchers and the women, as a sin belonging to the category of transgression against a sexual prohibition, defiles the land.[51] According to Num. 35.33 murder defiles the land;[52] in several instances the Mosaic laws condemn the sin of sorcery (in one instance, Lev. 19.26, together with the consumption of blood; according to Deut. 18.9-14 the Canaanites are driven out by Yahweh before the Israelites, and this is the reason

MMT, and furthermore the so called Mishmerot-texts contain various calendar texts with a differing system from that of the official calendar of Jerusalem. On the calendars of Qumran see Glessmer 1993.

49. See Dimant 1974: 23-72, who considers the relationship of the Watchers and the women, and the story of the giants, to be separate narratives.

50. According to Lev. 19.19, 'You must observe my statutes. You may not allow two different kinds of animals to mate together. You are not to plant your field with two kinds of seed, nor to wear a garment woven with two kinds of yarn.'

51. Lev. 19.29: 'The land is not to play the prostitute and be full of lewdness.'

52. Purification takes place when somebody is killed. If the murderer is unknown the inhabitants have to take care of purification; cf. Deut. 21.1-9; also in the case of someone who died in war, Num. 31.19-20.

why they lose their land). The sins committed against animals may mean the violation of dietary laws, that is consumption of animals of the land, water or air considered to be unclean, or the consumption of clean animals under circumstances considered to be unclean, for example that of a fallen animal or an animal torn by beasts (cf. Lev. 11.39-40; 17.15; 22.8); and the consumption of meat without draining the blood (cf. Lev. 17.13-14).[53] Prohibition against the consumption of blood appears separately and emphatically in several places, once among the Noahide laws (Gen. 9.4; Lev. 19.26; etc.). In the apocryphal works known from the Qumran library—from which we know the Aramaic texts of *1 Enoch*—and from elsewhere similar prescriptions played an especially significant role; special emphasis was placed on the prohibition against the consumption of blood, and the requirement of strictly observing the sabbath and the dietary laws. It seems that the pseudo-myth of the Watchers created from Mesopotamian elements is about this: in the view of the author of the story of the Watchers the 'sinners' are a group of people using a different calendrical tradition from that of the group transmitting *1 Enoch*; they do not follow the dietary laws, and engage in forbidden practices and magical practices. This behaviour is made to appear as the origin of evil and the sin which brought the punishment of the Flood onto humankind. Thus then the Watchers tradition also serves as self-definition, the tradition of a distinctive group. In the light of their written tradition it is clear that members of the Qumran community believed themselves to have lived in an age which was soon to be ended by divine judgment: these people saw a parallel between their own era and that of Enoch, between themselves and and the 'righteous' Enoch.[54] The traditions dealing with the Flood and the preceding age—which to us seem mythical but in the eyes of the group transmitting the *Book of Enoch* constituted a historical analogy—were extremely popular and in all likelihood played a very significant role in the world-view of the community. The antecedents of the *Book of Enoch* were not of Qumranite origin, or at least

53. The latter is an especially severe prescription; its punishment is that 'whoever eats it is to be cut off', while transgressing against the former merely makes the transgression unclean.

54. This tradition must have been very popular as in addition to the narrative of *1 En. 6–11* several other text fragments have been found at Qumran which are parallels of this narrative, or which may have served as its source. Thus for example the fragments of a work called the *Book of Noah* in Caves I and IV (1Q 19 = DJD I, pp. 84-86, Table XVI; see also 1Q 19; 4Q Mes. ar and 4Q180-81).

they did not belong to the spatially segregated settled community[55]—however, the work was clearly popular in the Qumran library, with regard to the number of manuscripts and also with respect to the frequent occurrence of works associated with certain traditions of the book.

The Afterlife of the Watchers Stories

The transformation of the tradition of the Watchers has already begun in the later tradition of the Enochic book. The text of *1 En.* 8.1-3, which also belongs to the Asa'el tradition, is nothing else but the reworking of the teachings told in 7.1d-e. In the version presented by the author of *1 En.* 8.1-3 the list of the teachings of the Watchers is longer and more varied than the enumeration of the earlier tradition. According to this the Watchers taught people weapon-making, metallurgy and the making of cosmetics, and the author also mentions here the teachings already familiar from the Shemihazah narrative: 'cutting of roots', magic, and sorcery. Finally the text enumerates the various areas of the interpretation of omina, which the same Watchers taught to the people.

Those parts of the Enochic tradition which came into being later, and those pieces of the apocryphal and pseudepigraphic literature also known from Qumran which were familiar with this tradition, show changes in their interpretation of the tradition about the origin of evil. The text of *1 En.* 15.8-12 complements the Shemihazah tradition.[56] According to this the descendants of the Watchers and the daughters of men are evil spirits, demons (Ethiopian *nafsat*, Greek *pneumata*, *1 En.* 15.8). These beings are spiritual in nature, following their fathers' characteristics: they do not eat, they are not thirsty and know no obstacles. Their destructiveness first and foremost affects children and women, as they were born of women. This is a kind of complementary explanation to the tradition of chs. 6–7 of the text.

Chapters 65 and 69 of the Enochic collection are of later origin than the sections discussed so far.[57] These are also based on the narrative of

55. For archaeological proof of the existence of the settlement from the middle of the second century BCE see Laperrousaz 1976. G.W.E. Nickelsburg dates the tradition of the Watchers to between 400 and 165, which also antedates the foundation of the Qumran community; see Nickelsburg 1991.

56. This part of the text is only known from Ethiopian and Greek translations; judging by the tiny fragments of 4Q En. ar./c, however, it definitely belonged to the Enoch tradition, which was created before the second century BCE.

57. On the questions of the dating see Schürer 1973–79: III.1, 257-59.

1 Enoch 6–11—they constitute complementary information, embellishments and explanations. These texts merely repeat the earlier motifs associated with the teachings, enlarging the list of the names of the Watchers. *1 Enoch* 65 supplements the list of the teachings of Asa'el by adding that the Watchers also taught people the making of cast metal statues and the changing of the qualities of metals. According to *1 Enoch* 69 a Watcher named Pinem'e taught people writing and the use of ink and papyrus—things that later could be the source of several misunderstandings.

The other narratives of the Enochic tradition mentioning the Watchers are the so-called 'Animal Apocalypses' of chs. 85–89 and the text, only known from Qumran, denoted by 4Q180-81, does not provide anything new about the teachings of the Watchers. The tradition which relates the appearance of the Watchers on earth to the origin of evil, and which classifies the nature of 'evil' disappears from the texts originating in the first half of the second century BCE. The next time we find the tradition of the Watchers is in the *Book of Jubilees* written at the turn of the second and first centuries BCE in a quite conscious and radical revision (see Chapter 4 below).

Chapter 3

DANIELIC AND ENOCHIC TRADITION ON THE EVE OF THE MACCABEAN REVOLT

The middle of the second century BCE, the mid-60s, is the age of the re-evaluation and the recreation of former tradition among Palestinian Jewry. Re-evaluation and revision were made timely by historical events. Following 198 BCE Palestine changed hands, becoming part of the Seleucid empire having been part of the Ptolemaic empire. Its position, at least to begin with, was no less favourable than before.[1] From the reign of Antiochus IV Epiphanes (175–164 BCE), however, Jewish opinion, which had always been loyal towards the Ptolemaic rulers,[2] evaluated the Seleucid ruling house very differently. The Jews were especially offended by the policies of Antiochus IV Epiphanes which disregarded local characteristics and traditions:[3] the Maccabean revolt broke out during his reign, which, at least at the beginning, was supported by the Hasidic groups, who practised religion according to their own special

1. Under Antiochus III it was markedly good and the ruler granted them various favours; see Bickerman 1935; 1955. During the reign of Antiochus III the Seleucid empire was overwhelmed by Rome. The financial burdens of Rome loaded the inhabitants of the Seleucid empire with increasing taxes. The problematic politics and personality of Antiochus IV called forth the opposition of the Jewish population; see the excellent analyses of E. Will: Will 1972–75: II, 391-420; 1966–67: II, 253-98

2. The best expression of this sentiment is the Aristeas letter from the second half of the second century BCE (Pelletier 1962), which tells of the preparation of the Greek tradition of the Old Testament, with many legendary elements, and transmitted in the spirit of absolute loyalty towards Ptolemaios Philadelphos, the ruler.

3. Bickerman (1937: 8) stresses the role of the priestly groups in the escalation of the crisis. As a consequence of the decree of 168 BCE against the Jewish religion, the former upper class, that is the members of the senate, the Elders, and the new class of wealthy people seized properties of those sentenced to punishment with the support of the Seleucid powers. The withdrawal of the decree Nov.–Dec. 165 BCE (2 Macc. 11.27-33) did not imply the return of the properties of the priests. This was the reason why the Maccabeans—also a priestly family—continued the struggle even after the Temple had been restored and purified; see Hyldahl 1990.

precepts.[4] Questions relating to the historical period and the future were formulated during the reign of Antiochus Epiphanes, who was considered to be an arrogant and cruel tyrant.[5] These questions are basically similar to the ones formulated after 568 BCE: what will be the fate of the chosen people? Will God punish their oppressors? How can the present rule be interpreted: as failure or a period of assigned punishment? Works of the era very often answer these questions with reinterpretations of the earlier prophetic—or pseudo-prophetic—tradition.

Daniel 7, 8–12

The collection of Daniel 7 and 8–12 also ties in with the earlier part of the Danielic collection, primarily with the tradition of ch. 2. On the basis of its language and literary characteristics, Daniel 7 is related to the collection beginning with ch. 2 but I will discuss it in conjunction with chs. 8–12 because of the time of its creation and its message, which is a vision and prophecy of the downfall of Antiochus Epiphanes. In a literary sense then it is the conclusion of the Aramaic collection of chs. 2–7.[6] From the point of view of Jewish attitudes to history, however, it constitutes a beginning and a model for certain forms of the vision-and-prophecy literature of the second century. Beginning with ch. 8 the language of the book of Daniel is Hebrew, but the subsequent pieces are contemporaneous with Daniel 7. One explanation for the change of language may be that a Hebrew collection came into being following the Aramaic Daniel tradition, partly after the manner of the Aramaic, but with many differences and characteristics springing from individual variation or from another tradition. This retains many of the characteristics of the Aramaic section, but does not use the language, and there are other differences as well. In any case, the collection of chs. 8–12 has been linked with the Aramaic part, which probably ended with Daniel 7. The first piece of the later Danielic collection (which most likely is also

4. 1 and 2 Maccabees chronicle the reign of Antiochus and the beginnings of the revolt from a Jewish perspective. On the background of the policies and propaganda of Antiochus and on the various rebel groups see Bickerman 1937; Bringmann 1983; Mörkholm 1963: 17-20; Mörkholm 1966: 130-34. On the meaning of the word 'Hasid' and on questions of its identification with various social groups see Lightstone 1983.

5. Antiochus strongly emphasized his own divine status. See Mörkholm 1963; 1966.

6. See Miller 1991.

the first in chronological order), the narrative of ch. 7, follows the theme and formal arrangement of ch. 2, and most likely was created with that as a model. Chapter 7 also describes a vision seen in a dream. The person seeing the vision is Daniel—he is also the interpreter of the dream—and after the dream he himself records the vision (7.1). In Daniel's vision, he 'saw the Great Sea churned up by the four winds of heaven, and four great beasts rising out of the sea, each one different from the others' (7.2-3). The three animals of the vision—endowed not only with great size but fantastic attributes as well—were the lion, bear and leopard. The author of Daniel 7 does not name the fourth animal, but provides its description: 'I saw a fourth beast, fearsome and grisly and exceedingly strong, with great iron teeth. It devoured and crunched, and trampled underfoot what was left. It was different from all the beasts which went before it, and had ten horns' (7.7).

A little horn emerges from among the ten horns, and 'three of the first horns were uprooted to make room for it' (7.8-9); in the parts following the vision is about the fate of the little horn and about the destruction of the fourth beast (7.11-12), but wedged into the description of the emergence of the little horn, its fate and the text of the interpretation of the vision about the four animals, is the description of another vision in two parts. In this Daniel sees thrones: 'thrones were set in place and the Ancient in Years took his seat', whose hair is like wool, his throne is constituted of flames, and a river of fire springs from under it. The first part of the throne vision concludes with the image of judgment: 'The court sat, and the books were opened' (7.9-10). This is followed by the destruction of the fourth beast, after which the previous vision resumes: 'I saw one like a human being coming with the clouds of the heaven; he approached the Ancient in Years and was presented to him. Sovereignty and glory and kingly power were given to him, so that all peoples and nations of every language should serve him; his sovereignty was to be an everlasting sovereignty...and his kingly power was never to be destroyed' (7.13-14).

The vision of the beasts and the throne vision may have been separate texts originally, which belonged to different traditions. The description of the visions is followed by their interpretation, the פשר, which is given to Daniel by 'one of those who were standing there'; here, however, the elements of the two visions merge. The description of the tenth horn of the fourth beast is completed by a comment which alludes to the figure of the Ancient in Years of the second vision: 'this horn was waging war on the holy ones and proving too strong for them until the Ancient in Years came. The judgment was pronounced in favour of the holy ones of the Most High, and the time came when the holy ones gained possession of the kingly power' (7.21-22). Subsequently the interpretation of the figure of the fourth animal is resolved with the interpretation of the vision of the throne and the judgment (7.25-27).

The beasts mentioned in the text, like certain elements of the statue vision of Daniel 2, signify 'empires' or rather reigns (מלכו) (cf. the פשר of the vision of Dan. 2), and the horns refer to kings (7.23-24). However, despite all the similarities in the structure and style of the vision about the four beasts and the vision of Daniel 2, we have no reason to suppose that the meaning of this vision would be exactly the same as that of Daniel 2 (whether we are thinking of the probable Persian period meaning of Daniel 2 or of the Hellenistic reinterpretation of the revised text). In fact we have reason to suppose that the author of the text may have intended to change the interpretation of the historical prophecy given by the author of Daniel 2, or to supplement it, and to adapt it somehow to his own era. The fact that, most probably consciously, he uses the vision of Daniel 2 as a model, only shows that Daniel 2, as a work expressing a certain kind of historical consciousness, may have been very popular and respected in the intellectual milieu in which the author of Daniel 7 lived.

The beasts of the vision of Daniel 7 have symbolic value. The attributes of the beasts (wings, the number of heads, the description of the characteristics) allow us to identify them with the concrete representatives of territories, or their rulers. The identification is not easy, however. In the course of centuries the text had been commented upon by numerous ecclesiastical authors and scholars who attempted to identify the four kingdoms with historical periods and rulers. The conclusion varies greatly from one interpretation to another.[7] In any case the work of Jerome (fourth century CE), which is the most significant ancient commentary on the book of Daniel was determinant for subsequent identifications and interpretations. Jerome identified the four kingdoms analogously with the interpretation of the prophecy of Daniel 2, in a diachronic system. In the first kingdom, symbolized by the lion, he saw the Neo-Babylonian empire. He identified the bear with the Persian

7. On the interpretations see Braverman 1978. On the identification of the kingdoms and relating them to different eras see Goez 1958: 366-77; Koch 1980: 182-99.

kingdom, the leopard with Macedonian rule, and the fourth beast with the Roman empire.[8] Jerome's identification reflects the Christian interpretation of his age, an interpretation made to fit his own era, which is no longer accepted today; it is well known that the *terminus ante quem* of the compilation, or writing, of certain parts of the Danielic collection must have been 165 BCE. Jerome's method—of looking for the kingdoms with which to identify the four beasts in a diachronic historical system—is still, however, alive and well. Current opinion accepts the identification of the kingdoms mentioned in the text with the Neo-Babylonian, Medean, Persian, and Greek empires (i.e. with the successor states of Alexander the Great). This is similar to the interpretation of Daniel 2 in the Hellenistic period. On the basis of the similarities of the fourfold schema (four 'reigns') and of the language (Aramaic) some scholars consider chs. 2 and 7 to belong to the same layer of the Danielic tradition, that is, they think that both narratives came into being in the Neo-Babylonian–Persian period.[9] However, the schema, the language and other shared features (e.g. the circumstances of the vision, the method of dating, the similarity of the method of the *pesher*, i.e. of the interpretation) do not necessarily prove that the two narratives are contemporaneous and that they belong to the same layer of tradition: the common features may also be the result of conscious imitation—and most likely they are. In addition, Daniel 7 contains elements which cannot be found in Daniel 2. In Daniel 7 the vision about the 'four beasts', and its *pesher* is intercalated by another vision and its interpretation: that of the Ancient of Days (7.9-13, 13-14). The style of this section, however, is more akin to the descriptions of the visions of Ezekiel: the throne, and the figure sitting on it, the spring originating under the throne (cf. Ezek. 1; 10.4-6).[10]

8. Jerome, *Commentar libri Danielis*, cols. 528–30. Interestingly, Jerome relates the three ribs in the mouth to the events recounted in the book of Esther, to the time when during the reign of Ahasuerus they wanted to annihilate the Jews; cf. *ibid*., col. 529.

9. Noth 1926; Eerdmans 1947.

10. On the connections of Ezekiel with other works of the Jewish tradition of the Neo-Babylonian and Persian periods see Baltzer 1971. Most likely the description of Enoch's throne vision in the Enochic tradition (*1 En.* 14) also uses Ezekiel; the similarity of its motifs and vocabulary has already been noted by Charles (1893: 33-35) and by Beer (in Kautzsch 1900: II, 244-46). For its detailed analysis see Black 1976; Gruenwald 1980: 32-37. The Qumran Songs for the Sabbath Sacrifice describes a similar locale; see Strugnell 1960: 335-45; the complete critical edition of the text in Newsom 1985.

The symbols representing the four 'reigns' in the narrative of Daniel 7 are different from the statue symbol of Daniel 2—and they may originate from a different body of tradition. In Daniel 2 four parts of one statue represent the four מלכו. In Daniel 7 four figures represent the same; it may be important that the four beasts appear *at the same time*; thus a synchronic explanation for the מלכו may also be possible.[11] The beasts of Daniel 7—as already mentioned—always appear with some kind of attribute, on the basis of which they may be identified with concrete eras; henceforth they do not function as symbols, but as allusions. Thus the lion had eagle's wings, the bear had three ribs between its teeth, the leopard had four heads and 'four wings like those of a bird on its back', and the fourth beast had ten horns, and an eleventh little horn which grew out after the others. In addition we find other references to the age and milieu symbolized by the animals. The system of complementary attributes is only clear in the case of the fourth beast: we may identify the ten horns of the animal with the succession of Seleucid rulers, and the eleventh horn and 'the mouth that uttered bombast' (Dan. 7.8) with Antiochus IV Epiphanes. Staub has identified the beast itself—which is not named by the text—with the battle elephant.[12] This animal—which in the ancient Near East was used only by the Seleucid army—appears several times on the coins issued by the Seleucid rulers. The fourth beast, then, is a characteristic symbolic reference to the Seleucid period. Reference to a state in terms of some characteristic (in this case as an instrument of war) is an emblematic symbol. Assuming that the symbols of the vision constitute a coherent system, we may also interpret the other animals using the same logic.[13]

It is customary to identify the first of the other animals—the lion, whose 'wings...were plucked' first, and then 'it was lifted up from the

11. Eerdmans argued in this manner too, but he placed it in a Babylonian-Persian milieu; he identifies the 11th horn with Nabuna'id; see Rowley 1935: 169.

12. Staub 1978.

13. So far the beasts of Dan. 7 have been interpreted according to different systems: as mythical animals, or the chaos monsters of Mesopotamian myths; Gunkel 1895: 239; Hölscher 1922: 192, A.32. Others suppose them to have originated from a tradition of the interpretation of the constellations of stars in Babylonian astrology: Caquot 1955: 9ff.; Zevit 1968: 385ff. According to P.A. Porter, the antecedents of the animal figures of Dan. 7–8 would be the Babylonian animal omens ('summa izbu'-texts); see Porter 1983. Herzfeld (1947: 831-33) sees the memory of later Achaemenid animal representations in them; Eerdmans (1932) supposes Persian period symbols, while Beek (1935: 49) holds them to be the symbols of Persian kings.

earth, and made stand upon the feet as a man, and a man's heart was given to it' (7.4)—with the Neo-Babylonian empire, partly on the basis of the fourfold schema of Daniel 2, and partly on the basis of the section of Dan. 4.25-34 about the madness and recovery of Nebuchadnezzar. This identification is not necessarily well-founded, partly because the analogy with Daniel 2 is not conclusive, and partly because the motifs of the narrative of Dan. 4.25-34 and the references of Dan. 7.4 do not entirely correspond. Similarly, the identification of the second and third beasts with the Medean and Persian empires is uncertain.

Hanhart[14] answers the question very convincingly. His starting point is the text of Dan. 7.2-3, which, with regard to the appearance of the beasts merely says that: 'I saw the Great Sea churned up by the four winds of heaven, and four great beasts rising (יעלו) out of the sea...' without noting their order of appearance. Hanhart attempts to identify the third animal of the vision, the leopard, on the basis of a vision in the Revelation of John (Rev. 13). This part of Revelation consciously builds on the vision of Daniel 7, making use of its elements and of the animal symbolism. It is not impossible (though neither is it an established fact, but we may make it our hypothetical starting point) that the author of the above-mentioned vision of Revelation also followed the interpretation of the animal symbolism of the author of Daniel 7, which by now has become obscure for us. In the first vision in ch. 13 of Revelation (13.1-10), a beast appears from the sea. This animal is similar to a leopard and has numerous attributes referring to various animals. The animal of the vision of Rev. 13.1-10 may be identified unequivocally with Rome. It may be supposed that the author chose the leopard as the symbol of Rome because he knew this to be the meaning of the leopard of Daniel 7. It is not unimaginable then—indeed, it is rather probable—that the author of Daniel 7 had Rome in mind at the time of the creation of the symbol of the leopard and its attributes. By the time of the reign of Antiochus IV Epiphanes (the last, little, horn of the fourth animal may be clearly identified with him, as the prophecy came into being during his time), during the first half of the second century BCE, Rome already exerted a very significant influence in the eastern basin of the Mediterranean Sea. Therefore it could, justifiably, appear in the vision of a Jewish author surveying the significant powers of the age.

Hanhart identifies the other two animals of Daniel 7 with Egypt (lion) and the Parthian kingdom (bear). The attributes of the beasts may also be

14. Hanhart 1981.

related to the events of the first half of the second century BCE; the lifting up of the lion may be linked to the changes taking place at the Ptolemaic court.[15] The three ribs in the mouth of the bear may be related to the three successive Iranian kingdoms—Medean, Persian and Parthian.[16]

The possibility of a synchronic interpretation is supported by the introductory words of Daniel 7 prior to the vision, which mention the 'four winds' (Dan. 7.2). The 'four winds' expression may be of Mesopotamian origin. In Mesopotamian texts the expression usually serves to denote the four points of the compass, but it also has a special mantic role as well: in one of Nabuna'id's inscriptions Marduk roused whirlwinds from the four cardinal points to remove the sands which covered the Ebabbar, thus disclosing its old foundations.[17] Here, the winds appearing from the four points of the compass have revelatory power; according to the legend, they reveal the foundations of the old building to the king, so that he can build the new temple on them. It is not accidental that the author of Daniel 7 mentions the four cardinal points in the introduction to his vision, since the four states—here interpreted as synchronous—appear according to these: Egypt (south), Parthian kingdom (east), Rome (west), Seleucid kingdom (north). The centre, from which the seer of the vision views the 'reigns' (מלכו), is Palestine.

Based on the above it may be concluded that the symbolism of the vision of Daniel 7 derives from a different principle and was created later than the symbolism of ch. 2, which made use of the motifs of the prophetic tradition preceding the Babylonian exile.[18] The symbolism of ch. 7 reflects the realities of the age of the author as much as the vision of ch. 2 does, but this reality is completely different: Daniel 7, unlike the visions of the earlier section, reflects the world and the symbols of the Hellenistic kingdoms. The figure of the winged lion representing Egypt was most likely inspired by the sphinx. The bear cannot be defined so precisely. It is an image known from the prophetic tradition, repre-

15. The plucking of the wings of the lion means the reduction of the power of the state symbolized by the animal. This may be a reference to the changes taking place at the turn of the third and second centuries, when Ptolemaic Egypt lost its power over Palestine. The lifting up and the bestowing of a human heart in all likelihood refer to the occasionally occurring pro-Jewish tendencies, most likely to the pro-Jewish policies of Ptolemy Philometor (181–146 BC) and his wife, Cleopatra (cf. Josephus, *Ant.* 12.4 ff.).

16. Hanhart 1981.

17. Langdon 1912: 288-97 (Nabonidus, Nr. 9); see Beaulieu 1989: 56.

18. See the conclusions of the previous chapter.

senting a wild, strong, and barbaric invader, and the author of Daniel 7 may have used its figure to represent the Parthians who were considered to be all three. Based on a similar logic the leopard became the symbol of the resolute and strong Rome. The elephant is the only one, which—as the battle animal used in the Seleucid army—refers directly and unequivocally to its referent.

The vision, then, is an overview of the powers in existence in the basin of the Mediterranean Sea, and it is a prophecy of the downfall of one of them, the Seleucid empire. This downfall, according to the author of the text will take place during the time of Antiochus Epiphanes (175–164 BCE): based on this, it is likely that the author of Daniel 7 wrote his work during the reign of Antiochus Epiphanes, before the latter's death, at a time when, according to the evidence of contemporary sources (Dan. 9; 10–12; *1 En.* 85–89; 93; 91), change was awaited with great impatience.[19]

The author of Daniel 7 uses the fourfold schema of an earlier work, Daniel 2. It is possible that this schema, which by the second–first century BCE had become very popular, could have had variants already in the earlier period of Hellenism. There had been similarly structured political prophecies prior to the second century BCE—however, we do not know if the interpretation of the schema had changed, or how. In any case, the author of Daniel 7 used the tradition of the fourfold schema in a different, reinterpretive way.

Most likely the narrative of Daniel 7 originated in popular tradition. This is attested by the fact that its author wrote it in Aramaic which had been the vernacular of the area of Mesopotamia and Syria since the Persian era. Formally it continues the same Aramaic language tradition, the tradition of Daniel 2 and the first half of the Danielic collection. Like Daniel 2 the narrative describes a vision and gives its interpretation, or *pesher*. However, while the text may have been written in the Hellenistic period, there is no internal evidence that it was a Hellenistic revision of an earlier prophecy, like Daniel 2. The author of Daniel 7 also refers to another tradition, that of the throne vision of Ezekiel, and links this to the motif of the judgment, in which, after the fall of the fourth מלכו, the eternal kingdom of the 'saints' will follow. He does not use the Watchers tradition, nor does he deal with the age of the Flood—nevertheless the

19. Fischer's interpretation—the Son of Man stands for Judas Maccabeus—seems to be highly probable, for the oracle refers to events on the eve of the Maccabean revolt and reflects expectations of the same era; see Fischer 1980.

tradition of *1 Enoch* is present in Daniel 7, in several instances. On the one hand this work also uses the tradition of the Ezechielic throne vision and we do not know what kind of links may have existed between *1 Enoch* 14 and Daniel 7. On the other hand, in Daniel 7 the announcement of the eternal kingdom of the 'saints' and the cosmic judgment and the downfall of the fourth empire are followed by words invoking the introductory part of *1 Enoch*, in which Enoch tells a historical parable to the righteous elect (בחירין קשיטין), who 'will be present on the day of tribulation to remove all the enemies and the righteous will be delivered' (*1 En.* 1.1).

The genre of vision and *pesher* is not only used in Daniel 7, but also flourishes in chs. 8–12—all of which were created during the first half of the second century BCE. The prophecies of ch. 8 are also communicated in this form by its author. Animal figures appear in this vision as well. The prophecy reviews the history of the Persian empire, the empire of Alexander the Great and the Seleucid empire, up to the age of Antiochus Epiphanes.[20] The author of the prophecy expects the death of Antiochus in the near future. According to the calculations of the text 'For two thousand three hundred evenings and mornings; then the Holy Place will be restored' (Dan. 8.14); that is, the predicted event, the cleansing of the Temple, will take place three and a half years after the decree of Antiochus in 167 BCE, which elicited strong opposition. This did indeed take place at the end of 164 BCE subsequent to the successful battles of Judas Maccabeus. It is to this that the prophecy of Daniel 8 refers, so that it must have been written soon after 164.

Daniel 8 shows the influence of Daniel 7 in every respect, although their language differs; the author of Daniel 8 uses Hebrew, which was considered to be more elevated and literary. The method of the vision and interpretation (*pesher*) and the animal symbolism are, however, the same. The two-horned ram, which thrusts west, north and south with its horns symbolizes the conquests of the Persian empire (8.2-4, 20). The text calls the he-goat coming from the west 'the king of Yawan' (8.21)—this animal represents the Macedonian ('Grecian') kingdom. The little

20. In the vision, a he-goat arriving from the west represents Alexander the Great, or rather the conquering Macedonian state, and the ram, Persia, the Persian empire. The animals are the symbols of states; their horns represent rulers. The size of the horns and their fate (they grow, break off) symbolize changes in the power of the rulers. The vision does not provide a detailed overview of the fate of the *diadochoi*. The author is only concerned with the role and fate of Antiochus Epiphanes.

horn between the horns of the he-goat stands for Alexander the Great (8.5-8).

The author of Daniel 8 is also familiar with the schema of the four 'reigns'. Here too, the schema suggests contemporaneous kingdoms, 'four prominent horns pointing towards the four quarters of heaven' (8.8). The four kingdoms emerging at the same time can only be interpreted as the successor states of the empire of Alexander the Great. The text of Daniel 8 is a good example of how the schema overrules reality, how the author of the prophecy insists on the number four even when it no longer reflects reality.[21]

The origin of the symbolism of Daniel 8 is debated.[22] One widely held view is that the symbolic animal figures derive from the zodiac signs (Aries and Capricorn).[23] It is much more likely that we should look for the origin of the symbols in the biblical tradition. The shepherd simile of Ezek. 34.17 and 39.18 and the vision of Zech. 2.1-4 about the horns symbolizing conquering states may have been the forerunners of the tradition of Daniel 8 (Zechariah is also familiar with the historical fourfold schema).

In chs. 7–8 of Daniel there also appears a feature which, in the later apocalyptic, becomes a characteristic motif: the *pesher* of the revelation is received by the addressee through the mediation of a heavenly being, an angel (7.15-16; 8.15-16). In the Danielic tradition the intermediary heavenly being is the angel Gabriel.[24] This motif further underscores the characteristic revelatory nature of the *pesher*-s of the Danielic tradition. The Danielic visions can have one interpretation only, and this interpretation is based on divine revelation. The interpretation cannot be arrived at through learning (cf. the Mesopotamian handbooks of dream interpretation). Only a chosen person may receive it, from the revelator,

21. See Koch 1980: 116: 'die Vierzahl der Diadochenreiche durch cap. 2.7 hervorgerufen'.

22. Gunkel (1895: 331-55) identifies the monsters of Dan. 7 and 8 with the so-called chaos monsters of the creation stories of the ancient Near East. According to Eissfeldt (1932: 25-27) these figures may be traced back to another mythological figure, Typhon; others (e.g. Ferch 1980) originate them in figures of monsters of Ugaritic mythology. The most general view is that they come from astrological symbols; see Cumont 1909: 263ff.

23. Cumont 1909: 273; Bentzen 1952; Hengel 1969: 336-40; Collins 1977: 107; Porteus 1979: 122. Sahlin (1969: 52) interprets it as an 'Astralisierte Israel-Vorstellung'.

24. Dan. 8.16, 'Gabriel'; Dan. 9.21, 'the man Gabriel'.

through an intermediary.[25] In the Danielic collection the tradition of the narratives of vision and its interpretation continues with the vision of chs. 10–11 and its *pesher*. Daniel receives the revelation described here from a man: 'his face shone like lightning, his eyes flamed like torch...' (10.5-6). The style of the introduction and the description is similar to those of the introductions of Daniel 2–6 and the book of Ezekiel. The vision is revealed only to Daniel, and to no one else who was with him (10.6-7). The source of the vision is God, the intermediary is an angel who even refers to the 'Book of Truth' (10.21) as the source of the revelation. The author of Daniel 10–11 imagines history—the revelation is about historical events—as a process which God had determined, and put in writing, in advance.[26]

The revelation presents an overview of history from the beginning of the Persian rule to the age of the author. The text mentions four Persian rulers: the last among them 'who will far surpass all the others in wealth; and when by his wealth he has extended his power, he will mobilize the whole empire against the kingdom of Greece (Yawan)' (11.2). This text is about Xerxes (484–464 BCE) and the second half of the Greco-Persian war (Yawan = Hellas). The second ruler mentioned is 'a warrior king, who will rule a vast kingdom and do whatever he pleases', but 'once he [is] established, his kingdom will be broken up and divided to the four quarters of heaven. It will not pass to his descendants...' (11.3-4). These references relate to the empire of Alexander the Great, except for the detail according to which, following its breakup, Alexander's empire was divided 'to the four quarters of heaven' (11.34). Here, just as in the introductory lines of the chapter, the formulation of the text of Daniel 10–11 is influenced by the fourfold schema of four empires. The text mentions only four kings in the line of Persian rulers (most likely those whom the author of Daniel 10–11 considered to be the most significant). Similarly, in the case of Alexander the Great it also says that his realm disintegrated into four (cf. Dan. 8.8), even though the one-time empire

25. The *pesher* of the vision is always divine revelation; therefore the vision can only have one meaning, one interpretation—and this is only known to those who belong to the group transmitting the vision literature.

26. The Enochic tradition, which shows many literary parallels with the Danielic cycle, mentions Enoch in several instances, as he sits at future judgments and checks the history of humankind and bears witness against the sinners from tablets which he has with him and which had been written before the beginning of human history. The idea that history is something that may be read from heavenly tablets written in advance is of Mesopotamian origin.

of Alexander the Great was eventually survived by three large successor states.

In the next segment we can read about the union of 'the king of the south' and 'the king of the north' and its unravelling (11.5-9). The events depicted here may be identified with the familiar events of 252–242 BCE: the marriage of Antiochus with Berenice, the daughter of Ptolemy II, which took place in 252 BCE (11.6). This event is the beginning of the same series to which the insertion of Daniel 2 in the Hellenistic period (2.43) refers. This text, however, enumerates in much greater detail—albeit without names—the events leading to the conflict. It alludes to the death of Berenice, of her child and her retinue, furthermore to Ptolemy III's war against Antiochus.[27] The overview of events continues with the description of the military campaign of Antiochus III (223–187 BCE) and Seleucus IV (187–175 BCE) against Egypt (11.10-20). The text mentions that Antiochus III invaded Palestine (11.16), and ends with a description of the events taking place at the time of Antiochus IV (175–164 BCE). Dan. 11.30-35 mentions the king's sojourn in Jerusalem and that Antiochus put an end to the offering of sacrifices in the Temple (167 BCE). Dan. 11.40-45 describes the military campaign of Antiochus Epiphanes against Egypt in the form of a prophecy, and attaches to the events a genuine prophecy about the 'end of times'.[28] The text then, with the exception of the concluding v. 45, is a *vaticinium ex eventu*, that is, a record of the events of the recent past in the form of a prophecy for the future. The concluding verse, however—the foretelling of the death of Antiochus Epiphanes—is a genuine prophecy, from a time before his death. The genuineness of the prophecy is guaranteed by the subsequent unfolding of events. The events prophesied in Dan. 11.45 do not happen, or rather do not happen in the manner foretold. Antiochus did die soon, but not at the time and not under the circumstances prophesied by the version of Daniel 10–11. According to the prophecy the king ought to have died in Jerusalem, on his way back from the Egyptian campaign of 165 BCE—whereas his death took place somewhat later, in 163 BCE, at Elam.[29]

27. The detailed historical references of the text point to the fact that the author of the unusual historical survey used for his short outline excellent historical sources; see Smend 1885: 241; Koch 1980: 118.

28. The southern military expedition of Antiochus IV is evaluated in the Egyptian sources as the height of the arrogance of the king; see Lebram 1975: 760.

29. Cf. the legendary narrative of 1 Macc. 6.1-6 on the illness and death of the

The author of the text does not provide an interpretation to the historical overview of Daniel 10–11, but leaves it to the reader. The key to the interpretation is provided by the names occurring in the text. These names fall into three categories. The first category contains the so-called synchronic names, that is geographical names, in the form and with the meaning used at the time of the author. In fact these names also constitute the key to the interpretation of the other names as well. Such are פרס–Persia (11.2), מצרים–Egypt (11.8, 43), לבים and כשים–Libya and Kush, or rather, the inhabitants of these lands (11.44).

To the second category belong those proper names designating peoples which had already appeared in the earlier tradition of the Bible. These names are actualized by the author of Daniel 10–12; he endows the names with new meanings relevant for his own age. In the earlier tradition these names appear in the book of Genesis. The author of Daniel 10–12 transposes the names for the states and peoples of his own era. Thus Daniel 10–11 applies the name יון (11.2)—which up to then had traditionally denoted the Ionians of Asia Minor (cf. Gen. 10.2, 4; 1.Chron. 1.5, 7 *et passim*)—to the 'Greek' Seleucid state. The term כתיים in the tradition of Genesis is Kition, that is, Cyprus (cf. Gen. 10.4; Isa. 23.10, 12 etc.). In Daniel 10–12, however, it refers to the Romans. The first meaning then is expanded to include all of the Seleucid state as well as the coastal region of Asia Minor, whereas the second name no longer means the island itself, but those arriving from the sea—from the direction of Cyprus—to Palestine.

The third group of names are those which had been created on the basis of some typical or peculiar characteristic of the person denoted ('symbolic names'). The terms 'the king of the south' and 'the king of the north' stand for the Seleucid and Ptolemaic rulers. The basis for the names is the position of the Seleucid and Ptolemaic state viewed from Palestine. The expression 'despicable creature', נבזה (11.21) denotes Antiochus Epiphanes, and refers to the aggressive anti-Jewish policies of the king. In the text the things which are most important to the author also appear in symbolic names: thus the expressions ארץ הצבי ('the fairest of all lands', i.e. Palestine, 11.16), מקדש המעוז ('the sanctuary and citadel', the Temple of Jerusalem, 11.31), and ברית קדש (the holy covenant—probably the 'elect', the religious group to which the author belongs, 11.28). Within the community the משכילי עם ('wise leaders of the nation' or those who 'will give guidance to the people at large') constitute a

king. On these events and the sources see Bickerman 1937: 83-84.

separate group (11.33). The text contrasts them with the other group referred to as מרשיעי ברית ('those who are ready to violate the covenant', 11.32). From the context it seems probable that the author considers himself to be one of the משכילי עם. They are the ones who, possessing special knowledge, engage in teaching (יבינו) (11.33). According to Dan. 11.35 not all of them can live up to the special requirements—some of them 'fall victims for a time, so that they may be tested, refined, and made shining white; for an end is yet to be at the appointed time' (יכשלו לצרוף בהם ולברר וללבן עד־עת קץ כי־עוד למועד).

The historical overviews of the second part (chs. 7–12) of the book of Daniel show a significant change in the view of the historical periods as compared to the overviews of the first part (chs. 2–6). The presentation of the 'fourth reign' had changed: in Daniel 2, it was the weakest of the reigns—by contrast, in Daniel 7 it is represented as an aggressive, arrogant rule. In the overview of Daniel 10–12 the presentation of the Seleucid rulers ends similarly; the last one (Antiochus IV Epiphanes) is portrayed as a symbol of violence and arrogance, and the absolute negative of the holy Israel. In terms of the notion of 'holy war', his fall means the victory of the 'saints of the Most High'.[30]

Historical Consciousness in the Second Century BCE*: The Later Enochic Tradition*

A similar preoccupation (the wish to present a historical overview) and a similar method (vision-like form, but without interpretation and with symbolic names) characterize the *Animal Apocalypse* (*1 En.* 85–90) and the *Apocalypse of the Weeks* (*1 En.* 93 and 91) of the *Ethiopic Book of Enoch*, the two works which are more or less contemporaneous with the second part of the Danielic collection, the description of Daniel 10–11.[31] In the *Animal Apocalypse* the patriarch Enoch tells his son,

30. Veerkamp 1991; Heard 1986.

31. Charlesworth, summarizing and systematizing research up to his time (1983-85, I: 6-7), gives the following definitions: the *Apocalypse of the Weeks* (*1 En.* 93 and 91) is 'early pre-Maccabean'; the *Animal Apocalypse* (*1 En.* 85–90) may have come into being between 165–161 BCE. The re-evaluation of the elements of the Enochic tradition has been going on since the finding and publication of the Qumran Aramaic fragments; the *Animal Apocalypse* and the *Apocalypse of the Weeks* is only contained in the manuscript tradition beginning from the end of the second century BCE; see Milik 1976: 41 On the dating of the pieces of the Enochic collection see Charlesworth 1983–85: I, 6-7; Schürer 1973–79: III.1, 254-60; Nickelsburg 1981a: 48-55.

Metushelah, of his dream (85.1-2). The concluding event of the dream is the outbreak of the Maccabean revolt. Thus, then, the *Apocalypse* is a brief treatment of the historical tradition of the Old Testament: the tradition of the age of the patriarchs, the history of the unified, then divided kingdom, of captivity and deliverance, and of the Persian, then the Seleucid rule. The final part of the narrative recalls the Maccabean revolt. We find the key to the symbols of the text—the depiction of the historical events—in the books of the Maccabeans, as well as in the historical books of Josephus (*Ant.* 12.6–13.6). The omissions and emphases of the condensed historical tradition are deliberate. The author of the *Apocalypse* highlights certain biblical events and elsewhere tells of events which differ from the biblical tradition. The most efficient tool for expressing and stressing his views is the system of symbols, which he employs systematically throughout the course of the narrative. This use of symbols deriving from a very long tradition automatically enriches the meaning of the narrative by expanding its connotations. The reader familiar with this tradition interprets the text on the basis of this background meaning of the symbol, by recalling analogies from the past traditions of the meaning of the symbol.

In *1 Enoch* 85–90 the white bull symbolizes the 'righteous' and the 'elect'. Adam (85.8-10), Noah (89.1), Sem (89.10), Abraham (89.11) and Isaac (89.11) appear in this form. Among the list of the elect Noah stands out (cf. Gen. 6.8). After an angel reveals to him the secret of the approaching Flood, the white bull (Noah) becomes human, and in the remainder of the narrative he continues to appear as a human being (89.1-9). (He is the only one among the characters of the narrative to reach this form, which is obviously rated as a higher order by the author.) The text of the *Apocalypse*, however, also mentions black bulls and cows who descend from Eve. The colour black distinguishes those similar to Cain (subsequently not merely those descended through blood, but also those deemed to be sinners). According to the author of the text, humankind prior to the Flood was dualistically divided into the righteous (Seth and his descendants) and the evil ones (Cain and his descendants and the other children descending from Adam and Eve, 85.9). In the eyes of the author righteous ones descend only from the family of Seth; therefore their place in the world is determined. According to the author of the *Animal Apocalypse*, it is the women descending from the—non-Sethite—'evil' half of humanity who, immediately prior to the Flood, come into contact with the angels, whom the

Aramaic fragments of the text call כוכבים, 'stars'.[32] (This meaning supports the etymology of the beings called עירין in Genesis 6; that is, that both their names and forms are associated with the stars.) Upon seeing the black cows the stars fall to earth; at first they graze with the cattle, and later mate with them. From their union elephants, camels and donkeys are born (86.1-6). A pure white heavenly being in human form binds the stars (in ch. 87, in Enoch's vision, four such heavenly beings appear; they may be identified with the four archangels) and the animals begin to destroy each other (88.1-3).

Another colour, red, also appears in the symbolic system of the *Apocalypse*. This may symbolize various groups. Abel appears in the narrative as a red bull (85.3-4), as does Noah's second son, Ham (89.9). The image of the red bull does not continue in the text; the descendants of Ham and Jafet are represented by wild beasts and birds, just like the descendants of the angels and the daughters of men (86.1-6). From there the system of the *Animal Apocalypse* becomes dichotomous. Various nations—more precisely theinhabitants of historical state formations ('empires')—appear, who are symbolized by beasts: donkeys (Medeans), wolves (Egyptians), dogs (Philistines), foxes (Ammonites), wild boars (Edomites), lions (Assyrians), leopards (Babylonians), hyenas (Ethiopians?), falcons (Greeks, more precisely Macedonians), hawks (Egypt of the Ptolemaic period), crows (Syrians), and dogs (Samaritans).[33]

In the biblical tradition Ishmael and his descendants, considered to be relatives of Israel (cf. Gen. 16), were symbolized by the wild donkey (89.11), and Esau and his descendants by the wild boar (89.12, cf. Gen. 16; 25.19-26).

The system of symbols changes when the narrative reaches the story of the immediate ancestors of the twelve tribes. The figure of the bull disappears from the text, and a new symbol appears in its stead: that of the sheep. Jacob is represented by a white lamb, from whom twelve lambs originate. The descendants of the twelve lambs become a large herd (89.14). A ram (in the Aramaic fragment אמרה) represents Moses (89.30 *et passim*). Yahweh's metaphoric place in this system is that he is Lord of the Sheep, that is to say, he is the owner of the herd (89.30 *et passim*). The text also represents leaders of the people as rams who had

32. *1 En.* 86.1, sixth copy; see Milik 1976: 245; cf. 88.3, fifth copy; see Milik 1976: 238.

33. On the identification of the animals with various peoples see Schreiner 1969: 97.

stepped into the place of the ram that fell asleep (i.e. Moses), and lead the sheep (89.38-39). The text mentions Samuel (89.41), Saul (89.42) and, David (דכרא, 'lamb', later ram) (89.45-46) in this capacity. Elijah and the prophets are such rams who had been sent by the Lord of the Sheep (89.51, 53). According to the *Apocalypse*, after them the herd is lead not by rams, but by shepherds. Here the text talks of the activities of 70 shepherds (89.59), whom the Lord of the Sheep had appointed to graze the herd. At the end of their tenure, the shepherds have to account for the size of the herd and they have to hand over the account to their successor (89.60-64). In heaven Enoch bears witness as to how each of them had fulfilled their duties (89.65-66).

The shepherds guard the herd carelessly. The majority of the sheep perish because they had been exposed to the wild beasts. The beasts, after having slaughtered most of the herd, finally ruin the house (89.69). The story refers to the events of the year 586 BCE, the beginning of the Babylonian exile, following the destruction of the Temple of Jerusalem and the cessation of the independent Judean kingdom. Subsequently, further shepherds guard the sheep for '12 hours' consecutively (89.72). During this time 'three of those sheep' return and begin building the house. Although the beasts interfere the house is finally built (89.72-73). This part refers to the period following the Babylonian exile, to the building of the so-called Second Temple, which began under Persian rule, and was completed in 516 BCE.

In the next section of the narrative the herd is guarded by 35 successive shepherds (90.1). During their tenure birds of prey appear, under the leadership of eagles and they snatch sheep (90.2). In the following era 23 shepherds take care of the herd, through 23 'times' (90.5). At this time white lambs appear among the herd, who begin to open the eyes of the blind and lost sheep. Some white lambs grow horns. A large-horned white ram appears—based on the text and the historical tradition, his figure may be identified with the first leader of the Maccabean revolt, Judas Maccabeus (90.6-12).

According to the conception of the author of the *Apocalypse*, the period of the 23 shepherds will be followed by the judgment (90.15-26), when the Lord of the Sheep will sit in judgment over the stars and the shepherds and will punish them (90.24-26). At this time the figure of the white bull appears again—here symbolizing the messiah—and the sheep themselves turn into white bulls and cows (90.37-38)—with this metamorphosis essentially the descendents of Seth return, as an the elect group of white bulls and cows.

In the text of the overview the separate biblical traditions and historical events in general are easily identifiable. The section about the time of the shepherds is somewhat more problematic, since here the author is not so much guided by real events (which regarding this period are in any case little known even from historical sources), but rather by the wish to accommodate himself to numbers which had predetermined symbolic value. Within the era of the shepherds, two periods may be identified as follows: the time of the shepherds begins with the end of the era of Elijah and the prophets—according to the Jewish tradition the cessation of prophecy coincides with the beginning of the Babylonian exile, 586 BCE. The era of the twelve shepherds lasts until the completion of the 'second house', that is, the Second Temple, that is to say until 516 BCE. The author does not characterize the era of the 35 shepherds specifically. Based on the context and the known historical data this period may be identified with the historical period lasting from 516 BCE until the time of the Seleucid conquest (Antiochus III seized Palestine from the Ptolemaic rulers in 198 BCE). The last period is the rule of the 23 shepherds—this may refer to the Seleucid period, the time that had elapsed from 198 BCE until the beginning of the Maccabean revolt (164 BCE). By no means does the number of the shepherds (12 + 35 + 23 = 70) refer to the actual leaders and rulers of these historical periods; these numbers cannot be reconciled with known historical facts. The rule of the 70 shepherds lasted altogether 70 'hours' or 'times' (80.71-72; 9.1, 5), from the destruction of the Temple of Jerusalem (586 BCE) until the beginning of the Maccabean revolt (164 BCE). The 70 units of time do not denote actual time;[34] the tradition of the number alludes to one of the prophecies of Jeremiah (25.11-12; cf. 29.10), his prophecy about the seventy-year Babylonian exile. The author of the *Animal Apocalypse* reinterprets this tradition and regards as 'exile' the period between 586 BCE and 166 BCE. It is this that he divides into 'hours' or 'times'—most likely, year-weeks.

The sheep symbolism derives from one of the poetic images of the prophetic literature. In Jer. 23.1-7, in the words of the prophet who speaks in the name of Yahweh, 'The pastors that feed my people' and let the sheep scatter refers to the kings[35] of the period preceding the exile. This prophecy of Jeremiah also foretells exile, following which,

34. Cf. the expression שבעה עדנין 'seven times' in Dan. 4.13, 20, 22, 29.
35. Cf. Ezek. 34 where the same symbolism appears.

after an unspecified amount of time, Yahweh collects the remainder of his herd from the countries where he scattered them and drives them back to the pasture. The author of *1 En.* 85–90 elaborates on this image and fits it into the chronology of his own overview.

Dividing up the text on the basis of the systems of the narrative, we may discern the following phases of human history in the *Animal Apocalypse*:

1. The age of the first people, up to the Flood. The author divides the people of this age into three (but practically only into two) groups. The transgression of the 'black ones' with the angels brings about a catastrophic punishment, the Flood, coming upon the whole of humanity.
2. The age following the Flood which shows parallels with the first one. The author again delineates three groups, the groups of the 'blacks', 'reds' (the first two groups practically constitute one group in this era as well), and the group of 'whites'. The descendants of the 'blacks' and 'reds' become wild beasts; in the narratives these symbolize the peoples hostile to Israel. Unlike the biblical tradition, which links the surrounding peoples to the twelve tribes by ties of kinship (see Gen. 10, the so-called *tol^{e}dôt*—list of generations—and the patriarch narratives of Genesis) the author of the *Animal Apocalypse* stresses the separateness of the alien peoples and Israel when for example he derives the Ishmaelites and the Edomites from wild beasts (89.12).
3. The third age begins with the time of Jacob; this era essentially coincides with the history of Israel. At this point in the narrative a new symbol appears, that of the sheep, which represent Jacob and his descendants, the ancestors of the twelve tribes. The end of the period is not defined precisely. The last characters mentioned in this section are Elijah and the prophets. Like the antediluvian period, this era closes with a sin committed against Yahweh and its punishment.
4. The fourth age begins with the destruction of the Temple and lasts 70 'times' (probably 70 year-weeks = 490 years, i.e. 10 jubilees). According to the author of the Apocalypse, the end of this period is the Maccabean revolt (166 BCE).
5. The last, fifth age begins with the success of the revolt. The description of the victory in all likelihood is a product of the

> imagination. From here on the text is a genuine prophecy. The victory is due to divine help (90.11-19). Most probably the author of the *Apocalypse* supposed that the fifth period would last until the seventieth year after the beginning of the revolt (586–166 = 420 years = 69 year-weeks), and with the passing of the 70 year-weeks—as he interprets Jeremiah's year-week—the prophetic oracle would be fulfilled. This would be the actual end of 'exile', which he probably hoped be followed by with the coming of a messianic kingdom.

The historical schema of the author of the *Animal Apocalypse* blends certain schemas of the Danielic tradition with the prophecies of Jeremiah. The author basically divides the historical periods according to a fourfold schema (from the Beginning to the beginning of the Maccabean revolt). The fifth age is not historical but is situated in the future. This is a completely different kind of era, which sees the return of the Beginning and the onset of a new history (the return of the symbolism of the white bull in the narrative refers to this).

The author of the *Animal Apocalypse* combines this schema with the schema of 70 year-weeks of the prophecies of Jeremiah, which appears in several places in the foretelling of the Babylonian exile lasting for 70 years. He considers this period to last until his own era, that is, in his view the exile did not end in 516 BCE as Jewish tradition held it in general.[36] Along with many other features, this attitude, evident also in the chronological system, proves that the second century BCE author of the *Animal Apocalypse* was a member of the group of Hasidim, that is the 'righteous', and thus represented his group's particular point of view in this respect as well.

The author of the *Animal Apocalypse* wishes to prove that the period of the Babylonian exile did not end even in the first half of the second century BCE. For his proof he uses Jeremiah's prophetic authority in such a way that he reinterprets the chronology of Jeremiah's prophecy, and calculates the time prophesied by Jeremiah not in years, but year-weeks (1 year-week = 7 years). Thus, the period of the exile lasts exactly until the beginning of the Maccabean revolt (586–166 = 420). He divides the schema of 70 year-weeks into another fourfold system (the reign of the 70 shepherds divides into the reign of 12 + 23 + 23 + 12 shepherds). This schema, however, has nothing to do with historical reality.

36. Hanson 1975.

The Hasidic position is also represented in the other apocalypse of the Enochic collection, the so-called *Apocalypse of the Weeks* (*1 En.* 93 and 91) created in the second century BCE at the same time and within the same circle as the former. The full text can only be read in the Ethiopian version. The apocalypse provides a historical overview, which is divided into ten 'weeks'. Seven of these periods represent genuine historical eras, and three refer to the future from the point of view of the age of the author.[37]

The description of the historical eras begins with the age of Enoch. The author of the text makes no mention of the creation of the world, nor of Adam—important in the tradition of Genesis. His work may be classified as typically belonging to the circle of the so-called Enochic tradition, though this attitude would be recognizable even if it had not survived in the Enochic collection. The first period is hallmarked by the name of Enoch, 'while justice and righteousness still lasted' (93.3). The second week is the age of evil, from which 'one man' escapes—based on the tradition of Genesis he is identified with Noah (93.4). The third week is again the age of evil, the age of the violation of the Law. Only one man survives this age—the reader may identify him with Abraham. He will be the elect of the 'plant of righteousness for ever' (93.5). In the fourth week 'a law for all generations' (93.6) appears. Based on the biblical tradition this age may be identified with the time of Moses. At the end of this period 'a house of glory and of sovereignty will be built for ever', that is, the Temple of Jerusalem, at the time of Solomon (970–931 BCE) (93.7). In the sixth week, people become blind, and at the end of the week 'the house of sovereignty will be burnt with fire', and 'the whole race of the chosen root will be scattered' (93.8). Here the symbolism refers to the destruction of the Temple of Jerusalem in 586 BCE and to the Babylonian exile. The age of the seventh week is 'the generation of evil'. The author does not characterize this period with a historical reference, but merely notes that at the end of the week the righteous will be chosen for 'the plant of righteousness' (93.9-10). According to the author, the restoration of judgment and righteousness will take place soon, already at the end of this week. The mention of the 'righteous', of those who will be chosen at the end of the age, in all likelihood refers to the group of which the author of the *Apocalypse* considers himself a member: the god-fearing Jews, the upholders of the Law, the group who in contemporary sources are referred to as Hasidim.

37. Eissfeldt 1964: 838.

The division of time into 'weeks' in the *Apocalypse* has a basis in reality. In the text the basis for the periodization is always the activity of some outstanding individual or some outstanding event. The action of this person, or the event, characterizes the entire era (Noah, Abraham, the building of the Solomonic Temple, the two kingdoms). The only exception is the contrast between the character of Enoch and that of his age. Thus the length of the eras is not identical numerically. The number of years is not defined in the text—thus the 'week' is not defined numerically either, it simply means 'period of time'. In the narrative an alternation of the nature of the ages may be observed: the age of Enoch, a good age, is followed by two ages of evil. In both only one person escapes the communal punishment, or becomes elect. The events of the fourth and fifth age are 'good' (Moses receives the Law; the building of the Temple). The sixth and seventh week are the age of blindness and sin. With the eighth week, the series of good times begins again—these, however, are ages in the future.

The *Apocalypse of the Weeks* presents a less complex view of history which is chronologically less elaborate than that of the *Animal Apocalypse*. However, the two are similar and spring from the same source. Whereas the author of the former attempts to reconcile the traditional fourfold schema with the schema of 70 year-weeks associated with the exile and his own expectations, the author of the latter primarily wishes to parade the 'righteous' who had appeared in the course of history, and who, through the example of their continuous deliverance keep alive their own and their group's consciousness of their own elect status, thus keeping alive hope for the future.

Chapter 4

THE BEGINNINGS OF THE TRADITION OF THE 'REWRITTEN BIBLES': HISTORIOGRAPHY IN THE *BOOK OF JUBILEES*

It is difficult to place the *Book of Jubilees* within the continuity of Jewish tradition, as the narrative gives no clues to the events of the author's era, and not even the original text of the work survives. The only complete extant text of *Jubilees* is the Ethiopian translation.[1] In addition, a fragmentary Latin translation[2] and a few Greek quotations from the work are also known.[3] The latter most likely belong to the text from which the Latin translation had been prepared.[4] It has long been supposed that the original of the work may have been in Hebrew—and this theory was proved correct when Hebrew fragments of *Jubilees* were identified among the manuscripts found in the Qumran caves.[5] The perspective and religious views of *Jubilees* have been the subject of numerous analyses already; these have proposed a wide variety of spiritual backgrounds for the work.[6] The spiritual milieu from which *Jubilees* emerged

1. Charles 1895.

2. Ceriani 1861: I.1, 15-54.

3. For a systematic presentation of these texts see Denis 1970: 150-62.

4. The Greek translation was made from the Hebrew original, and from this in turn the Latin (and directly from the Greek the Ethiopian). See VanderKam 1977: 6.

5. The *Book of Jubilees* must have played an important role in the life of the Qumran community; 12 fragmentary copies of the *Book of Jubilees* were found at Qumran; see VanderKam 1977: 258-82. The earliest of them are late Hasmonean, dated around 100 BCE. On the fragments see Schürer 1973–79: III.1, 309, n. 1. Editions since 1979 include: Kister 1987: 529-36; VanderKam and Milik 1991: 243-70; 1992: 62-83.

6. The earlier analyses primarily attempted to define the circle of authors and not the time of creation—with greatly diverging conclusions. Jellinek (1855) considered it an Essenea work; Beer (1856) supposed a Samaritan origin; Frankel (1856) considered it to be a Jewish work with a Hellenistic viewpoint; Charles (1902) supposed a Pharisaic priest as the author; Singer (1898) defined it as a Jewish Christian work; Leszynsky (1912) thought it to be Sadducean.

was, in all probability, the prehistory of the Qumran community, before the establishment of the Qumran settlement. Beside the striking similarities of the calendar of *Jubilees* and of some calendrical Qumranic texts[7] there is a similarity between *Jubilees* and various literary texts from Qumran.[8]

The dating of the book is not an easy task, and it has led to various theories: the suggested dates for the creation of *Jubilees* range between the third and first centuries BCE.[9] Based on the later manuscript tradition it may be supposed that the work was written in the first half of the second century BCE; it has definitely came into being before the turn of the second and first centuries BCE.[10]

The *Book of Jubilees* is probably the earliest example of a rewritten

7. On the relationship of the calendar of *Jubilees* and that of the Qumran community see Jaubert 1953; 1957; Morgenstern 1955; Baumgarten 1958; Zeitlin 1959; Kutsch 1961; Cazelles 1962; Hoenig 1979; Baumgarten 1982; VanderKam 1982; 1979; Baumgarten 1987.

8. On this see Noack 1957–58; Skehan 1975; VanderKam 1978; Grelot 1981; Knibb 1989; Tyloch 1988; Lignée 1988.

9. The text does not contain historical references, and no long excerpt has survived from the original text. The *terminus ante quem* of the dating is Damascus Document 16.3-4 which mentions 'the book of the divisions of the times according to their jubilees and their weeks' and Qumran fragments of *Jubilees*—both from around 100 BCE. *Terminus a quo* is *1 Enoch*, which is very much used in *Jubilees*; cf. Charles 1893: 34-35; 1902: 36-37. On the pre-Qumran history of research on *Jubilees*, see Endres 1987. Charles's works on *Jubilees* exerted significant influence on current opinion; he dated the work to the end of the second century; see Charles 1973, II: 6. Today a second-century dating is generally agreed, but opinions differ in precise dating of the work: pre-Maccabean (175–167 BCE), according to Finkelstein 1943; between 169–167 BCE, according to Goldstein 1983b; around 168 BCE, according to Nickelsburg 1981a: 73-80; pre-Maccabean times, without precise dating, due to the uncertainty of the historical allusions, Doran 1989. Others assign the work to the reigns of various Hasmonean rulers: John Hyrcanus (Charles 1973: lviii-lxvi; Milik 1976: 58); Jonathan and Simon (Berger 1981: 300); the middle of the second century BCE (Schwarz 1982). For a high-Maccabean date (161–140 BCE) see VanderKam 1977: 254, 84; age of Judas: Davenport 1971: 15 (3 redactional layers). However, the dating of Testuz (1960) of 110 BCE is not acceptable; similarly Zeitlin 1939–40; 1945–46; 1957–78. Vermes (see Schürer 1973–79: III.1, 311-12) originates it in the Maccabean era.

10. The earliest Hebrew fragments have been defined as 'late Hasmonean', and as such they are dated to between 100–175 BCE. As the writing of the fragments is semicursive, according to VanderKam they must have been preceded by an earlier written tradition; see VanderKam 1977: 215-17.

Bible: a work which systematically adapts the material of the biblical narrative tradition, sometimes supplementing, sometimes contracting it, or leaving out certain parts.[11] In point of fact there are two historical overviews in the work, two adaptations of the biblical tradition. The first of these is a divine revelation about history, from the time of Moses to the time of the author of *Jubilees*, given to Moses on Mount Sinai[12] before the handing over of the tablets of the Law (i.e. relative to the time of Moses this is a revelation about the future) (*Jub*. 1.1-25). According to the revelation, God will lead the people back to the land, which at one time he had promised to Abraham, Isaac and Jacob. There, however, the people turn away from him; they will not listen to the witnesses whom God has sent to them, and persecute and even kill them (*Jub*. 1.12)—for all these reasons 'I shall give them over to the power of the nations to be captive'. After this, however, a turning point will arrive. The exiled will turn their hearts towards God, who will gather them together from among the nations. God will settle the returnees 'as a righteous plant';[13] he will build up his Temple among them, he will live among them, and they will be his people.[14]

The 'witnesses' of the revelation are the prophets of the period of the kingdom; the giving over to the power of the nations refers to the Babylonian captivity. In the overview of *Jubilees* the 'righteous plant' means those who return from the exile, or rather one group of them ('they will turn to me from among the nations with all their heart and with all their soul'),[15] and the author identifies them with the 'righteous'—in all likelihood his own circle. They are the ones, who, due

11. 'Revealed histories' are very popular between 200 BCE and 130 BCE; see Hall 1991. 'Rewritten Bibles' are the result of earlier interpretative traditions; on this see Vermes 1961; Attridge 1976; Endres 1987. Wright (1966: 133) called these texts 'narrative midrash'. On Genesis Apocryphon as 'narrative midrash', see Weimar 1973. Recently Dimant (1991) has examined the functioning of biblical items in later texts, and she defined two major kinds: *pesharim*, explications of explicit quotations, and narrative discourses, in which biblical texts are alluded to, or used thematically.

12. Moses appears here as mediator of a revelation. On similar roles of Moses in non-canonical Jewish writing see Hafemann 1990.

13. Translation of Charlesworth 1983–85: II, 53; Vermes 1987: 83

14. Cf. *1 En.* 90.1-20; CD 1.8-11; 7.10-11 where the emergence of a separatist, reformist sect is to be traced; on this see Kister 1986–87.

15. Cf. the Damascus Document which refers to a group of the elect, members of a distinctive community, by a similar name (שורש מטעת). The author of the Document considers himself also to be one of them; see CD 1.7.

to their faith in God, repossess the land promised to Abraham and given, but later lost because of the faithlessness of the people. The key to the first overview is the connection between the land and the observation of the Law; those unfaithful to the Law lose the land, those who return to God may return to the land.

The other overview—constituting the remainder of the work—is about the history preceding the age of Moses (relative to the time of Moses, it is about the past). Historical revelation about the past—and not the future—is a new phenomenon; its goal is not to inform the reader about the events of the past (as theoretically the past is already known to the person receiving the revelation, and also to the reader) but to present that special image and chronological system of the past that can only be known from the revelation—in this case from the *Book of Jubilees*. This revealed history is not identical to the tradition known from Genesis, but is its paraphrase, its adaptation to a set of particular points of view.

The beginning of history revealed in *Jubilees* is Adam's time, and its end is the period following the Egyptian exodus, the time of law-giving on Mount Sinai. The narrative, then, includes the entire material of Genesis and Exodus. It ends with that scene to which the introduction referred: Moses receives the tablets of the Law. Thus, then, the narrative of *Jubilees* is not unfinished, ending abruptly, but rather a very consciously edited structure in which the narrative returns to the beginning, to the era of the frame of the story.

The story of creation—as in the narrative of Genesis—includes both the six-day creation story, and the traditional telling of the creation of Adam and Eve. In the story of the first day (*Jub.* 2.2), we also read that in addition to the creation of the heavens, the earth and the waters,[16] God created 'all of the spirits which minister before him' (*Jub.* 2.2), namely 'the angels of the presence, and the angels of sanctification, and the angels of the spirit of fire, and the angels of the spirit of the winds' etc. The names of the functions of the angels for the most part coincide with the meanings of the Aramaic names of the Watchers known from the early part of the Enochic tradition (*1 En.* 1–11).[17] The author of the *Book of Jubilees* also uses the Watchers tradition of *1 Enoch* later on, partly in accordance with the biblical tradition and the tradition of

16. Gen. 1.6-8 is about the separation of the heavens and earth, and of the waters above and below the firmament.

17. Cf. *1 En.* 6.9 and the teachings of the Watchers in the Shemihazah tradition, which gives an interpretation of the planets and of natural phenomena.

1 Enoch, in the story of the events leading up to the Flood, and partly in an independently developed form, as a story of demons active in the world, who according to *Jubilees* are the descendants of the fallen angels.

The sabbath following the six-day creation story gains a special significance in *Jubilees*. The sabbath is the sign of the covenant made upon the completion of the act of creation; it is also a day of rest according to the tradition of Genesis (Gen. 1.28–2.4a).[18] In the text of *Jubilees* the sabbath also appears as a feast, 'sign', which according to divine will has to be observed by two groups of angels, the angels of the presence and the angels of sanctification, and later by those people whom God 'shall separate...from among all the nations' (*Jub.* 2.16).

From the history of humankind, the author of the *Jubilees* presents the tradition of the antediluvian period solely in the form of genealogies, (just as do the books of Chronicles, compiled in the Persian period). On the one hand, these genealogies are much richer in names than the text of either Genesis or Chronicles, since the *Book of Jubilees* systematically provides the names of the wives of the patriarchs as well.[19] On the other hand, it does not contain details of the time before Abraham which appear in Genesis.

The narrative proper in the *Book of Jubilees* begins with the events leading up to the Flood. As I mentioned above, the author of *Jubilees* discusses the tradition of Gen. 6.1-4 from a point of view similar to that of the Enochic collection (*Jub.* 5.1-19). At the same time there are also significant variations from this tradition: according to *Jubilees* the children born to the angels and the daughters of men are giants; however, they have nothing to do with the proliferation of sins following their birth (*Jub.* 5.1-2).[20] The strife and bloodshed—which according to the Enochic narrative is brought upon the earth by the appearance of the giants[21]—in the narrative of *Jubilees* only takes place after the punishment of the

18. In the narrative of the redactor of the priestly codex the act of creation is concluded by a covenant-like section (although the word 'covenant' [ברית] does not appear). Since Wellhausen, based on the context, this is regarded as the first element of the series of covenants of Genesis. The other covenants are the covenant with Noah after the Flood (Gen. 9.9-17), the covenant with Abraham (Gen. 17), and finally the covenant with Moses at the time of the handing over of the 'tablets of the Law' (Exod. 19–20).

19. Rook (1990) reconstructs the names on the basis of the Ethiopic text of *Jubilees*.

20. Neither is this so in the tradition of Genesis, see Gen. 6.4.

21. Cf. *1 En.* 6–11.

fallen angels and the limitation of the lifespan of humans to 120 years (*Jub.* 5.7-8) upon divine order ('and he [i.e. God] sent his sword among them', *Jub.* 5.9).

In the narrative of *Jubilees*, Enoch—as in the tradition of *1 Enoch*—is an eyewitness who testifies against the 'watchers', that is, against the beings here referred to as angels (4.21-22). The text highlights the 'righteousness' of Enoch. Evidently the author of the *Book of Jubilees* was familiar with the tradition of the Enochic circle, as he refers to one of its pieces, the work known as the *Letter of Enoch* in one instance (*Jub.* 4.17). He also describes the fate of Enoch after his life on earth in a manner similar to that of the Enochic collection: Enoch is carried off to Eden, and there he writes about the judgment and fate of the world (*Jub.* 4.23).[22] In the *Book of Jubilees* his figure is contrasted with the corruption of his age, his elect status is the result of his merits.

Similarly to the treatment of the figure of Enoch, the text of the *Book of Jubilees* enlarges on the biblical tradition in both the case of the figure of Noah, and the figures of the later 'righteous ones', thereby emphasizing certain of their characteristics. By highlighting the characteristics of Enoch, the author of *Jubilees* makes the Enochic period into a much more significant age than it had been in the biblical tradition. That is to say, according to the *Book of Jubilees* the time of Enoch is an independent historical age, associated with two characteristics: one is that it was at this time that the upper limit of the human lifespan was defined as 120 years (cf. Gen. 6.3), and the other that at the end of the period there will be a judgment and the destruction of the world will follow (5.7-8, 9-10).

The description of the period immediately preceding the Flood and of the figure of Enoch plays an emphatic role in the narrative of *Jubilees*. By comparison the narrative about the Flood itself receives relatively little attention. Several elements of the narrative of Genesis—the building of the ark, the stages of the Flood, details of the escape—only appear in a cursory form. The description of the covenant made with Noah is similar to that in Genesis (*Jub.* 6.4-16; cf. Gen. 8.20–9.17). Accordingly, by keeping the covenant henceforth, the earth will not be destroyed, and the seasons will follow in set order. Meat, the food assigned to humans, is also one of the elements of the covenant made with Noah (*Jub.* 5.6-8; cf. Gen. 9.9-11). The sign of the covenant is the rainbow (*Jub.* 6.15-16; cf. Gen. 9.12-17). In addition to all of these, as a conclusion to the story

22. The image is based on Gen. 5.24.

of the Flood, we are told about the determination of the order of the feasts and of the calendar. The Flood ends at the time of the 'feast of the weeks', therefore this feast will become the reminder of the deliverance of the 'righteous' Noah from the cataclysm. It is also this calendar defined at the end of the Flood which organizes the year into 364 days.[23] The author of the work considers this calendrical system to be the result of divine revelation and the only possible correct system (*Jub.* 6.27-38).

In connection with the Flood and the tradition of the covenant with Noah, the author of *Jubilees* consciously uses materials diverging from the tradition of Genesis. The basis of his narrative is in Genesis, but in addition to the elements appearing there, he also incorporates into his own narrative the tradition of the Watchers from the Enochic circle, and the calendrical system known from the Enochic tradition, and from other works known from the Qumran library.[24] The mention of the definition of feasts and of the calendar is not simply an addendum in the narrative; in the world-view of the author of *Jubilees*, the calendar means a new system of determining time, a new basis for the restoration of the world order. These two additions give the covenant with Noah following the Flood outstanding significance, and grant them a special place in the historical system of the work.[25]

In *Jubilees* the description of the period after the Flood essentially follows the narrative of Genesis, expanding it by numerous additions.[26] At the same time certain types of additions serve to highlight certain figures from among the participants in the patriarch stories. The stories about Abraham in the narrative of *Jubilees* are not only enriched by new elements, but the significance of the entire figure of Abraham himself is different from the tradition of Genesis.[27] According to the *Book of*

23. The year consisting of 364 days is the basis of the calendrical system of the Enoch-tradition; the calendar of the Temple Scroll and of 4QMMT has the same system as well.

24. See Jaubert 1953; 1957.

25. According to Endres the covenant made with Noah is much more significant than the later covenant concluded with Abraham; see Endres 1987: 7-10.

26. Due to considerations of space the vast number of additions to the biblical tradition in the *Book of Jubilees* cannot be discussed here in great detail. Therefore I will restrict the discussion to those features which are of special significance for the world historical overview.

27. The changing of the significance of the characters is a general characteristic of the *Jubilees*; for example Rebecca's role is upgraded; Esau's presentation is more negative here than in the Bible; see Endres 1987: 49.

Jubilees, at the time of Abraham the world was ruled by unclean demons, whose leader was Mastema.[28] In the eyes of the author of *Jubilees* these demons are the descendants of the 'fallen angels' (cf. *Jub.* 19.8-10). Abraham has power over the demons. The source of his power is his 'righteousness'.[29] In the city of Ur, Abraham is not only unwilling to sacrifice to idols, but he also takes action against them; he sets 'the house of idols' on fire (*Jub.* 12.12).[30] It is also at this time that he begins to speak in Hebrew, the 'language of the covenant' (12.23-27). In the *Book of Jubilees*, then, Abraham is the embodiment of the archetype of the 'righteous', a person who observes the Law even before its revelation—that is to say before the appearance of Moses.

The next outstanding figure of the *Book of Jubilees* is Jacob.[31] His figure also displays characteristics which are not mentioned in the tradition of Genesis, and which prove Jacob's elect status. According to the tradition of *Jubilees*, Jacob is the favourite of the aged Abraham (19.14-16), and Abraham bestows upon him 'all the blessings with which he [God] blessed Adam and Enoch and Noah and Shem' (19.27).

Eventually, four patriarchs play an outstanding role in the *Book of Jubilees*: Enoch, Noah, Abraham and Jacob. In connection with them, the author not only supplements the biblical tradition, but also makes the figures of the elect uniform and typical, that is to say, he endows them with typical, characteristic features. The four figures are united by the common feature that all of them, under all circumstances *observe the Torah, the prescriptions of the Mosaic Laws*. This also reflects the special attitude of the author of *Jubilees* towards the Torah: he considers the Torah to be timeless, to have existed since the Beginning—since the time of creation.

The other common feature uniting the four is *knowledge*, the fact that

28. The name originates from the Hebrew verb שטם 'bear a grudge, cherish animosity, against' (Ar. שטן).

29. This viewpoint is similar to that of the Qumran community. In their view, the demons causing illness can be chased away by certain people with special powers, through the laying on of hands, and the 'release' of sins; cf. Jesus' *dynamis*, that is to say, power to heal, see e.g. Mk 6.2, 14; *Acts* 8.10, 19.

30. In the book of Judith, in Achior's speech (5.6-9) Abraham has to leave Mesopotamia because he refuses to worship the local deities. The core of this legend most likely came into being at the end of the second century BCE.

31. According to the analysis of Endres (1987: 228-31) in *Jubilees* the figure of Jacob is central to the covenants made with God by the patriarchs, and Jacob's figure is more significant than that of Abraham.

they are handing down a certain tradition and knowledge. The *Book of Jubilees* attributes the invention of writing to Enoch (4.17); Noah is said to be knowledgeable about medicinal herbs, having received this knowledge from the angels (10.10-15); Abraham is the first human who speaks Hebrew (12.23-27); Jacob studies the Law (19.14). As for the list of the elect, the fifth figure cannot be ignored either. This is Moses, who appears in the introduction of the book, which serves as its frame. According to the *Book of Jubilees*, Moses not only receives the Torah in the revelation, but the entire story of his ancestors—that version of their story which is described in the *Book of Jubilees*, and which differs from the tradition of Genesis. It is not identical to the tradition which is customarily associated with Moses. In the *Book of Jubilees* then, the concept of 'knowledge' also means familiarity with and transmission of such a tradition, the content of which is not identical to that generally attributed to Moses.[32]

Beside focusing on and modifying the presentation of the above-mentioned characters the author of the *Book of Jubilees* also modifies certain traditions associated with the patriarchs. The lifespan of the patriarchs according to the *Book of Jubilees* is longer than that given in Genesis—thus their life stories do not constitute a series of consecutive biographies but a single flow of events the constituents of which are intertwined. Adam lives to see the birth of Noah (*Jub.* 4.28-29; cf. Gen. 5.3-28), Abraham blesses his grandsons (*Jub.* 23.1), Isaac also lives to see his grandsons grow up and blesses Levi and Judah (*Jub.* 31; cf. Gen. 27). This system of blessings transmitted over the distance of several generations completely 'overlaps' with the period of the patriarchs; the blessing is continuously valid through the age of each generation, it is present in the life of the elect group.

The author of the *Book of Jubilees* sets up correspondences between the events described by him and the laws of his religion. Thus for example certain periods of the Flood, according to the author of *Jubilees*, come

32. I would once again refer to the point of view of the Qumran community, which claimed esoteric knowledge for itself and interpreted the texts of the psalms and of the prophets according to its own methods. According to the Habakkuk *pesher* God did not reveal everything to the prophets, and the proper interpretation to the revelation is contained in the commentaries. This knowledge, this type of interpretation belongs to the community, and is at variance with those of outsiders. Furthermore, it is noticeable that the number 22 has a special significance in the *Book of Jubilees*; this feature also relates to knowledge, to the written tradition, since it is the number of letters in the Hebrew alphabet (*Jub.* 2.2).

to an end on the dates of the yearly festivals; thus the origin of the feasts is made to appear as memorial days of certain periods of the Flood (5.29-32). The memorial days concluding the various phases of the year-long Flood provide all the annual feasts. The Flood ends with the feast of the weeks, *shebuot* (שבעות). In the view of the author of *Jubilees* this is the most important feast.[33]

Incidentally, this perspective is similar to that of the *Book of Enoch*. The earliest pieces of the Enochic circle, dating from the third–second centuries BCE, deal with the antediluvian period. They regard the sins of that age as analogous to those of their own era, and they await the punishment of the sinners, and the deliverance of the 'righteous' (themselves).[34] The system of analogies in *Jubilees* is based on the coming punishment, the Flood, or rather on certain phases of the Flood. The feasts indicate the end of the individual phases, and the *shebuot* signals the completion of the entire period of punishment, the conclusion of the Flood. In addition to the fact that with the already discussed typical features Noah belongs to the characteristic group of the four patriarchs, the role of the covenant made with Noah is of special importance in *Jubilees*. The covenant with Noah is the apex of *Jubilees*.

As well as the above-mentioned reasons, there are further motives for the modification and supplementation of the biblical tradition in the *Book of Jubilees*. At times the insertions are due to the author's views on retributive justice;[35] thus for example in the description of Cain's death we find that Cain was killed by a stone (*Jub.* 4.31-32), because Cain also killed Abel with a stone. A similar reasoning can be found in the version of the exodus story in *Jubilees*: the Egyptians pursuing the Israelites drown in the Red Sea because earlier they had drowned the children of the Hebrews in the river (*Jub.* 48.14).

The other characteristic running through the narrative of *Jubilees* is sublimation; that is to say the author relegates to the background everything in the biographies of the highlighted protagonists—especially in the

33. The feast is of great significance in the calendar of the Temple Scroll; in the calendar of 4QMMT, and it was also the most important feast of one of the subgroups of the Essene community, the Egyptian community of the therapeutae; on this see Philo, *Vit. Cont.* 65; *Spec. Leg.* 2.176-77. On the feasts of the therapeutae, and on the significance of the *shebuot* see Yelisarova 1966; 1972: 78-80.

34. This is well demonstrated by the *Animal Apocalypse* and the *Apocalypse of the Weeks*, which tell of events up until the age of the authors, and expect decisive changes to take place during this age.

35. Endres 1987: 231-33.

biographies of the four patriarchs—that might cast the person in a negative light. Thus, Noah's drunkenness (Gen. 9.20-27) is only cursorily mentioned (*Jub.* 7.6-8),[36] and we are told how Sarah was taken away from Abraham in a drastically shortened form (*Jub.* 13.11-13; cf. Gen. 12.10-20 and also 20.1-18, 26.1-11). The story of the binding of Isaac (*aqedah*) is also reformulated by the author of *Jubilees*: according to him the entire attempt at sacrifice happens upon the request of Mastema. He is the one who asks God to test Abraham's faith. It is interesting, and most probably not without significance, that the author of *Jubilees* does not omit the story, as a negative element, but rather reformulates it with the insertion of the figure of Mastema (*Jub.* 17.16).

The author of *Jubilees* makes certain things seem eternal, or at least older than the tradition of Genesis considers them to be. I have already mentioned the 'timelessness' of the Torah in the narrative of *Jubilees*. Similarly, according to the narrative, Israel has been chosen since the creation of the world (*Jub.* 2.19-20); Adam toiled in Eden from the first, and he was taught to work by the angels (*Jub.* 3.15). At the same time this view constitutes the negation of the theology of the Fall, in Genesis; 'the first to call the name of the Lord upon the Earth' was Enos, the fourth descendant of Adam (*Jub.* 4.12); the prescription of the feast of the weeks has been in existence since the era following the Flood (*Jub.* 6.17-18); furthermore the text notes several times that the patriarchs who lived before Moses also observed the prescriptions of the Law.

Beside focusing on the figures of the patriarchs, the author of *Jubilees* especially stresses the significance of Judah and Levi from among the sons of Jacob.[37] At the same time *Jubilees* speaks negatively about Gentiles, and identifies the negative characters of the stories with the historical neighbours of Israel. According to the *Book of Jubilees*, the giants born of the angels and the daughters of men (רפים; see Gen. 6.1-4 and the Aramaic fragments of *1 Enoch*) were in point of fact Amorites—the inhabitants of historical Canaan (*Jub.* 29.7-11). Certain remarks in the *Book of Jubilees* regarding geographical places reflect an anti-

36. According to Gen. 9.21 'He drank so much of the wine that he became drunk and lay naked inside his tent' (וישת מן־היין וישכר ויתגל בתוך אהלה); according to the narrative of *Jubilees* here referred to, however, Noah's nakedness is not really caused by his drunkenness, but rather he uncovers himself in his sleep; 'he entered in his tent and lay down drunk. And he slept and was uncovered in his tent as he was sleeping.'

37. In *Jubilees* heroes are always descendants of Levi and Judah. This can be considered as a forerunner of the concept of 'two messiahs'; see VanderKam 1988.

Samaritan tendency. The names of Shechem and Betel appear often in the text, always in connection with the patriarchs and their religion. According to the *Book of Jubilees*—in contrast to the tradition of Genesis—immediately after making the covenant with God, Abraham receives a revelation in Shechem, and sets up an altar nearby, between Bet-el and Ai (*Jub.* 13.1-9), where subsequently he receives a further revelation. Shechem and Bet-el were the holy places, cultic centres, of the Northern Kingdom and later of the Samaritan population. By making these the locale of revelations given to the patriarchs and of ancient cultic centres, the author of the *Book of Jubilees* had, as it were, appropriated these places for his own tradition. The stance taken by the *Book of Jubilees* regarding the Dinah story and the massacre of Shechem also reflects an anti-Samaritan tendency. The story (Gen. 34) tells of the unjust and cruel vengeance of the sons of Jacob against Shechem. The tradition of Genesis—referring to this episode—condemns the behaviour of the sons of Jacob, and among them especially that of Simeon and Levi—they were the instigators and leaders of the massacre. The tradition of Genesis explains the fact that the priestly tribe descending from Levi has no independent territory as a punishment for this deed. 'A curse be on their anger, for it was fierce; a curse on their wrath, for it was ruthless! I shall scatter them in Jacob, I shall disperse them in Israel' (Gen. 49.5-7).

The *Book of Jubilees*, however, recalls this event, most likely consciously, from a completely different point of view. It does not merely rehabilitate Levi, but places him above everyone. According to *Jubilees*, Levi was a high priest at Bethel (32.9). With the help of modifications and omissions, not only does the author prove that the ancestors of the twelve tribes were present at those places which later became the settlements and religious centres of the Samaritan population, but also that the patriarchs' sacrificial places and temples were precisely at these places—Shechem and Betel—and they received divine revelation here. All of this aims to prove the primacy of the Jewish presence and tradition over that of the Samaritans.

The focus on and re-evaluation of the figure of Levi also results in the elevation of the role of the Levites in the *Book of Jubilees*. The Levi image of the *Book of Jubilees*—in accordance with many other features—proves that the author of *Jubilees* intended to give a new perspective to the tradition of the history of Israel. His outline on the patriarchal period is focused on the idea of the continuity of the presence of the descendants of Abraham in the land of Canaan, the land which was promised to their forefather. In addition to the so-called anti-Samaritan tendencies other attributes may also be found which aim to prove a kind of historical priority over the Promised Land, and which cannot be found in the tradition of Genesis. According to the *Book of Jubilees* the sons of Jacob had been buried near the Makpelah cave, in the hills of Hebron (*Jub.* 46.9). Some of their descendants stayed here at the time of the Egyptian exile and did not go down to Egypt; one of them in fact was Amram, the future father of Moses, who went to Egypt only after the death of Joseph (*Jub.* 47.1).[38]

The great overview of the *Book of Jubilees*, the adaptation of the traditional history of Israel as a revelation given to Moses, exhibits several characteristics: on the one hand, it is a 'periodized history'—it is a historical tradition arranged according to the periods represented by the figures of the four patriarchs. At the same time the four figures, or rather the eras they represent, are not of equal significance: the apex and dividing line is the episode of the covenant made with Noah.[39] This is followed by the periods of the patriarchs receiving the Promised Land (among them, however, Jacob has the outstanding role as opposed to Abraham). These are followed by the story of Joseph, the description of the Egyptian exile and captivity based on Genesis, but with some additions. The conclusion of the overview is the description of the exodus and of the feast of Passover, the return to the land and the promise to set up the tabernacle of the Lord (*Jub.* 49.18).

On the other hand this is also an overarching attempt to combine the narrative tradition of Genesis and of other diverse traditions within the framework of a single historical overview. The 'other diverse traditions' derive from *1 Enoch* and the Essene calendrical traditions, and both of these are woven into the system of the overview. This is a comprehensive attempt at amalgamation: the author of *Jubilees* aims to reconcile both the Enochic theology and the Enochic historical perspective with

38. Between the death of Joseph and Amram's moving to Egypt one jubilee and two year-weeks, that is 63 years, pass. This number (= 70 – 7) appears often in the Jewish eschatological calculations.

39. According to Endres there is only a single covenant in the work and this is the covenant made with Noah—there 'never was a time when Israel's ancestors did not observe the customs and laws revealed at Sinai' (1987: 22-228). Within the story of this single covenant there are outstanding figures, the patriarchs Moses, Noah and Jacob.

the tradition of Genesis. The Enochic tradition of the fallen angels originally formulated the theory of the origin of evil differently from that of Genesis. The author of the *Book of Jubilees* uses this tradition (the demons who present temptation and who appear in several parts of the narrative are derived from the fallen angels), but he incorporates the elements of the story, without their original function, into his narrative (evil is not brought into the world by the giants descending from the fallen angels). This view is reinforced in one other instance as well: according to *Jubilees* the angels descending to the daughters of men originally descended to earth with the goal of teaching humanity, and this goal, despite themselves, became the source of evil.

Finally, the entire overview is interwoven with motifs of 'timelessness'. Partly these are examples given by the *Book of Jubilees* to demonstrate that the Law is observed prior to the giving of the Mosaic Law, thus illustrating its timelessness, and the permanence of its historical presence. The other recurring motif relates to continuity: the stories and insertions which may be referred to as anti-Samaritan, which aim to prove the continuous presence of the chosen people in the whole of the territory of Canaan, from the time of the patriarchs. The requirement of strict observance of the Law, and justification of the right to the land are motifs which were current themes of the author's time and were the subject of other works adapting the biblical tradition in diverse forms.

Chapter 5

HISTORICAL LEGENDS IN THE LITERATURE OF THE HASMONEAN PROPAGANDA: THE USE AND INFLUENCE OF A LITERARY PATTERN

The perspective and methods of court historiography initiated and supported by the Maccabean (Hasmonean) dynasty after its ascent to power due to the victory of the Maccabean revolt (160 BCE)—which had begun as a national war of liberation—is not only present in the demonstrably courtly dynastic chronicles, but also in other historicizing works (e.g. the book of Esther, the book of Judith). These do not directly refer to the Maccabean revolt or to the family either in their titles or in their texts; in fact these books adapt a historical and literary tradition which predates the revolt. Nonetheless, a closer analysis of these works allows us to conclude that they had also been written in the same 'public relations offices' as the official and semi-official chronicles, the only difference being that these are based on a different literary material. However, the goal of these works is the same as that of official historiography: the celebration of the victory of the founders of the dynasty, who had been the leaders of the revolt.

The schema according to which these works of the Hasmonean period are structured, a mixing of literary and historical elements in unequal proportions, is the same: armed resistance and victory of a vastly outnumbered Jewish group, a religious community, over an opposing power which wishes to oppress it and to suppress its religion. The Jews are aided in their resistance by God. This divine assistance is secured by the unfailing faith of the believers in their God. Incidentally, the story of the Maccabean revolt itself is also based on this schema. Religion, and the practices and decrees violating the religious beliefs of the Jews, were among the root causes of the rebellion, and due to the inner weakness of the Seleucid empire—perhaps even surprising the Maccabeans themselves—it ended in victory.

One official chronicle of the successful revolt has survived, and in addition, several other works also express the same basic message, albeit in a form which is seemingly less authentic historically, or through the medium of a different historical tradition. The work referred to as the First Book of Maccabees is the product of Hasmonean court historiography. It is not a contemporary report of events, but rather it is a memorial created by the dynasty at the height of its power. The original language of the book is most likely to have been Hebrew; however, it has only survived in Greek translation.[1] Its author probably wrote during the reign of Alexandros Jannaios (103–176 BCE).[2]

The author of the book consciously employed archaic devices,[3] so that his work might appear to be a continuation of the book of Judges and the book of Kings, which preserved the history of the political institutions of Israel. He is especially fond of using the stylistic devices of the book of Judges. No doubt such connecting—or rather dividing—inserts between descriptions of events, as 'the land was at peace for two years...' (cf. Judg. 3.11, etc.) derive from this model. As indicated above, the inserts serve rather to divide than to connect. In 1 Maccabees events are disjointed. They are not in a causative relationship with each other. This discontinuity and the dichotomy characterizing the relationship of the protagonists are among the most important characteristics of the work.[4] In the stories 'Israel' and the 'nations' (cf. the book of Judges) are always opposed to one another. Israel is personified by the rebels, more precisely by the Maccabeans who first led the revolt and later founded the kingdom. The author of 1 Maccabees counts the 'pagans' among the 'nations' and considers them to be the representatives of the Seleucid government; their military attacks are seen as actions instigated by the Seleucid empire. The attackers are always Gentiles. 'Israel' is blameless; they represent the 'right' way, both in a religious and a moral sense. When the author is obliged to speak of deviance from religious laws, he refers to those who violate the law as 'apostates', and in essence does not consider them to belong to 'Israel' (3.8). According to the author of 1 Maccabees, the downfall of the attacking Gentiles is caused by their *hubris*. To prove his point by way of analogy he inserts a historical

1. See Bickerman 1937: 27; Abel 1949: xxiii; Goldstein 1976: 14.

2. The book is conventionally (and convincingly) dated around 100 BCE (not later than 90); see Goldstein 1976: 62-64. Recently Schwarz (1991) has proposed an earlier date (about 130 BCE).

3. Goldstein 1976: 6-7.

4. Bickerman 1937: 27-32.

legend into the text: he brings up the example of Sanherib, who attacked Jerusalem, but was miraculously obliged to withdraw (Isa. 37). The story has a basis in reality, the 701 BCE military campaign of the Assyrian ruler, Sanherib, against Jerusalem. The Assyrian, after having defeated the territories of Phoenicia and Canaan, also besieged Jerusalem. The besieged city offered him an enormous ransom. Finally (or perhaps at the end of a second campaign?—because of the disorder of the sources, the events of the campaign or campaigns and the reasons for the withdrawal can only be reconstructed hypothetically) he withdrew from the city, probably because of the breakout of pestilence in the Assyrian camp.[5] The record of this event which survived in the book of Isaiah does not derive from the prophet, but from a later author. Already this source refers to the withdrawal as the result of divine intervention, a historical example of deliverance, in the course of which 'The angel of the Lord went out and struck down a hundred and eighty-five thousand men in the Assyrian camp' (Isa. 37.36). The author of 1 Maccabees, recalling the deliverance tradition, connects the failure of the attacker with the motif of the divine punishment of *hubris*.

The work referred to as the Second Book of Maccabees, which is also a part of the historical propaganda of the Hasmonean dynasty, was probably created not long after 1 Maccabees, at the end of the second century BCE.[6] It adapts the same historical tradition (or rather one part of it, up to the period preceding the death of Judas Maccabeus, at the end of 161 BCE) as 1 Maccabees, and the history of its transmission is also similar to that of 1 Maccabees (both works were preserved in the canon of LXX, and based on this the Catholic church accepts both of them as deuterocanonical books). 2 Maccabees, however, aims at a different audience, and thus uses different devices than 1 Maccabees. This book was meant for a Jewish audience living in the diaspora, and reading Greek. The aim of the author in fact is not the provision of historical information, but rather the presentation of a historical example through the recounting of legendary events.[7] In 2 Maccabees the legendary element overwhelms the historical. All of the legends told in the narrative are somehow connected to the Temple of Jerusalem.

The author has several goals with the creation of historical legends. One of them is to prove the continuity of the existence of the Temple of

5. On the theory of the two campaigns, see Bright 1972: 296-308.
6. Goldstein 1983a: 63.
7. Bickerman 1937: 27-32.

Jerusalem, from 586 through the era of Nehemiah to the author's age. This purpose is served by the legend of the holy fire in the introductory part of the work. According to 2 Macc. 1.18-23, at the beginning of the exile the priests hid a fire from the sacrificial altar in a well-like pit. No stranger knew about the fire. Upon returning, on the order of Nehemiah, they sought it out, but in the assigned place they found only water. After prayer when the water was poured over 'some great stones' (2 Macc. 1.31) the fire started burning again. This is the holy fire in which the men of Nehemiah burn the sacrifices brought with them and thus re-dedicate the Temple. One of the literary forerunners of the legend of the holy fire may have been the legend of the rivalry of Elijah and the prophets of Baal (1 Kgs 18.20-40), while the statements and terminology relating to fire originate in the Persian tradition of fire-worship.

The author of 2 Maccabees also recounts another, in many respects similar, legend about the holy objects (the Tent of Meeting and the Ark of the Covenant) hidden by Jeremiah in a cave. Later no one can find the place where he had hidden the objects, and it will remain hidden 'until God finally gathers his people together and shows them his favour' (2 Macc. 2.7).

The expectation of finding the holy objects of the First Temple was still current at the time of the author: in all likelihood he expected them to be found during the Hasmonean era. In any case, the events described in the work, all of which concern the Temple, including the report of its recovery and re-dedication, serve as a preamble to this anticipated final 'gathering together'.

In the narrative of 2 Maccabees Jeremiah, who hides the objects, emerges as a figure similar to Moses: he presents the Law to those going into exile, and then, under divine inspiration, he goes up the same mountain Moses had climbed to view the Promised Land (2 Macc. 2.4). In the prophecy of Jeremiah, God's future glory appears in the form of a cloud—just as in the tradition of Moses wandering in the wilderness (2 Macc. 2.8).

The other historical legends in 2 Maccabees relate to the rather meagre historical material of the Maccabean era. These legends are intended to prove, through a series of 'historical' examples, that all those who violate the integrity of the Temple will be punished. These examples are interconnected through the identity of the characters appearing in them, or through the relationships between them, and constitute a series throughout the work. The first piece of the series is the well-known

Heliodorus episode, which takes place at the time of the reigns of the Seleucid ruler, Seleucus IV, and the high priest Onias III. The narrative recounts how Heliodorus, the general of the king, entered the Temple of Jerusalem in order to steal from it. His king had heard of the extraordinary wealth of the Temple, and wished to acquire some of its treasures. The arrogant intruder, who despite warnings does not desist from his plan to pillage the sanctuary, is struck down by a vision of divine origin, so that he is paralysed and only recovers when he acknowledges the power of the God of the sanctuary.[8] His ruler is only the immediate cause of the act of Heliodorus. The danger of robbery is brought upon the city by Simon, a disgruntled priest of Jerusalem, who having lost in a quarrel with the high priest, Onias, has betrayed the extraordinary wealth of the Temple to the governor, Apollonius, and it is this information which awakens the greed of the king.

The Simon–Onias conflict, or rather its consequences, recurs in further legendary episodes. In the following, Menelaus, whom the text refers to as the brother of Simon, hires a man named Andronicus, with valuable vessels stolen from the Temple, to kill Onias, who had escaped to Daphne near Antioch (2 Macc. 4.30-35). Menelaus also acts as an intermediary in another event related to the violation of the Temple when the new ruler, Antiochus IV Epiphanes, defiles the Temple of Jerusalem (2 Macc. 4.11-20). According to the legend the Lord delivered up the Temple to Antiochus because of the sins committed by the inhabitants of the city, although only for a short period.

In what follows, a whole series of legends illustrate the cruelty of Antiochus during this time, and the heroism of the inhabitants of the city and their adherence to the laws of their religion (among others there are the legends of the martyrdom of Eleazar, and the seven brothers and their mother, 2 Macc. 6–7). These legends justify, as it were, the first victories of the revolt, soon to take place (2 Macc. 8). Then we find another legend about the illness and death of Antiochus (2 Macc. 9). During his illness the king is broken, and, according to the legend, in order to get well he vows to return the vessels of the Temple of Jerusalem, to pay the expenses of the Temple from his own income, and even to convert to Judaism.[9] This legend is followed by a section which

8. On the story of 2 Maccabees see Bickerman 1939–44. Legends about temple robberies were widely popular in the Hellenistic Near East; see Stokholm 1968. On the Greek elements of the Heliodorus legend, see Fischer 1991: 122-33.

9. On the type of the legend and its spread see Nestle 1936.

is modelled on historical documents, on a letter in which the ruler appoints his son as his successor.[10] The author of 2 Maccabees attached the legend about the penitence and conversion of the king as a preface to this letter and made the legend part of the series of legends about the Temple. Incidentally, the literary precedent and model of the legend may have been the story in Daniel 4 about the illness and conversion of Nebuchadnezzar.[11] Another event of the history of the revolt is followed by the narrative about the death of Menelaus in which a typical motif associated with the Temple recurs. Menelaus's death takes place after the first victories of the Maccabeans, the recapture and re-dedication of the Temple, but before the final clash with Nicanor. The author of 2 Maccabees considers the death of Menelaus to be the fulfilment of divine will. He describes the machinations of Menelaus to secure the trust of Antiochus V, then continues thus: 'The King of Kings, however, stirred up the anger of Antiochus against this wicked man, and when Lysias produced evidence that Menelaus was responsible for all the troubles, the king ordered him to be taken to Beroea and there executed in the manner customary at that place' (2 Macc. 13.4). Menelaus dies in burning embers and in connection with this, the author of 2 Maccabees refers to the holy fire of the Temple, the fire of that Temple the sanctity of which Menelaus defiled time after time (13.7-8).

The author of 2 Maccabees attaches another legend to the story of the victory over Nicanor, which was the final victory of the revolt. Once again he draws upon the motifs of the legends associated with the Temple. Before the battle against Nicanor Judas Maccabeus sees a dream: the high priest Onias appears before him in the company of the prophet, Jeremiah, and they present him with a golden sword and assure him of his victory.[12] In a speech before the battle Judas Maccabeus cites another

10. On the authenticity of the letter see Doran 1981: 60; Habicht 1976.

11. 1 Macc. 6.1-16, where the illness and death of Antiochus serve as punishment for the earlier deeds of the king—the stealing of the silver and golden vessels from the Temple of Jerusalem. In mentioning the taking away of the vessels the text consciously alludes to the Danielic tradition, which is associated with the sin and punishment of Nebuchadnezzar; cf. Dan. 5.2. The words of Antiochus, recalling his one-time greatness, also refer to this; cf. Dan. 4.27. Like Antiochus and Nebuchadnezzar, Heliodorus is also punished by illness for the violation of the Temple (2 Macc. 3).

12. The giving of a weapon (sword) is a widespread motif in the ancient Near East; for parallels of the motif see Doran 1981: 73; for general parallels see Thompson 1955–58: 1000.

event of historical origin, which, however, in the Jewish tradition only survived in legendary form. He recalls as an analogy Sanherib's unsuccessful attack on Jerusalem—this is the same event, to which 1 Maccabees (7.39-42) also refers in connection with the battle against Nicanor. It seems that reference to this legend was a constant feature of the Hasmonean propaganda. Judas Maccabeus recaptured and cleansed the Temple and its surroundings after the 161 BCE victory over Nicanor, and introduced the feast of Hanukkah to commemorate the restoration of the cult. In effect, 2 Maccabees is the hagiographical narrative of this feast.[13] Incidentally, the text's introduction makes a reference to the fact that at the end of 143 BCE the Jewish community of Jerusalem addressed a letter to the community of Egyptian Jews, calling upon them to celebrate the feast of Hanukkah (2 Macc. 1.7). Maybe this chronicle-like work—which intertwines the historical traditions of the beginning of the revolt with the circle of legends describing the transgressions against the cult, and its restoration—was necessitated by a need to popularize this feast among the Egyptian Jewry.

In searching for the intellectual background and origin of the author, it has to be stressed that the focus of the narrative of 2 Maccabees is the Temple and the fight fought for it, and thus the traditions relating to Maccabeans and their leaders.[14] Whereas in the narrative of 1 Maccabees Mattatiah and his sons personally confront the Seleucid officials and soldiers who wish to force them to perform a pagan sacrifice, this motif is entirely missing in the narrative of 2 Maccabees, and the author of the latter only talks of the violence committed against the Temple and against the Jerusalemites and the fight waged against this. In 2 Maccabees the starting point of events is the attempted robbery against the Temple, and the entire revolt is fought for the Temple, for its recapture and cleansing.

Another feature of the Temple-centred legend series should be mentioned here. According to the text of LXX, those Jews who for selfish reasons became the enemies of the Temple—Simon and his brother, Menelaus—were from the tribe of Benjamin. The translation of the Vetus Latina changes this (2 Macc. 3.4): here the aforementioned belong to the family of Bilga, from the descendants of Aaron. According to the biblical tradition Bilga (1 Chron. 24.14) was a priest at the time of David,

13. Bunge 1971; Momigliano 1975a. Doran (1981: 105-106) does not accept the term *Festlegende*, but does not propose another term.

14. The motif 'the defence of the temple' is of Greek origin; see Fischer 1991: 122-33. For an analysis of the motif in 2 Maccabees, see Doran 1981: 63-76.

from the Ithamar family of the generation of Aaron. The book of Nehemiah also mentions a similarly named priest (כהן) (Neh. 12.5, 18) among those who returned with Zerubbabel. It is possible that the Vetus Latina preserved a more logical tradition, which fits the narrative better: the betrayers of Onias, the last Zadokite high priest, were not of Zadokite origin, but from the Ithamar family who were relegated to the background in the postexilic Temple hierarchy.

The history of the works inspired by the propagandistically inclined historiography of the Hasmonean period does not end with 1 and 2 Maccabees. There are several other works which are one way or another connected to this propaganda. It is not entirely clear what prompted these works and who their authors were—however, their connections are far too obvious to ignore. The book of Judith is clearly connected to 2 Maccabees, since this historicizing narrative also provides an aetiology of the feast of Hanukkah, from a similar viewpoint as 2 Maccabees.

The other historicizing narrative is the book of Esther. This narrative also contains the aetiology of a feast. This feast, however, is not related to the Maccabean revolt; originally it did not commemorate a historical event, although the narrative makes it appear to be so. Purim, the feast of the book of Esther, in all likelihood was a feast brought back to Palestine by those returning from a Persian milieu. The feast became popular in Palestine, and due to this popularity it had to be legitimated by inclusion in the series of Jewish feasts. The compiler of the book of Esther performs this task. The book shows numerous features which justify its discussion among the documents which came into being under the influence of Hasmonean propaganda.

Judith

The book of Judith may be the most enigmatic among the pseudo-historical works. The work was not included in the Masoretic canon;[15] its Greek text is known from the LXX.[16] The work also has a Latin textual tradition[17] and is also part of Jerome's Vulgate; the text of the

15. On questions of the canonicity see Skehan 1962.

16. In addition to the *textus receptus* published in the LXX three other Greek versions of the text are also known. For textual criticism see Hanhart 1978. A new edition of the Greek text is Hanhart 1979.

17. The texts appearing in the collection of the Vetus Latina exhibit significant differences. On the Vetus Latina see Schürer 1973–79: III.1, 221.

Vulgate, however, according to the foreword of the translator, does not precisely follow the previous Latin or Greek textual tradition.[18] In addition to the Greek and Latin texts a Syriac[19] and an Ethiopian version of the book of Judith is also known. The Syriac text also differs from the Greek.[20] The narrative of the book of Judith incidentally also appears, in a shorter version, in several medieval Hebrew midrashim.[21] It would be fruitful to compare in detail all these narratives; however, this task is beyond the scope of the present work: my analysis follows the text of the LXX, and I will only refer to the midrashim in as much as they can be of use in connection with problems arising in the LXX text.[22]

The supposed original language of the work is Hebrew or Aramaic;[23] however, not even minute fragments survived of such a text. No fragments of the book of Judith have been found among the Qumran texts (where otherwise fragments of numerous apocryphal texts survived in their original language).[24] In view of certain features of the work this is not surprising; it is understandable that the community that did not

18. According to his Prologus (2–8), Jerome was aware of the Aramaic tradition of the work: *chaldeo tamen sermone conscriptus inter historias conputatur*. His translation, however, as he says, is not a faithful translation of an Aramaic text, but rather a paraphrase, which was probably prepared from not one, but several variants of text.

19. Lagarde 1861: 744-90.

20. Prat 1903: col. 1825.

21. Jellinek 1853-57, I: 130-31; II: 12-22; Gaster 1892. A collected edition of the medieval Hebrew texts of the story is Dubarle 1966. For other editions see Schürer 1973–79: III.1, 219.

22. Dubarle considers the midrashim (especially text B) to be the result of a Hebrew textual tradition; everyone else sees them to be a translation prepared from the well-known tradition; see Grintz 1957; 1971. In any case, there are differences between the content of the midrashim and the other known versions. Among the narratives of the midrashim the one entitled 'The story of Judith' (מעשה יהודית) deserves notice, the so-called Hanukkah midrash, which was read on the feast of the victory of the Maccabean revolt, Hannukkah; this gave rise to its title as well. Their editions: Jellinek 1853–57: I, 130-131, II, 12-22; Dubarle 1966: II, 140-42, nos. 8-9.

23. Most scholars are of this view; see Dancey 1972: 71; Enslin and Zeitlin 1972: 40; Skehan 1966: 348; Zenger 1981: 430-31. According to Dubarle, there is a Hebrew textual tradition, which is independent of both the Greek text and of the textual tradition of the Vulgate; see Dubarle 1966: 48-74.

24. For example the Aramaic and Hebrew fragments of the book of Tobit, the Hebrew fragments of the book of Ben Sira and of the *Book of Jubilees*, and the Aramaic fragments of *1 Enoch*, have been found. See Milik 1959: 31-34; 1976.

transmit the book of Esther, did not show any interest in the story of Judith either. Neither did any quotes survive in the rabbinical literature, which could be identified with parts of the Greek or the Latin text.[25] It seems that Josephus is not familiar with the story of Judith either, and the other works of the Hellenistic Jewish literature are also silent about it. Among the Christian church fathers Clement of Rome (1 *Clem.* 55.4) is the first patristic reference.[26] The earliest known text fragment from the work originates in the third century CE.[27]

Based on the Hebraisms present in both the lexicon and the syntax of the work,[28] it had earlier been supposed that the original text of the work may have been Hebrew.[29] These characteristics, however, only prove that the native language of the author may have been Aramaic or Hebrew. Other characteristics indicate that the author used Greek[30] sources, and it is likely that the text of the book of Judith surviving in the LXX had also been written in Greek.

In the narrative of the LXX the plot of the book begins in the twelfth year of the rule of Nebuchadnezzar. The text mentions Nebuchadnezzar as someone 'who ruled the Assyrians from his great city of Nineveh'

25. The Talmud quotes amply from other works which did not become part of the rabbinical canon—thus e.g. the book of Jesus Ben Sira—which supports the statement of the Prologue of the Greek Book of Jesus ben Sira that the text had been translated from Hebrew. The Hebrew Ben Sira text, found at Masada, containing approximately two-thirds of the text, clearly proved this supposition right. The text of the book of Judith does not state anywhere that the book was a translation.

26. See Dubarle 1959; Schürer 1973–79: III.1, 220; Prat 1903: col. 1833

27. An ostracon, representing fragments of Jdt. 15.1-7; see Schwartz 1946.

28. ...*kai epetaksen*...*en stomati romphaias* (1.27), which is a literal translation of the expression ויך לפי חרב (i.e. הרג) 'delivered to the mouth of the sword' (that is, killed him) which is quite frequent in the Bible (cf. Gen. 34.26; Num. 21.24; Josh. 8.24; Judg. 1.25), or the expression *kathōs areston esti tō prosōpō sou* (3.2), which is also a mirror translation of the Hebrew כטוב לפנך ('as it is good in front of you', that is, as you like it). For similar Hebraisms see Grintz 1957: 56-61 *et passim*.

29. See Eissfeldt 1964: 587; Zimmermann 1938; Grintz 1957: 56-63.

30. In the biblical quotations the author follows distinctive LXX readings; see Engel 1992. According to Zenger, it is certain that the entire text of the book is not a translation, but a work written in Greek; see Zenger 1981: 430. Similarly, Craven also states that 'it seems equally plausible that the Greek text could have been written from the outset in elegant hebraicized Greek' (1983: 5). In addition to the above, in the use of sources familiarity with Greek historiographers, thus for example with Diodorus, also seems probable. Naturally, certain traditions narrated in the book might have had Semitic (Aramaic) precedents in the written tradition.

(1.1). The ruler first attacked and defeated Arphaxad, the Medean king, 'in the great plain on the borders of Ragau' (1.5); then he

> sent a summons to all the inhabitants of Persia, and to all who lived in the west: the inhabitants of Cilicia and Damascus, all who lived along the coast, the peoples in Carmel and Gilead, Upper Galilee, and the great plain of Esdraelon, all who were in Samaria and its cities, and those to the west of the Jordan as far as Jerusalem, Betane, Chelus, Kadesh, and the wadi of Egypt, those who lived in in Tahpanhes, Rameses, and the whole land of Goshen as far as Tanis and Memphis, and all the inhabitants of Egypt as far as the borders of Ethiopia (Jdt. 1.7-10).

In the seventeenth year he once again clashed with and defeated Arphaxad, occupied Ecbatana, then 'in the mountains of Ragau' captured and killed Arphaxad (1.13-15). On the 22nd day of the 1st month of the 18th year he decided to punish those living in the western territories, who had not taken part in his previous military campaign. He appointed as the commander of the new campaign a certain Holophernes, 'who was second only to himself' (2.4). Holophernes, setting out from Nineveh with an army of 120,000 marched through Asia Minor and Syria, and occupied the cities lying on the eastern shore of the Mediterranean Sea (2.4–3.8). He set up garrisons in the coastal cities which had surrendered to him, and took from the inhabitants of the cities 'picked men to serve as auxiliaries' (3.6); in addition, he 'demolished all their sanctuaries and cut down their sacred groves, for his commission was to destroy all the gods of the land, so that Nebuchadnezzar alone should be worshipped by every nation, and he alone be invoked as a god by men of every tongue and tribe' (3.8). Upon the news that Holophernes 'had despoiled all the temples of the nations and razed them to the ground' (4.1) the Judeans, who 'had just returned from captivity' (4.3) sent warnings all over the territory of Samaria. Joiakim, the high priest of Jerusalem, wrote to the inhabitants of Bethulia[31] and Bethomesthaim,[32] that they should close off the mountain passes through which Judea can be reached. The sons of Israel repented and the Jerusalemites atoned and prayed in front of the Temple (5.9-15). Hearing this, Holophernes called together 'all the rulers (*arkhontas*) of Moab and the Ammonite generals (*stratēgows*) and all the governors (*satrapas*) of the coastal region' (5.2-4), and talked to them about the inhabitants of the Judean mountain region. His speech

31. In the text of the LXX the Baithuloua, Betuloua, Baitouloua forms appear; the Vulgate calls the city Bethulia.

32. LXX: Baitomesthaim.

was answered by the 'commander (*hēgoumenos*) of the Ammonites', Achior. He recounted the origin and history of the inhabitants of the mountains. In his speech, alluding to the tradition of the exodus, he warned Holophernes not to attack these people, because their god, if the people had not committed a sin, would save them from danger (5.5-24). The enraged Holophernes ordered Achior to be delivered up to 'the sons of Israel' (6.10). They bound and left the commander at the foot of that mountain on which the city of Bethulia lay. The inhabitants of the city took Achior in (6.11-21). This incident is followed by the description of the siege of the city and the familiar events: the desperate city—the enemy had stopped up its external water supply, a spring—is saved by Judith's bold plan. Judith, the beautiful and pious widow, goes with her maidservant to the enemy camp and enchants Holophernes with her beauty. He invites her to a feast, and at the end of the feast the woman kills the intoxicated man and flees back to the city. In the morning, from the city wall, she shows the besieging army the severed head of their commander. Upon seeing this the besieging army flees. The Bethulians pursue them as far as Damascus (15.15). The narrative concludes with a description of the victory feast and thanksgiving hymns (16.1-17).[33]

33. The texts of the midrashim—although it cannot be proved that they represent an independent tradition—exhibit certain common characteristics which differ from the versions of the LXX and the Vulgate. Thus for example they do not mention Nebuchadnezzar and his eastern and western campaigns; only the character corresponding to Holophernes appears in them, but he is mentioned not as a commander, but as the king of Yawan, who personally leads the campaign (the texts of several midrashim mention the attacker only as 'king'). All the narratives begin with the siege of the city. The city, however, is not called Bethulia, but Jerusalem. According to the midrashim the saviour of the city is a beautiful widow or maiden, who goes to the camp of the enemy, claiming that she is fleeing from the besieged city. According to one version (Jellinek 1853–57: I, 130; Dubarle 1966: II, 110-13), she promises to marry the king and only begs him to wait until the period of her uncleanness (נדה) passes. She succeeds in killing the king, then together with her maidservant she returns to the city. The guards, however, fearing treason, do not want to admit them. A man bears witness on behalf of the maiden. Earlier he had been the commander (שר) of the king; however, because he had continually warned the king not to attack Jerusalem, the king had ordered that him to be hanged opposite the gate of the city.

In addition to the already mentioned Jerusalem, only one specific geographical name appears in the narrative: the besieging army, after the death of its leader, flees to Antioch. Although the dating of the midrash is impossible for lack of sufficient data, nonetheless there is no reason to suppose that the medieval translators would have made up the names: it is much more likely that the midrash preserves an earlier tradition.

Based on its contents, the story, as it appears in the LXX, may be divided into three larger units, which are also differentiated from each other by formal characteristics.[34] The three parts are:

1. Nebuchadnezzar's eastern military campaign against Arphaxad; the western campaign against the cities, under the leadership of Holophernes; Nebuchadnezzar wishes to be worshipped as a god (chs. 1–3).
2. The Temple of Jerusalem is in danger; the plan for its protection and the formulation of the theology of deliverance (chs. 4–7).
3. The story of Judith—the justification of the theology of deliverance; thanksgiving for the deliverance, followed by sacrifice at the Temple of Jerusalem and jubilation (chs. 8–15).

The entire story—the three parts combined—is about *hybris* and its downfall: Nebuchadnezzar wishes to be worshipped as a god; however, the inhabitants of Bethulia, with the help of Judith's plan, hold up Nebuchadnezzar's army, and save the Temple of Jerusalem. Since the final outcome and apex of the story is not the deliverance of Bethulia, but of the whole of Israel and of the Temple of Jerusalem,[35] just as much as the locale of the sacrifice following the victory and the jubilation is also this city (Jdt. 18–20).[36] It is into this basic structure of the work that the various elements originating in diverse genres, eras and traditions are incorporated.

This multiplicity and variety in the text is the reason why not many people have attempted to comment upon the book of Judith. It is not an accident that no church father has commented on the book; its first commentator was Hrabanus Maurus, and after him only those who were commenting on the entirety of the Bible, or on almost the entire collection, dealt with the book.[37]

The assessment of the origin and dating of the narrative material constituted in the book of Judith is very varied in the literature. Due to its anachronisms the work has been considered to be a seventeenth–

34. Engel 1992.

35. Although the framework of the third part of the narrative is provided by the biographical data of Judith (see 8.1-8 and 16.21-25) the apex of the narrative is the description of the victory and the thanksgiving. The high priest arriving in Bethulia refers to Judith as the 'glory of Jerusalem' (15.9).

36. On the theological message of the narrative see Haag 1962; Zenger 1974.

37. Prat 1903: col. 1833.

nineteenth century rationalist fiction, which has no realistic basis. One group of nineteenth-century scholars considered the book to be a *roman à clef*, a story in which the system of the named characters and the events narrated contain references to people and events of a later age: the key to the story would have been provided by the identification of the name Nebuchadnezzar with the appropriate historical personage.[38]

Most scholars have considered the book of Judith to be a narrative which had a *historical core*, based on a tradition about some actual event—which later on, in the course of literary elaboration, has been further enriched by elements of different origins. Lewy has connected the events recounted in the book to the era of the historical Nabû-kudurri-usur.[39] The majority of scholars consider the historical core of the story to have been of the Persian period.[40] Most agree that the event which served as the basis for the narrative was the Persian military campaign[41] of 350 BCE, led at the time of Artaxerxes III Ochus (359–338 BCE) against Phoenicia and Egypt.[42] Heltzer relates the narrative to later Persian period names.[43] According to Colunga,[44] however, the story of Judith is nothing but a revision of the story of the battles of Judas Maccabeus against Antiochus Epiphanes (175–164 BCE); Prat also

38. There have been attempts to identify the Nebuchadnezzar of the book of Judith with a whole series of historical rulers from Merodach-Baladan, i.e. Marduk-apal-iddina, to Antiochus IV Epiphanes. Most scholars seem to agree that this key figure is the historical Ashurbanipal (688–626 BCE); see Prat 1903: col. 1830.

39. Lewy 1927.

40. According to Grintz (1957: 15-44) the narrative would have been a folk epic about Darius I. In Grintz's opinion the author of the epos lived at the time of Artaxerxes II (404–359 BCE); the geographical descriptions of the book also come from this era (Stummer 1947; Brunner 1940). According to Dubarle, the story is based on a Persian period story, which, however, cannot be identified more closely than this and which had been continually idealized by the tradition; see Dubarle 1966: I, 135-36.

41. For the description of the campaign see Diodorus Siculus, 16.43-47; 31.19.2-3. Among the commanders of the campaign are Orophernes and Bagoas, whose names may be identified with the names of certain characters of the Judith story. At an early date Sulpicius Severus (c. 360–420 CE) associated the description in the book of Judith with this military campaign (*Chron*. 2.14-16).

42. On opinions see Schürer 1973–79: III.1, 217-18.

43. Based on a name appearing on two ostraca which may be identified with the name of Judith; see Heltzer 1980.

44. Colunga 1948: 92-126.

associates the entire book with the Maccabean period.[45]

Approaching the work from the point of view of literary structure, several scholars have regarded it as an allegory, that is to say a literary pattern placed into a historical milieu. Thus, Bruns considers the narrative to be a revision of the biblical Yael story[46] and its transposition into a historical milieu. According to Haag[47] it is a parable which had been compiled from elements referring to various biblical figures.[48] The figure of Judith in the story is reminiscent of that of Judas Maccabeus.[49]

Bearing in mind the peculiarity of the work—that is to say, its 'historical' elements originate in different periods—Scholz[50] saw the work not as a simple allegory, but as an allegorical prophecy, a pseudo-historical work, which, with the help of traditions alluding to various eras, depicts the authors' expectations for the future. In the view of Lefèvre,[51] the author of the work proves the continuity of divine assistance in the history of his people using elements which originate in the historical traditions of different eras and compressing them into a single narrative.

When analysing the work we have to take into consideration that it uses traditions of historical origin, features alluding to a historical milieu, and deliberately chosen literary patterns. The entire narrative is defined by its message which is expressed in its very structure—that is to say, the story is about the *hybris* of Nebuchadnezzar and its downfall, the repelling of the attack against the Temple of Jerusalem. The author puts the literary patterns and the historical elements in the service of this message.

45. Prat 1903: col. 1830 (details of the nineteenth-century views are also given here).

46. Bruns 1954. The story of Yael is known from the Deborah song and its prose parallel; see Judg. 4–5.

47. Haag 1963; similarly Nickelsburg 1981a: 107.

48. The characters whose figures the Judith story evokes are partly biblical heroines, such as Miriam (Exod. 15.20-21), Deborah and Yael (Judg. 4–5), the woman of Tebez (Judg. 9.53-54) and the woman of Abel-beth-maacah (2 Sam. 20.14-22), and partly men, such as Simeon, whom the story mentions as an ancestor of Judith (Jdt. 9.2-3, 8-10), as well as David, who killed Goliath and beheaded him with the latter's own sword (1 Sam. 17).

49. Nickelsburg 1981a: 107, 151, n. 7. He sees Judith as a 'female counterpart of Judas Maccabaeus' (1981a: 152, n. 10).

50. Scholz 1885; 1896.

51. Lefèvre 1949: cols. 1315-1321; Lefèvre, apud Robert and Feuillet 1959: 746-52.

In the work the names of certain characters and the geographical descriptions of military campaigns recall historical events. From this point of view the existence of a Mesopotamian layer of tradition can be demonstrated in the narrative; however, this appears to be rather incoherent. First of all, it is noteworthy that Nebuchadnezzar—the name can only refer to Nebuchadnezzar II, the greatest ruler of the Neo-Babylonian empire who ruled between 605–562 BCE—is referred to as the ruler of Assyria, whose seat is in Nineveh (Jdt. 1.1). Nor can the Medean campaign be reconciled with the person of the historical Nebuchadnezzar. Arphaxad, also mentioned in the same place, cannot be identified with any Medean king either. The mention of Assyria, Nineveh and Medea may refer to personages and events of the eighth–seventh centuries BCE; that of Nebuchadnezzar, however, refers to the first half of the sixth century BCE.

Other elements refer to events or the milieu of the Persian period. The names of the commanders, Holophernes and Bagoas, are genuine Persian names, and most likely they found their way into the narrative from some Persian period source. Another Persian element is that Holophernes, as a sign of surrender, demands earth (*gēn kai hōdur*) and water from the coastal cities. The motif of the 120-day feast also indicates a Persian milieu, as does the denotation of Holophernes' rank as being 'second only to himself' (that is to Nebuchadnezzar) (Jdt. 2.4).

The third well-distinguishable group of motifs in the narrative, from the point of view of historical references, reflects the attitude and customs of the Maccabean period. The emphasis on strict adherence to religious prescriptions and on the righteousness of Judith, the frequent mention of fasts, the text of the prayers provided in the narrative, as well as the religious fanaticism reflected throughout the book all point to this period—and this is definitely when the final compilation of the book took place. In connection with the elements referring to different periods the question automatically arises: from what sources do these originate and what is their meaning? What was the objective of the author in combining these elements of diverse origin?

As I already mentioned it is customary to criticize the narrative for the strange and crass mistake of calling Nebuchadnezzar the ruler of Assyria, with Nineveh as his seat. It is unlikely that either a Persian period, or even a later, Jewish author would have been unaware of exactly which state Nebuchadnezzar ruled, since his figure—both that of the historical figure and the character of legends—had been commemorated in several books of the Bible. Furthermore, the figure of 'Nebuchadnezzar, the king of Babel' had become the epitome of arrogance, *hubris*, in the Jewish tradition of the Persian period, and as such he became the symbol of the Neo-Babylonian empire, which forced the Jews into captivity. In other parts of his work the author of the book of Judith demonstrates in several instances that he is extremely knowledgeable about the biblical tradition. The fact that Nebuchadnezzar appears as Assyrian ruler in the book can only be deliberate; the author of the book of Judith most likely attempted to compile a story, which—with the help of historical material taken from diverse eras—would justify his belief in divine assistance and deliverance, which is the basic message of the story.

The names of the characters are not genuine: in the book of Judith Nebuchadnezzar is also the embodiment of *hubris*, of arrogance towards God.[52] The *hubris* of Nebuchadnezzar manifests itself in that the king has the altars and sacred groves of the cities destroyed and wishes to be worshipped as a god—however, this is no longer the Nebuchadnezzar of Daniel 4, but is similar to the Antiochus figure of the later Danielic tradition of the second century BCE (Dan. 7–12).[53] Incidentally, this section no longer refers to the king as Nebuchadnezzar; however, the interpretations of the visions are always about the *hubris* of the king and its punishment. According to the image preserved about Antiochus in the second-century Danielic tradition, he is the 'eleventh horn', who '[he] will hurl defiance at the Most High', and 'He will have it in mind to alter the festival seasons and religious laws', 'But when the court sits, he will be deprived of his sovereignty' (Dan. 7.24-27). He is the 'little horn' whose heart swells, and kills many and even attacks the Prince of Princes [prince of the host?], 'but he shall be broken without hand' (8.9-14, 23-26); and 'he will put a stop to sacrifice and offering. And in the train of these abominations will come the perpetrator of desolation'; this is why he is punished (9.27). He is also the 'king of the north' who 'will exalt and magnify himself above every god, and against the God of gods he will utter monstrous blasphemies' (Dan. 11.36), and for this he will also be punished. Like the name Nebuchadnezzar, the name of the heroine in the book of Judith is also typological:[54] it stands for Judea and the Temple.

52. The key to the meaning of the name is found in the book of Daniel, where Nebuchadnezzar's madness occurs at the height of his power, and lasts until he realizes 'that the most High is sovereign over the realm of humanity', Dan. 4.25.

53. Brunner (1940) identifies him with Antiochus Epiphanes.

54. יהודית 'Judean woman', 'Jewess'.

The figure of Nebuchadnezzar, then, most probably represents the figure of Antiochus Epiphanes as he has been commemorated in historical legends. This introductory sketch presented with the help of symbolic names immediately at the beginning of the story indicates the true background of the narrative, the historical context of the period of the Maccabean revolt. It only becomes clear with this identification in mind why the military campaign against Arphaxad appears in the narrative at all, since it plays no role whatsoever in the later unfolding of events. The name of the enemy, Arphaxad, does not denote a genuine historical person,[55] but rather it is also a typological name, based on Genesis, where it had been used to denote the Persians, and later the Parthians.[56] This meaning of the name is further supported in the book of Judith by the use of the place names, Ecbatana and Ragau, which are supposed to lie on Iranian territory. The historical Nebuchadnezzar had not led a Persian military campaign, whereas the historical Antiochus did lead a campaign to the east, against the Parthians, in 166 BCE, in the year of the beginning of the Maccabean revolt (1 Macc. 3.27-37).[57]

The question of the campaign led by Holophernes and its route is another element which can be identified from historical sources. The history of the western campaign of the Persian ruler, Artaxerxes III Ochus (359–337 BCE), can be found in the work of Diodorus Siculus (*Diod.* 16.43-47). In Diodorus, Orophernes (Holophernes) and Bagoas also appear among the commanders of the campaign. Artaxerxes led a campaign to the territory of the rebellious Syria and Egypt, and therefore the route led across the territory of Syria and the coast. The itinerary described in Diodorus coincides with the tradition of the book of Judith,[58] although some of the geographical and personal names of

55. Several scholars have attempted to identify the name with a historical figure; these identifications, however, are not convincing; see Priebatsch 1974: 58; Lewy 1927.

56. The name appears on the tablet of generations of Genesis (see Gen. 10.22, 24; 11.11-13), and it is also mentioned in 1 Chron. 1.18. According to Genesis, Arphaxad is one of the descendants of Shem; however, like all the other names appearing on the tablet of generations, it does not refer to a person, but to a people—the Persians and the Parthians.

57. On the question of the Parthian military campaign of Antiochus and the military campaign of the book of Judith against Arphaxad see Diakonov 1956: 41.

58. Diodorus Siculus 16.43-47. Artaxerxes III Ochus set out against Phoenicia from Babylon. Tennes, the ruler of Sidon (*dēnastus*, 16.43; *basileus*, 16.42.2) surrendered; nevertheless Artaxerxes devastated the city. Then he divided his army into three and appointed Bagoas as its commander. Orophernes, the ruler of Cappadocia,

the narrative of the book of Judith cannot be identified from this source. Diodorus mentions the siege of Sidon, which also took place during this campaign, in 351–350 BCE.

Based on the particulars of the campaign and in view of the geographical and personal names used in the book of Judith, it may be supposed that the author used some chronicle of the campaign of Artaxerxes.[59] In all likelihood the historical tradition from the Persian period was intended to support the historical authenticity of the complex narrative of the book of Judith. There is no evidence in the Assyrian or later sources of an event that would confirm the siege and deliverance of Bethulia. It has also proved impossible to identify the Bethulia place name although there have been several attempts to do so.[60] It is a much-debated question why the LXX, Lucian's Greek text and the narrative of the Vulgate choose Bethulua or Bethulia as the locale of the plot.[61] The Bethulua or Bethulia name is not known from any other source. Based on the descriptions of the above-mentioned Greek texts and the narrative of the Vulgate the city lies southwest of the Esdraelon plain (plain of Jezreel), in the vicinity of Dothaim (Dothan). There have been several unsuccessful attempts to correlate the locality of the place with several fortifications and settlements of the vicinity of Dothan.[62] The texts mention two details in connection with Bethulia, which theoretically make the identification

also took part in this campaign. Following the campaign, Artaxerxes decorated him for his bravery. After the campaign, Orophernes returned to Cappadocia; see Diodorus Siculus 21.19.2-3; cf. Olmstead 1948: 436.

59. According to Priebatsch (1974: 56-57) the author of Judith most probably used Kleitarchos's Greek narrative.

60. A place name or a geographical name that could be definitively identified with it is not known from any other source either. On the identification see Stummer 1947. Most earlier scholars identify it with Shechem: Torrey 1899; 1945: 91-93; Dalman 1935: 115, n. 2; Abel 1933–38: II, 283; Steuernagel 1943. Based on the description of the location of the city in the book of Judith (Jdt. 4.6, 'opposite Esdraelon, facing the plain near Dothan') some identify it with Qubatiya lying near Dothan; see Free 1962; Eissfeldt 1964: 586 and n. 4. According to Priebatsch (1974) the name is the conflation of two geographical names, 'Bethel and Ai'.

61. The Hebrew midrashim—if they mention any name at all—mention Jerusalem as the besieged city.

62. Steuernagel (1943: 232-45) identified the place with Qubatiya lying east of the present-day Dothan. According to Stummer (1947: 40) it might be a nearby hill in the same vicinity. Grintz (1957) also identifies the locality similarly. However, none of these localities correspond to the characteristics of Bethulia described in the book of Judith: a city built on a hill, with a spring outside the city and with a water supply.

of the locality possible, or probable. One is that the city lies southwest of the plain, behind an extremely narrow pass. Only one road leads through the pass, which makes it easily defensible. Based on the particulars of the description, it is in the vicinity of Shechem where Bethulia should be sought.

The other detail which may help in the identification is that the water supply of the city is provided by a hidden spring, which lies outside the walls of the city; from here an underground pipe carries the water to the city. The inhabitants of Bethulia are in extreme peril—and this is when Judith resolves to take the decisive step—when the enemy discovers the spring and blocks it off. Several Judean and Israelite fortifications had an underground water system. Such systems have also been excavated in Megiddo and Jerusalem. Such a system is not known from Shechem. It is possible, then, that in the narrative traditions which were known to the authors of the Greek or Latin versions, the besieged city would have been Jerusalem, and the narrative referred to the water supply system of that city. The Greek and Latin versions, however, have changed the locality and transferred it to the north, to the vicinity of Dothan—however, they left unchanged the other element of the story, the tradition about the spring outside the city walls and the water supply, which plays a crucial part in the narrative.

We may have to accept the fact that the name of the city is not a genuine place name,[63] and that, in keeping with the message of the story, it constitutes a theological cryptogram symbolizing Jerusalem.[64] On the siege and deliverance of Jerusalem, however, there is a historical legendary tradition which may have played a role in the formulation of the story of the book of Judith. This is the siege of Jerusalem in 701 BCE, at the time of Hezekiah, the story of which is recounted in two parallel sources: in 2 Kings 18–20, as well as in a chronicle-like section of Isaiah (Isa. 36–39). In these texts Sanherib is the Assyrian ruler. It is certain that this biblical narrative tradition is based on actual events. This is proved by the names of the characters, by references to earlier historical events and the speeches in the text which bear witness to a thorough knowledge of Assyrian diplomaticpractices. At the same time both sources present the events rather obscurely. Bright, separating the sources into two narratives, has concluded that in point of fact the texts record two separate events, two military campaigns. One is Sanherib's 701 BCE

63. Thus Avi-Yonah 1971: col. 749.
64. Zenger 1981: 435.

campaign against Judea, in the course of which he besieged Jerusalem, and the city only escaped upon paying a substantial ransom. According to Bright, the siege was most probably repeated a few years later, around 688 BCE. The city was saved from its hopeless situation by an unexpected event, most likely an outbreak of the plague in the Assyrian camp, as a result of which the besieging army withdrew.[65] The two narratives, although they contain historical data, do not constitute a chronicle even in the above-mentioned sources; their goal is not the presentation of events, but rather, the presentation of Hezekiah as the righteous ruler, whose beliefs had been justified by the events. According to the two texts (2 Kgs 19.35; Isa. 37.36), in the course of the second attack supposed by Bright the departure of the Assyrian army happened as a result of the influence of supernatural forces: 'That night the angel of the Lord went out and struck down a hundred and eighty-five thousand in the Assyrian camp; when morning dawned, there they all lay dead.'

This legendary tradition of the deliverance of Jerusalem from the Assyrian siege remained a living tradition in the later Jewish literature as well. The book of Ben Sira (48.18-21) and the books of the Maccabees (1 Macc. 7.40-42; 2 Macc. 15.22-24), as well as *3 Maccabees* (6.2-5) (which, incidentally, only belongs to the books of the Maccabees on the basis of its title inscription) are familiar with it and refer to it.[66] One of the Judith midrashim[67] also indicates that this may have been the model which the author of the Judith story had in mind, when creating the story of the miraculous deliverance of the besieged city. According to the text, the king besieging the city (which in this case is Jerusalem) is warned by a 'captive king' not to attack the city because he will fare like the earlier kings, who had raised their hand against Israel 'like the pharaoh, and Sanherib and the other kings' (פרעה וסנחריב ויתר המלכים). In other words, it recalls the deliverance stories commemorated by the historical tradition, the deliverance story of the exodus and the deliverance tradition associated with Sanherib from the history of Jerusalem.

When formulating his narrative the author of the story of Judith also incorporated other salvation traditions of the Old Testament, primarily the tradition of the Deborah song (Judg. 4–5). These two chapters of the book of Judges contain two parallel narratives about the same event: the

65. Bright 1972: 196-308.
66. Zenger 1981: 442.
67. Jellinek 1853-57: II, 12.

battle fought at the waters of Merom and the death of Sisera, the enemy commander. The events take place at the time of the settling down of the Israelite tribes, probably in the thirteenth century BCE. Not only is the tradition ancient, but the text of the Deborah song, which is the first formulation of the tradition, also belongs to the oldest layer of the biblical text. According to the Deborah song, Sisera, the commander of the enemy, is obliged to flee, and in the course of his escape he seeks refuge in the tent of 'Heber, the Kenite'. Heber's wife, Yael, feigning friendship, takes Sisera in; she offers him milk, and then she kills the exhausted, sleeping man. The stories of Yael and Judith show similarities in several instances, and it is clear that the story of Yael also served as a model for the story of Judith.[68] Both women kill the commander of the enemy, both feign friendship (Judith feigns love) towards the man. Both kill their adversary in his sleep, and both receive the accolades due to a hero. In the thanksgiving hymn of the concluding part of the book of Judith the literary influence of the Deborah song is clearly felt (Jdt. 16.1-17; cf. Judg. 1.24-31).

Thus there are two larger legendary historical traditions in the background of the narrative about Judith. In addition to these, certain elements of the story recall numerous other biblical traditions. There is a deliberately created similarity between Judith's thanksgiving song (Jdt. 16.2-17) and the Deborah song (Judg. 5) and the song of Miriam (Exod. 15.20-21). Certain details of the story also refer to yet other biblical traditions: the image of Judith beheading Holophernes with the man's own sword is reminiscent of David beheading Goliath with his own sword (1 Sam. 17.50-51).[69] The story of Judith recalls two other women, the woman of Thebez, who kills Abimelech with a stone hewn from above (Judg. 9.53-54) and the woman of Abel-beth-maacah who saved her city from the general Joab (2 Sam. 20.14-22). With this systematic practice of alluding to books of the Bible the author of the book of Judith intends to enhance his own message.[70]

Why had the author of the Judith story chosen these stories as models for the formulation of his own narrative? Most probably because he saw

68. On the similarities of the two narratives, and the parallels between the figures of Yael and Judith, see Bruns 1954; 1956.

69. Cf. 2 Macc. 15.35: 'Judas hung Nicanor's head from the citadel, as a clear proof of the Lord's help for everyone to see'; according to Abel (1949: 479) this is not a historical, but a literary feature.

70. Alonso-Schökel 1975.

some kind of analogy between these traditions and the historical event which he himself wished to preserve, so that by buttressing the commemoration with these historical analogies it should seem to be of eternal validity.[71] The literary allusions and the legendary tradition about the deliverance of Jerusalem have a common feature: it is always the weak, the one in a hopeless situation, who is unexpectedly victorious—and the narrative attributes the victory to divine assistance. A similar situation, a seemingly miraculous, unexpected deliverance, occurred at the time of the Maccabean revolt when the Maccabees clashed several times with the troops of the Seleucid ruler. At the outbreak of the revolt, in 166 BCE, Antiochus Epiphanes, who was otherwise engaged with his Parthian campaign, entrusted Lysias, his commander, with the leading of a military campaign to Judea. Lysias sent three armies, under three generals (1 Macc. 3.27-37). The generals—Ptolemy, Nicanor and Gorgias—had set up camp in the vicinity of Emmaus. Judas Maccabeus, though vastly outnumbered, soundly defeated the enemy army (1 Macc. 3.42–4.25). In 164 BCE Lysias set out on a campaign with an even larger army. Judas defeated him for the second time at Beth-Zur. Following the victory Judas went to Jerusalem, ousted the Seleucid garrison from the citadel, and cleansed the Temple of Jerusalem, which in December (Kislev 25) 164 BCE was re-dedicated (1 Macc. 4.36-61; 2 Macc. 10.1-8). The third unexpected victory in a hopeless fight constituted a turning point in the history of the revolt. In addition, it also meant the recapturing and renewed use of the Temple, the symbol of one-time statehood and later religious unity.

Although final victory only came with the victory over Nicanor in 161 BCE (Nicanor himself fell in the battle), the celebration of the victory, Hanukkah, was placed on 25 Kislev, the memorial day of the rededication of the Temple. Before the retaking of the Temple the situation of the Maccabees was clearly reminiscent of the situation of defenders of the besieged Jerusalem, of the situation depicted by sources describing the Assyrian siege.

Faith, strict observation of the laws, and hope in divine salvation are the fundamental ideas of the book. The additional details only serve to complement and enhance this; thus for example the figure of the high priest, Joiakim. In the work, Joiakim's position as high priest is greatly emphasized (*ho hiereus ho megas*), and he is one of the main moving forces of the plot. His figure was doubtless created after a Hellenistic

71. Abel and Starcky 1961: 320.

model, since in Hellenistic times high priests, or certain high priests, also played a politically significant role.[72] (A person called Joiakim is also known from the time of the rule of Hezekiah, although he was not a high priest).[73]

What could have been the purpose of changing the locale of the story? Bethulia lay on the territory of the one-time kingdom of Israel, in the area which later became Samaritan territory. According to the book of Judith, then, Jerusalem's deliverance comes from Samaria. The origin of the Bethulia name may be Bethel. This is where at one time the Temple rival to that of Jerusalem stood, which had been destroyed by Josiah.[74] The Judaization of Samaria in the story, the 'annexation' of a territory with a rival tradition, is not surprising, since an anti-Samaritan tendency is noticeable in other features of the story as well; that is, the author transforms the traditions relating to places associated with the Samaritans, evaluating them according to his own viewpoint.

According to the book of Judith, Judith descends from the tribe of Simeon (9.2). The text does make a reference to the story of the daughter of Jacob, Dinah (Gen. 34). In this story Simeon, one of the sons of Jacob, plays a significant role. In the biblical story it is he who together with his brother, Levi, incites the sons of Jacob to unconscionable bloody vengeance, to avenge their sister's, Dinah's, rape. It is with reference to this event that the text of the Jacob blessing (Gen. 49.5-7)

72. The Zadokite dynasty ends with the assassination of Onias III; the high priests following him are not considered to be legitimate. Members of the Hasmonean dynasty held the title of high priest from 142 BCE, although because of their origins they were not entitled to it. Nevertheless, in sources discussing the history of the family, during the rule of the dynasty, the priestly origin of the family receives great emphasis. Hasmonean historiography also wished to emphasize that the struggle led by the Maccabeans took place in defence of the Temple.

73. Joiakim is the second high priest of the postexilic Temple; see Neh. 12.10-12. Lewy supposes a high priest called Joiakim at the time of Nebuchadnezzar; see Lewy 1927. Under Hezekiah a certain Eliakim was the prefect of the palace (על הבית אשר) (2 Kgs 18.18; Isa. 36.3-11). Prat (1903: col. 1831) regards him as the model for the figure of the high priest in the book of Judith. In my view, the name Joiakim may also be regarded as a programmatic name (its meaning is 'God sets up') and thus it is not necessary to seek a historical figure behind the figure of the high priest. Joiakim is the other protagonist of the narrative, beside Judith ('Judean woman'), who symbolizes the country and the nation. In point of fact, together the two protagonists constitute a prophetic oracle.

74. 2 Kgs 23.15-20.

condemns Simeon and Levi for their bloodthirstiness.[75] The book of Judith, however, does not condemn Simeon, but rather it makes him the ancestor of the heroine who saves her people.

The author of the narrative needs the Simeonite continuity because Shechem lay on Samaritan territory, on a land into which at the end of the eighth century BCE the Assyrians settled alien groups, the population which was later called Samaritan, to replace the Israelites, who had been taken into captivity. Although the newcomers, albeit with certain modifications, adopted the Jewish religious traditions, nevertheless they remained aliens in the eyes of the Jews. Describing the resettlement after the exile, the book of Ezra also considers it important to mention that those returnees went back to the cities of Bethel and Ai (Ezra 2.28). The narrative of the book of Judith also attempts to prove the continuity of Israel even in the face of reality. The changing of the locale of the siege, the use of the name Bethulia in the narrative is among the elements of the book's anti-Samaritan tendencies.

Beside the Simeonite tradition the book of Judith often refers to other biblical traditions as well. One of the characters of the narrative, Achior, who is the 'commander of the sons of Ammon', also refers to two such traditions. His speech mentions that he 'does not wish to serve Chaldean gods' (Jdt. 5.7), furthermore, he also refers to the story of the crossing of the Red Sea which appears in Exodus, as a deliverance story (5.11-13). The text of the book of Judith not only mentions the tradition associated with Abraham but supplements it by stating that Abraham

75. According to Priebatsch, the tradition associated with Simeon and Shechem may be the key to the mysterious locale of the Judith story as well; see Priebatsch 1974: 54-59. He quotes the poem of the Samaritan Theodotos about 'holy Shechem', which also refers to the place by this name. The poem survived in Eusebius (*Praep. Evang.* 9.22-23). According to Priebatsch, Bethulia may be the conflation of two geographical names, the contraction of the names of Bethel (ביתאל) and Ai (עי). According to the biblical tradition, Joshua tricks the inhabitants of Ai between Bethel and Ai (ביתאל ועי), next to a valley, and he occupies the city setting out from here (Josh. 8.9-10.). According to Priebatsch, however, Garizim, the holy mountain next to Shechem, was also referred to as Bethel in the Samaritan tradition. This Bethel-Shechem identity would also explain why the narrative of the Judith story (9.2-4) lays so much stress on the biblical Shechem tradition, on the above-mentioned story about the looting of Shechem, and on the deed of Simeon and Levi. The book of Judith also emphasizes the fact that after the revenge the ancestors of the Israelites took over the city (the biblical tradition does not mention this) from its earlier Canaanite inhabitants. Thus it makes Simeon and his brethren, the ancestors of the tribes of Israel, the founders of the Shechem of the Israelite period.

refused to serve foreign gods, which is not mentioned in the text of Genesis. This statement in the book of Judith became the kernel of numerous later apocryphal traditions associated with Abraham.[76]

The figure and role of Achior express an important idea in the narrative. Although the character—the king who is delivered up to the besieged city—may have been inspired by a historical precedent,[77] on the whole the episode provides an opportunity for the expression of the author's views on the gradations of elect status. Achior is similar to the figure of Bileam (cf. Num. 22–24), who, against his own interests, predicts the victory of an enemy people. In the narrative of the book of Judith Holophernes delivers Achior to the defenders of the besieged Bethulia. Incidentally, Achior's figure also appears in the midrashim. The shorter midrash of Jellinek mentions the figure of Holophernes as 'king of the peoples' (מלך הגוים);[78] the longer Hanukkah midrash, however, refers to him as 'Holophernes, the king of Yawan, great king'.[79] Beside Holophernes, an unnamed figure, 'a king' (מלך), also appears in the midrashim, whose function in the story is similar to that of Achior. He is the one who warns the king and urges him not to attack the Jews as their God is with them and will not let them fall into the hands of the enemy. He concludes his speech by saying 'Consider what He did with those who were before you, the alien kings and generals who had invaded Israel'.[80] The enraged Holophernes orders the king to be bound and hung alive next to the city gate (ולתלותו הי אצל שער העיר).[81] The heroine, whom the guards of the city are reluctant to admit at the gate, turns to the guards with the following words: 'if you do not believe me, this hanged man will recognize the head' (i.e. that of Holophernes). The hanged man, upon seeing the head, says: 'Blessed be the Lord who gave him in your hands, and who has saved us from this hand [i.e. danger]!'[82] In the midrash, then, this character has a specific role: he is the one who first predicts and then confirms the victory of the city, also spelling out the reason for the victory. In the texts of the LXX and the Vulgate

76. Ginzberg 1938: I, 202; V, 215.

77. Padi, the king of Ekron, was delivered up to the Jerusalemites by his city before the 701 BCE siege of Jerusalem; see Sanherib's inscription, third campaign, 65–75 in *ANET*, pp. 287-88.

78. Jellinek 1853–57: I, 130.

79. Jellinek 1853–57: II, 12.

80. Jellinek 1853–57: I, 131; II, 12.

81. Jellinek 1853–57: I, 131.

82. Jellinek 1853–57: I, 131.

Achior is the representative of the 'sons of Ammon', that is of the Ammonites—of a people, who according to the biblical tradition are the traditional enemies of Israel. In the narratives of the LXX and the Vulgate his function only extends to predicting the victory of the besieged, and in the latter part of the narrative Achior's figure fades away. The midrashim, however, consistently use the figure of the 'king', who fulfils the same function as Achior. At the same time the most important element expressing the book's historical perspective is found in Achior's speech. The basic principle—unconditional obedience to God, the observation at all times of the religious laws as the only condition of and key to success and deliverance—coincides with the main message of 1 Maccabees. In the book of Judith the people who observe the Law are pitched against their detractors, who are not only attacking them, but their God as well, and whose defeat is therefore inevitable. In between the two groups, however—and this is a novel element in the Jewish view of history—there is a third group: those who recognize this inevitability, but due to their origin do not belong to the 'chosen people'. Achior, 'the leader of the sons of Ammon' in the book of Judith, is such a figure. He is the first representative of the notion that electness may be graded in the Jewish tradition.

By using historical analogies the author of the book of Judith wishes to validate this principle. By citing historical analogies, examples of deliverance, Achior's speech also expresses this. In addition to concrete events, however, the author also employs another, very subtle and effective method, for the evocation of analogies. I have already discussed the similarities and basic structural analogies between the story of Judith and Holophernes, and that of Yael and Sisera. A similar structural analogy can be observed between the legend about Jerusalem's deliverance from the Assyrian siege and the story of the deliverance of Bethulia. In addition, numerous details of the book of Judith recall analogies from the biblical tradition. The analogies do not always concern the content. In several instances the author evokes an earlier literary tradition with the help of a selected literary motif or stylistic device. Thus the author amalgamates his material from historical, at times legendary, traditions of diverse eras from a specific point of view. He does not reconcile these constituents, nor does he reconcile the chronological contradictions. His method is not the result of mere carelessness or ignorance; rather through examples taken from and alluding to diverse periods, traditions or events he wishes to demonstrate his unconditional belief in divine assistance. The 'compression' of the historical perspective in the book—that is to say, the telescoping of traditions referring to the events of several larger eras into the history of a few years—is the result of this attitude and method.

Esther

The book of Esther takes place in the Persian period, in the Persian court. The narrative contains many Persian details: thus for example we know the appearance of the Persian festive tent (ביתן) from the book of Esther.[83] The material of the book preserves numerous Persian names, such as that of Ahasuerus (אחשורוש), which may be identified with the Persian name Xerxes (*hšayarša*).[84] The name Vashti is also of Persian origin, as well as the names of the court officials.[85] The author of the book is familiar with the topography of Susa, which serves as a backdrop for the action, with the royal court, and the customs of the harem.[86]

Despite all these details the book, which in many respects is a unique creation among the narratives connected with the lives of the Achaemenid kings, cannot be treated as an authentic source or as a historical narrative: it is not even contemporaneous with the events it recounts. A definite tendentiousness is evident in the work. Events are shown from the point of view of the Jews living in Babylonian exile under Persian rule. Even if it contains authentic material about certain matters, the book of Esther is nothing but the revision of Persian period material, from a definite point of view.[87] The only question is when and where the revision was made, and what could have been its raw material. This question has been answered in different ways by scholars working at different times.[88]

The surviving Masoretic text, the text of LXX, and the narrative of Josephus about Esther present different versions of the story. Compared

83. On festive occasions the tents were set up in the palace garden; see Est. 1.6.

84. Incidentally, the character appearing in the book is usually associated with Xerxes II (485–465 BCE).

85. Millard 1977: 481-88. On the Persian origin of the name Vashti, see Gehman 1924: 327; on the name Mordecai, see Driver 1957: 56. According to Zadok (1986) the resemblance of the orthography of the onomasticon of Esther to that of imperial Aramaic is demonstrable.

86. Paton 1908; Duchesne-Guillemin 1953: 105-108; Moore 1971; 1977: 62-79; Perrot 1989.

87. Similarly, Heltzer 1992.

88. See Bickerman 1967: 211-18.

to the Hebrew text the narrative of LXX contains insertions; however, there are internal contradictions even within the Hebrew text. The date of the feast of Purim for example is different at different points of the text: the Jews living in the provinces celebrate the feast on 14th Adar, whereas the Jews of Susa celebrate it on 15th Adar. Another internal contradiction is that, after having issued a decree against the Jews (3.12-13), the king rewards the Jewish Mordecai (6.1-12).

In the majority of cases the repetitions within the text have no function from the point of view of the narrative. There are repetitions in all of the three versions mentioned above (Masoretic text, LXX, Josephus); however, each version repeats different episodes. The Masoretic text repeats the statement that, Vashti having been chased away, beautiful maidens were gathered together for the king (2.2-4, 19). Esther does not betray her origin at the royal court (2.1, 20). She invites the king and Haman to a feast twice (5.4, 8).[89] In addition, the author doubles the motifs of the letters sent to the Jews by Esther or rather by Mordecai (9.29-32). He also mentions the bloody battle and the killing of the ten sons of Haman twice (9.5-10, 12-15). In the text of Josephus Esther sends the eunuch to Mordecai, to inquire after the cause of Mordecai's sorrow (*Ant.* 11.6, 7), and she invites the king and Haman to a feast twice (*Ant.* 11.6, 9-11). Similar repetitions can be found in the text of the LXX as well, only in other places and in a different order. For the most part the repetitions seem to be result of the contamination of textual materials of diverse origins, at least in the case of the Masoretic text and the narratives of LXX.[90]

As I have already indicated scholarly opinion on the book of Esther varies greatly. Earlier many considered it to be a unified narrative from the Persian era.[91] However, it is much more plausible that the book of

89. These and other duplications summoned explications from the Rabbis—on these see Adler 1990–91.

90. Usually the duplications indicate that the author of the narrative used various sources. See Moore 1975: 74-76; Bardtke 1963; Cazelles 1961: 17-29; Bickerman 1967: 171-88.

91. Jensen 1892: 47-70, 209-26; Willrich 1900: 1-28; Haupt 1906; Lévy 1949: 114ff.; Gunkel 1958: 28; Talmon 1963: 419-55. Many have considered the narrative to be a *roman à clef*; according to Willrich it recounts events that took place in Egypt in the court of Ptolemy II Euergetes. According to Haupt it deals with the events of the age of Alexandros Balas (150–145 BCE), Seleucid ruler. Most recently Littmann attempted to establish a connection between the material of the book and the events

Esther is the result of the contamination of various narratives, originally independent of each other.[92]

Those scholars who consider the book of Esther not to be a uniform creation agree that the main line of the narrative is constituted by the conflict of Esther's uncle, Mordecai, and his rival Haman. The names of the two protagonists, Mordecai and Haman, have proven to be of Mesopotamian and Elamite origin respectively.[93] The original story about them, which served as the basis for the adaptation of the author of the book of Esther, in all probability was about the discovery of a conspiracy against the life of the king by Mordecai, a royal courtier.[94] He reports the conspirators to the king. The culprits are executed and Mordecai's name is recorded in the 'the chronicle of memorable events'. 'All this was recorded in the court chronicle in the king's presence' (Est. 2.23)—that is to say in the court diaries—however, Mordecai does not receive a reward. In the meanwhile the king elevates to very high rank an official called Haman. Mordecai—probably aware of his own worth—refuses to bow to the higher-ranked Haman. The infuriated Haman reports Mordecai to the king. Mordecai escapes Haman's vengeance only accidentally since the king spends a sleepless night and asks to be read to from 'the chronicle of memorable events' (Est. 6.1). This is how he is informed that Mordecai who had saved his life has not received a reward for unmasking the conspiracy. He orders that Mordecai be decorated, and Haman who accused him be executed.[95] This may have

relating to the religious policies of Xerxes. These are only the best-known attempts at identification.

92. Bickerman 1967: 187-89; Bardtke 1963; Moore 1975: 74-75; Stiehl 1960: 195-213; Cazelles 1961: 17-23.

93. Driver 1957: 56; Millard 1977. The name *Marduka* is known as the name of a Persian royal official from the Persepolis Archives; see Delauney 1976: 17-18; Yamauchi 1992. Though the name is attested, the literary figure may still be fictitious; see Clines 1991. The name is attested also in a Ptolemaic funerary inscription (no later than 150 BCE); see Horbury 1991.

94. According to Est. 2.19 'Mordecai was in attendance in the court' (REB) every day (Hebrew: ומרדכי ישב בשער המלך). Gordis (1976), Bickerman (1967) and Moore (1975) take this to mean that Mordecai was a royal judge. It is well known that in the ancient Near East court cases and the conduct of official business took place at the gate; see Ruth 4.11; Job 31.21; Prov. 31.23. On the institution see de Vaux 1960: I, 245-50; Gordis 1976: 43-48; Moore 1975: 74-76; Bickerman 1967: 178.

95. Portnoy (1989–90) considers Ahasuerus as a weak character who asks for advice rather than acting on his own, and this weakness makes him the real villain. In point of fact, the figure of the king in the book of Esther is impartial; he is the medium

been the story, which has been termed the vizier story in literary theory after its protagonists, the rival court officials: it was this type of story that the author of the book of Esther used as one strand of his work.[96] First of all, of course, he Judaized the story, and he madc the wrongly accused official into a Jew.[97] This material was conflated with another story, the narrative about Vashti and Esther. In the case of the vizier story the Judaization of the narrative material merely consisted of presenting Mordecai as Jewish, and of implying that the vengeful Haman did not merely wish to destroy his rival, but the rival's entire nation—in other respects, however, the author did not even change the Mesopotamian or Elamite names of the protagonists of the text.[98] The internal contradictions of the text also bear witness to the *post facto* Judaizations; thus for example, after Haman has reported Mordecai to the king, the king must realize that Mordecai is Jewish. Nevertheless, the king rewards Mordecai, regardless of the fact that earlier he himself had decreed the destruction of the Jews (3.12-15; cf. 6.1ff.). The above-cited passages do not mention that the king would have rewarded Mordecai despite the

of the divine intervening which appears in the form of chance (the sleeplessness of the king). Portnoy's article called forth responses; Hyman 1991–92.

96. The literary ancestor was the story of 'Ahiqar, the wise', a high-ranking official who was falsely accused by his nephew, condemned to death, thereafter saved with the help of the hangman who recognized him for his former benefactor. The tradition about Ahiqar has a Mesopotamian origin: a list of post-diluvian sages found at Uruk mentions 'Aba-Enlil-dari, whom the Ahlamu [= Arameans] call Ahuqar'; see van Dijk 1962; 1963. An Aramaic manuscript of the story of Ahiqar was found in Egypt, Elephantine, at a Jewish military colony (fifth century BCE). The most convenient edition of the Aramaic text is Cowley 1923 (English translation by H.L. Ginzberg, in *ANET*, pp. 427-30). The story was widespread in the ancient Near East, and its variants survived in several languages; see Conybeare *et al.* 1913.

97. Mordecai is Benjaminite (2.5), while his rival, Haman is Agagite (3.1); they are stereotypes for Saul (a Benjaminite) and the enemy *par excellence* of Israel, Amalek (Agag was a king of the Amalekites, 1 Sam. 15.8). The rivalry of Mordecai and Haman is a kind of later replay of the Saul and Agag story in 1 Sam. 15.1-9, where Saul destroyed the Amalekites. The LXX does not seem to be familiar with the symbolism of the name; here Haman is a Macedonian, and 'a Gagite'; see Lacocque 1987.

98. Stories of Persian origin are present in Jewish literature, such as the fragments of a 'stories from the Persian court' from Qumran. Similar stories could have served as models for the book of Esther. On the Qumran fragments see Milik 1991. It is to be remarked that the book of Esther has not been found at Qumran, and, in all probability, was not part of the tradition of the community.

decree, or that he would have withdrawn the decree upon the rewarding of Mordecai, which proves that the decree against the nation must have been missing from the earlier version of the story.

Thus the career story of Mordecai contaminates the other story, that of Esther, which analogously to the former is also a kind of career and deliverance story. The two deliverance stories originally could not have had anything to do with each other. The story of Mordecai has a great number of parallels, not only in the Persian era Aramaic-language literature, but also in the literary material of the Old Testament from the Persian period. Similar career stories may be found in the book of Daniel, in the already discussed chs. 3 and 6. In these narratives, as already mentioned, Daniel or the Jews living in captivity (the three youths) are accused by their enemies, who are also court officials, to the king. The fate of the accused is determined by ordeal. The redactor of the book of Esther substitutes chance and irony for the motif of the ordeal (the life of the title character in the Ahiqar novel is also saved by chance).[99] The stories of the book of Daniel and of the book of Esther serve the purpose of religious propaganda. The book of Tobit not only is familiar with this type of story, but even makes a reference to the existence of the literary tradition of the story of Ahiqar (1.22; 11.17; 14.10). The basis of the literary tradition is the so-called Ahiqar novel, the earliest variant of which is of Mesopotamian origin (seventh century BCE). From the Persian era onwards the novel is known in numerous variants in the eastern literary tradition.

It is more difficult to trace the origin of the Vashti story.[100] The literature unequivocally considers the story of Vashti to be an introduction written to the story of Esther. Voltaire saw a parallel with a Herodotus

99. On the role of irony see Huey 1990; Goldman 1990; McAlpine 1987. The theme of coincidence is one of the key motifs of the book; see Lehman 1992. At the same time, coincidence is to be considered as a means of divine deliverance, as Segal (1989) argues; the absence of explicit references to God in the book is not to be attributed to a secularist world-view. Assuming the particular spelling of the word יהודים (as יהודיים) in the text of Esther as an acrostic of the divine name and a hidden allusion to God in the story (Fox 1989–90; Sabna 1992) seems to be speculative and not evident (no early manuscripts of the book are known).

100. Wright (1970) and Shea (1976: 240, n. 44) attempt to identify the name of Vashti with that of Amestris, but the reconciliation of the data found in Herodotus about Vashti and the narrative of the book of Esther is fraught with difficulties; on this question see Yamauchi 1990: 230-32.

novella in the narrative,[101] the narrative of the first book (1.8-12), about how Kandaules, king of Lydia wanted to show off the beauty of his wife to his guard, Gyges (cf. Est. 1.10-11). Although the elements of the two narratives do not show close parallels, the similarity nonetheless indicates that the author of the book of Esther, like Herodotus, may have used literary materials of Persian origin in his narrative.[102] Most probably in the original version the story of Vashti was no more than a simple preface to provide local colour. Incidentally, in the narrative of the LXX this detail does not appear as part of the introduction. Here the narrative begins with the story of Esther, and it is followed by the episode about the chasing away of Vashti, then the story returns to the later episodes of Esther's life (Esther gets to the court and becomes queen). In the text of the LXX the fates of Esther and Mordecai are intertwined with the story of the unmasking of the conspiracy. In this text the story of the conspiracy appears twice, and in the second version Queen Esther also plays a part. The LXX then conflates the originally independent material differently, in different order and with a different structure than the Masoretic text. The duplications appear at different places in the two texts.

Is it accidental that the narrator of LXX links the story of Vashti with that of Esther, and does not separate them as the narrative of the Masoretic text does? It is possible that the text of the LXX is based on a textual tradition which is familiar with two stories about women. The stories of the two women show certain similarities. The locale is the same, the Persian royal court at Susa, and the motif of the feast appears in both of them. Vashti refuses to appear at the feast of the men, at which Ahasuerus has ordered her to appear. Esther prepares two feasts for the king, and it is at the second one that she states her request (7.2-4).[103] Both Vashti and Esther are outstanding beauties; in Vashti's case

101. Bardtke 1963; Bickerman 1967: 185-86; Moore 1975: 74-76. On Voltaire, see Bickerman 1967: 185.

102. In connection with this question we may quote what Momigliano writes about Herodotus's historiography: the historiographer who otherwise 'had [a] bad reputation in [the] ancient world' used 'two types of historical research': he 'enquired and travelled; he had very few written documents to rely upon', and 'we are in [a] better position to judge him as a historian of the East than as historian of the Persian Wars'; Momigliano 1966: 12. It may be added that he was the most sensitive collector and transmitter of the popular literature of the East.

103. The theme of banquets reveals acts of empowering and disempowering in the story; see Craghan 1986.

the king wants to show off her beauty at the feast (1.12); in the case of Esther, her beauty catches the attention of Hegai, 'Hegai, who had charge of the women' (2.7-9). Both women disobey the king: despite the command of the king Vashti does not appear at the feast of the men (1.12); Esther despite the royal command enters the hall where the king is in judgment (4.11; 5.1-2). At the same time the fates of the two women are diametrically opposed. The king dismisses Vashti because of her disobedience (1.15-19), whereas even though Esther disobeys his order, the king fulfils her request (5.3). The narrative elements constituting the stories of the two women are similar, but their fates differ. The destinies of the two women—in contrast to the story about Mordecai—are not intertwined, they merely constitute two consecutive narratives. The stories of the two women are not about some kind of human conflict. Why then do the stories of the two women appear in the same narrative? There is no rational basis for chasing away Vashti for disobeying the king and rewarding Esther for doing the same. Their destinies only demonstrate the unpredictability of luck, of royal favour: one of the women is able to rule the king with her beauty, the other is not.[104]

Parables about the power of women appear in other Jewish works of the Persian era as well. The apocryphal *Book of Ezra* (*3 Ezra*) which survived in the corpus of the Vulgate, provides a similar type of narrative. The source here too is most likely the Persian narrative tradition. The protagonists of the story are three youths, who in front of Darius debate what is bigger and stronger than anything else in the world—wine, women, the king or the truth? With minor variations the same narrative can also be found in Josephus (*Ant.* 11.3.2-7).[105] According to Josephus's version Darius cannot sleep after a feast (cf. Est. 6.1, Ahasuerus's sleeplessness and its cure). In order to pass the time, he poses questions to his three guards: who or what has greater power wine, the king, women or the truth? The king promises a reward to the one who gives the best answer (cf. Est. 5.8-11). According to one of the three youths, the Jewish one, Zerubbabel, although women have great power the greatest power is that of truth (similarly *3 Ezra* 4.41: *magna veritas et praevalet*). This is the answer the king deems worthy of a reward. In all probability Zerubbabel's answer is an invention of Josephus: it may be

104. The motif of obedience/disobedience in relation to Vashti, Esther and Mordecai is also the subject of S.B. Berg's book; see Berg 1979: 72-93.

105. It is probably not an accident that this story appears shortly before the story of Esther in Josephus (*Ant.* 11.6.1-13).

supposed that in the original Persian version the motif of the power of truth had not yet appeared, and the greatest power was attributed to women.[106] The story serving as the parable of the power of women in Josephus is the following: 'Even the king, who is the lord of so many men, I once saw being slapped by his concubine Apame, the daughter of Rabezakos Themasios, and putting up with it when she took the diadem away from him and placed it on her own head...' (*Ant.* 11.3.5). In essence, the story of Esther is also a parable about the power of women over kings—a story similar to the parable mentioned in Josephus.

It is not known what Persian narrative sources the author of the book of Esther may have used in creating his narrative about Esther. Based on the authentic-seeming Persian milieu and his familiarity with the locale, Susa,[107] the story of Esther—like the story of Mordecai—seems to have been Judaized after the fact; the material which served as the basis of the narrative could have been Persian. This is indicated by the names of the characters appearing in the story of Esther, the twists of the plot, and the literary motifs of the narrative. The motif contributed by the author, which serves the purpose of Judaizing the narrative, is the motif of the deliverance of the Jews, that is to say the content of Esther's request. There is no trace of anti-semitism or persecution in the documents of the Achaemenid period, nor in the historical and literary sources of the era. The motif of deliverance in the story of Esther serves the same purpose as the decree issued against the Jews in the story of Mordecai.

The Persian origin of the narrative material is most obvious from the names appearing in the narrative. In Hebrew there is no earlier tradition of the Esther name, nor can its etymology be derived from Hebrew. However, the name may be originated from the Old Persian word *stri* meaning 'woman'.[108] This word constitutes one element of the Persian

106. The answers to the first three questions prove the power of concrete persons or things (wine, woman, king)—whereas the fourth one deals with an abstract concept (truth). Both the content of the fourth question and the style of the answer make it likely that this section was not part of the text originating in the Persian tradition. The speech of Zerubbabel in Josephus also differs in style from the previous sections recognizing the power of wine, the king, and women; Zerubbabel's speech was written in the style of Hellenistic oratory.

107. On Susa, see Yamauchi 1990: 279-303; on Esther and Susa: Moore 1971: xxxiv-xl; 1975.

108. *strī*—'Weib, in geschlechtlichem Sinn', Bartholomae 1904: II, col. 1069. An earlier popular etymology of the name was to originate from the Old Persian word meaning 'star' (cf. Greek *astēr* 'star'); see Moore 1975: 77.

name Amastri. One of the bearers of the name was the wife of Xerxes (Herodotus provides the name in the Amestris form). The meaning of the name is 'powerful woman', 'lady'. In relation to the name Esther, another name also appears in the narrative of the book, the name Hadassa, meaning 'myrtle', but this only appears once (2.7). It is certain that the double name Esther-Hadassa, like double names used in other narratives, indicates that the author is trying to substitute a more familiar name for a name from an alien tradition.[109]

The tradition of Vashti and Esther was in all likelihood richer than what appears in the text of the book of Esther. This view is supported by the fact that in the harem story of the Masoretic text there are many characters who play no role whatsoever in the further unfolding of the story: thus Hegai, 'who had charge of the women' (2.8), or other officials (1.10, 14, 16, 21, 4.5). Others only make an appearance at the end of the story—thus the ten sons of Haman, who are individually named in the text, and who according to the narrative are also killed after the murder of their father (9.7-10, 14). The names of all of these characters are of Persian origin, and it may be supposed that the story of Esther had a longer Persian narrative source.[110] The text does mention a possible source: 'the annals of the kings of Medea and Persia' (10.2). Most probably 'the annals of the kings of Medea and Persia' did not constitute an authentic chronicle, but rather a kind of *Volksbuch*, which was written in Aramaic, the *lingua franca* of the Persian empire, and which may have contained legend-like narratives about well-known personalities, and legendary historical traditions. Herodotus recorded

109. Similarly in the story of Joseph, the Egyptian origin of the elements of the story is indicated by Joseph's Egyptian name, Zaphenath-paneah, Gen. 41.45. See Janssen 1955–56: 63-72; Montet 1959: 15-23; Vergote 1959: 200-11. The Mesopotamian background of the stories and of the protagonist in the book of Daniel is similarly suggested by Daniel's other name, Belteshazzar.

110. Torrey 1944: 1-40; Bickerman 1967: 225. Bickerman also calls attention to the fact that the frescoes of the synagogue of Dura Europos present a version of the story somewhat different from the Masoretic text. The manuscript 4Q 550 from Qumran contains a narrative with Persian names. Earlier it was called Proto-Esther text by its editor, J.T. Milik. The story shows familiarity with Persian lore and with the Persian narrative literature. It may have originated from a Persian milieu. However, neither the names in the text, nor its contents are identical with those of the book of Esther. It is certain that the text passed on at Qumran was not a version of the book of Esther, but a narrative material of Persian origin similar in content. For the text see Milik 1991.

similar narratives in his historical work as well; travelling in the area he recorded stories he was told—most likely the sources of the stories were similar *Volksbücher*.[111]

Incidentally, Herodotus had also recorded historical folk traditions about Amestris: amongst others he tells the story of how Amestris took revenge on a supposed rival and her family (*Herod.* 9.108-113).[112] Herodotus's story about the cruel and bloody revenge of Amestris and

111. On the question of the legend literature associated with the Persian court see the novellas and legends of Persian origin appearing in Herodotus, such as the legend of the birth of Cyrus, the legend of Darius's rise to power, or the story of the Pseudo-Smerdis (Bardiya). These kinds of stories, containing Persian motifs most likely were transmitted through *Volksbücher*. Josephus, *Ant.* 11.5.1, 6-7 also contains legends about Xerxes.

112. According to Herodotus, Xerxes, in the course of a sojourn at Sardeis (in 479 BCE, and after the Battle of Salamis) fell in love with the wife of his brother, Masistes (Herodotus does not provide the name of the woman). After the woman refused the proposition of the great king, in order to create a better opportunity for his wooing Xerxes arranged that his son. Darius, should marry the daughter of Masistes and the woman. Following the wedding Xerxes travelled to Susa (which is also the locale of the story of Esther) where he presented at the court the young wife of Darius. From then on he lost interest in the wife of Masistes, but he wanted to win the new wife of Darius, who was called Artaynte. In time, however, Amestris, Xerxes' wife became suspicious, and for the following reason. Amestris had made an especially beautiful robe for Xerxes; on one occasion Xerxes visited Artaunte in this robe. The king promised Artaunte that he would fulfil all her wishes. Artaunte asked for the robe. Amestris found out who had received her gift to Xerxes; but she thought that Artaunte had received the robe from her mother, and therefore wanted to take her revenge on the mother. She waited until the banquet that the king gave once a year, on his birthday (*Herod.* 9.110). Herodotus calls the feast *tukta*, and he translates the word into Greek with the word τελειον, 'perfect', and adds that on this day the king makes gifts to the Persians. Amestris on the occasion of the feast asked the king to deliver to her the wife of Masistes. The king was reluctant but as Amestris persisted, and as on the day of the feast the king could not refuse any request, he finally agreed. However, he summoned his brother to him and endeavoured to convince him to divorce his wife. Masistes referred to the fact that he had grown children from the woman, and did not want to accept the daughter of Xerxes, whom the king offered to him as a wife. While Xerxes was in conference with his brother, Amestris sent soldiers to the wife of Masistes. On her order they horribly disfigured the woman. Following these events Masistes, with his sons and others, escaped to Baktria, to instigate a revolt. However, he never reached the land of Baktria: Xerxes, finding out about the plan, dispatched an army which defeated the army of Masistes. At this point Herodotus concludes the story which, unlike his other narratives, he does not date.

the story of Esther[113] show some similarities. Based on these, it may be supposed that the author of the book of Esther took his narrative from an Aramaic source, which also contained narratives about the life of Xerxes' court and relating to Amestris. The locale of the plot of both narratives is the royal harem in Susa. The protagonists are the same: Ahasuerus/Xerxes and Esther/Amestris. In both narratives a feast plays an important role. The book of Esther in essence is the aetiological story of a feast, that of Purim; and according to Herodotus, Amestris makes her request of the king on the occasion of a banquet which is held on a feast day, the birthday of the king, knowing that the king cannot refuse any requests on that day. At the feast, according to Herodotus, the king gives gifts to the Persians—the custom of sending gifts and food also appears among the customs of the feast of Purim. This may also have been the custom of the Persian New Year celebration (Est. 9.13). It is possible that what happened at the Persian court is also reflected in what all three versions of the narrative of Esther mention, that is, that the ten sons of the enemy, Haman, also paid with their lives. Herodotus also mentions the sons of Masistes—albeit, without mentioning their number—whom the soldiers killed together with their father.

It seems then that one of the sources of the book of Esther is a version of the so-called Ahiqar novel, which was a popular narrative in the Mesopotamian Aramaic literature—the other source was the narrative about the bloody family drama which took place at the Persian court. The latter may have been familiar to Jews living in Susa or Mesopotamia from the Aramaic folk tradition. The author of the book of Esther changed the origins of the characters; he Judaized the vizier story which is similar to the Ahiqar novel; and he conflated this narrative with another also modified, Judaized and remoralized story, which by then was not about a family drama, but about the power of women. In the wake of the modifications not only did the story of Mordecai become a career story, but so did the story of the heroine, Esther.[114] In the formulation

113. Luther also condemned sharply the cruelty evident in the revenge of the book of Esther: 'Ich bin dem Buch und Esther so feind, dass ich wollte, sie wären gar nicht vorhanden: denn sie judenzen zu sehr und haben viel heidnischen Unart' (Tischreden, No. 3391). It is also noteworthy that the book of Esther is missing from the Qumran tradition—on this question see Winter 1957: 16—despite the fact that a text similar to the narrative material of Esther was known at Qumran.

114. Career stories involving women (Judith, Esther) appear in Jewish literature in the postexilic age. On the question of the status of women in the postexilic era see Eskenazi 1992.

of this schema, the popularity of the Ahiqar novel most likely played a part,[115] but historical examples may also have influenced the formulation of the narrative, such as for example the career of Nehemiah at the Persian court. And last, but not least, another significant influence is also possible: the earlier tradition of the Old Testament, the story of Joseph in Genesis (Gen. 37.39-50), as well as the career stories of the book of Daniel, which also tell of the career of an outsider at the Egyptian court.[116] The extraordinary popularity of the story may also have played a part in the 'feminine side' of the book of Esther becoming a career story.

As already mentioned, the book of Esther at the same time also served as the aetiology of the feast of Purim. The tradition of the feast and its name probably originates in the tradition of the Persian New Year festival.[117] This is also indicated by the description of the festive customs in the book of Esther (9.17-19, 22). The Jews living in a Persian milieu have adopted the custom, and thus the origin of the feast needed no explanation in the Persian milieu. An explanation did become necessary when the carriers of the tradition returned to Judea, as the feast did not appear in the calendar of the Judean Jews.[118]

The redactor of the narrative of the book of Esther also employed another model, this time taken from the biblical tradition, for the final formulation of the story. It is not hard to discover elements of the story of the exodus (cf. Exod. 1–14) in the motif of the failed plan to destroy the Jews. This part of the story cannot under any circumstances be explained with the help of the Persian era literary material.[119] We are

115. This popularity is indicated by the text found at Elephantine, by the numerous ancient versions and translations of the text, by the narratives of the book of Daniel based on this schema, and by the book of Tobit which even interweaves the figure of Ahiqar into its story (1.21-22).

116. Dan. 1, 2, 3, 6. On this type of story see Lacocque 1987; Wills 1990.

117. Many have derived the word from the Akkadian word *pūru* the meaning of which is similar to the etymology found in the book of Esther, but the derivation has not proved to be valid. See Bea 1940. Lewy derives the name of the feast from the Persian feast of the dead, Farwadigan; see Lewy 1939: 127-51. According to Hutter (1988), the background of Purim is the Persian New Year festival.

118. Fox (1991) dates the story to the third century BCE and determines the genre of the present form of the story as a 'festival lection'. The feast is only mentioned at the end of the second century BCE in 2 Macc. 15.36 as the day of Mordecai which falls on the day before the victory over Nicanor.

119. The thesis of Gerleman that Esther is patterned after the exodus narrative

reminded of the story of the exodus in the part of the story of Esther in which we are told that not only did the Jews escape destruction, but they also managed to destroy their enemies. (Cf. Exod. 14, where the fugitives successfully cross the Red Sea which parts for them, while the waves closing behind them destroy their pursuers.)

The literature varies greatly on the dating of the book of Esther.[120] Some sections of the book seem to indicate that the composition is of late origin. According to Est. 9.27 the victory of the Jews is celebrated not only by them but by 'those who should join them' (הנלוים עליהם), that is to say the Proselytes also celebrated it. This statement can only refer to the era of the Hasmonean kingdom, the age of Aristobulos I (104–103 BCE) or Alexandros Jannaios (103–176 BCE): the aggressive religious policies of these two rulers are well known. Aristobulos and Alexandros converted the populations of entire provinces to Judaism (*Ant.* 13.11.3; 15.4), while earlier this practice was completely unknown. The other element indicating a rather later origin is that according to Est. 3.8 Haman speaks of the Jews as a people living in isolated groups scattered over the territory of the empire. According to Haman the laws of the Jews differ from those of the other peoples; they do not obey the edicts of the king—therefore the king has to destroy them. This way of thinking does not fit with what we know about the attitudes of the Persians to the Jews.[121] It is much more reminiscent of the ideology of 1 Maccabees, its dichotomous attitude which divides the world into Jews and 'nations' who are hostile towards them. The motif of the narrative according to which the vengeful Haman offers a large sum to the treasury to induce the king to issue the decree ordering the annihilation of the Jews does not reflect a Persian era practice either (Est. 3.8-9). A practice similar to this is, however, known from the time of the Seleucid rule, when under Antiochus Epiphanes the office of high priest is allocated to the candidate who offers the highest sum for it.[122] In all likelihood the

(1988) was later attacked by Clines (1984) and others. See also Moore 1987.

120. Third century BCE: Fox 1991; third–second century BCE: Bickerman 1967: 204-207. Paton (1908) and Pfeiffer (1957: 176-77) date it to somewhere after 135 BCE. Stiehl puts the creation of the work to between 165–145 BCE; see Stiehl 1960: II, 195-213.

121. As already mentioned, the various sources on the history of the Achaemenid empire, no matter what their point of view, show no indication of Persian anti-semitism, or of the persecution of Jews in the Achaemenid empire.

122. Jason (Joshua), the brother of the high priest, Onias, paid a high sum to Antiochus IV Epiphanes in 175 BCE to obtain his own appointment as high priest; see

motif of the general fast proposed by Esther also reflects a practice of the Maccabean period.[123] The emphasis on this element in the text also recalls 1 Maccabees, which has a predilection for stressing the connection between strict adherence to religious laws and the victory over the enemy. It is likely, then, that the final compilation of the book of Esther only took place during the Hasmonean era.[124] The book has another link to this era. 2 Macc. 15.36 commemorates the most famous victory of the Maccabean revolt, which was achieved by Judas Maccabeus over the forces of Nicanor, the Seleucid general, which vastly outnumbered the Maccabeans. The Jewish source refers to the day of the battle as the 'day of Nicanor'. This memorial day is only known from this source (2 Macc. 15.36), and there is no evidence elsewhere for its celebration. This same source, however, also mentions the 'day of Mordecai' (14th Adar), which is the day before the day of Nicanor. The author of 2 Maccabees may have been familiar with the feast of Purim of Persian origin, which it mentions as the 'day of Mordecai'—therefore the narrative of the book of Esther was compiled sometime in the Maccabean era, but before the compilation of 2 Maccabees.[125] The above-cited source of 2 Maccabees also leads us to suppose, that the Hasmonean rulers attempted to make use of the probable popularity of the feast of Purim in the celebration of the victory of the Maccabean revolt—and the date of Purim, which was only one day away from the day of victory, made it especially suitable for this.

With regard to its origin and literary raw material the book of Esther belongs to the genre of light literature.[126] At the same time the work is linked by almost invisible, but very strong, ties to the historical

2 Macc. 4.7-9. In the Seleucid empire candidates were appointed to office after paying a certain sum into the royal treasury; on this question see Bickerman 1938: and others.

123. Cf. the narratives of 1 Maccabees and 2 Maccabees, all of which emphasize strongly the necessity of observing religious laws, especially 1 Macc. 2.29-38.

124. Linguistic characteristics indicate diachronic developments of the text of Esther. Bergey (1984) pointed to the linguistic proximity of the Hebrew in Esther and in Tannaitic Hebrew. In a later article (Bergey 1988) he gave a diachronic approach to the linguistic characteristics (Early Biblical Hebrew, Late Biblical Hebrew, and characteristics which anticipate Tannaitic Hebrew).

125. The *terminus ante quem* would be the compilation of the books of Maccabees. According to Eissfeldt this is the last decade of the second century BCE; see Eissfeldt 1964: 785-87. Rost puts it later than this, to between 103–63 BCE; see Rost 1971: 58.

126. Lacocque 1987.

propaganda of the Maccabean period.[127] Overall, as a deliverance story the book sends the same message as the narratives describing the battles of the Maccabean revolt: the representatives of 'nations' who attack the Jews unjustly will be defeated by their own weapons, their plans will turn against them—the Lord of the Jews rescues his people, and the story of this deliverance and its memory becomes another parable in the Jewish historical tradition, of how God, not directly but in indirect ways, governs the course of history.[128]

The Third Book of Maccabees

The work entitled the *Third Book of Maccabees* appears in the canon of the LXX, in the Pravoslav canon and in the canon of the Syrian Peshitta. It is, however, missing from the canon of the Vulgate. The work may have been transmitted together with the two books of Maccabees accidentally, and it has been named after these, even though it has nothing to do either with the Maccabean family, or with the revolt associated with their name. The book had had an earlier, quite apt title, although by now this title had been forgotten: 'Ptolemaica', that is to say, something that happened under Ptolemaic rule—the title aptly describes the content of the book.[129]

Only a Greek text of *3 Maccabees* is known, and it is certain that the work had no Hebrew or Aramaic original. The book was written in Greek by its author, and in a Greek style which shows the influence of Polybius, although the style of the story is more bombastic than elegant.[130] The Jewish author writing in Greek, however, was also familiar with the special style of the Hebrew prayer—most likely from synagogal practice—and displayed this knowledge in the appropriate places of the work.[131]

127. Several authors point this out; most recently Berg 1979: 123-42; similarly, Wills 1990.

128. The Judeo-centred theology of the book is manifested in the use of the genealogies Saulite and Agagite; see Lacocque 1987. Behind 'coincidence' and 'irony' God is to be recognized; see Wiebe 1991; Lambert 1992. This is the message which, in the course of the later history of Jewry, linked lucky escapes from pogroms to the book of Esther and to the feast of Purim as the memorial days of such events are also called Purim. On the folkloristic parallels of Purim see Gaster 1950.

129. The tenth-century Synopsis Athanasii mentions it thus; see Emmett, apud Charles 1973: I, 162.

130. Tcherikover 1961; Eissfeldt 1964: 789; Rost 1971: 79.

131. Licht 1971: col. 299.

The basis of the narrative is provided by two legends. In the first one we can read of the visit of Ptolemy IV Philopator (221–205 BCE) to Jerusalem, which he made after defeating Antiochus III at Raphia, in 217 BCE (*3 Macc.* 1.8–2.18). Despite the well-known prohibition, the king dared to enter the innermost part of the Temple, called Holy of Holies, where only the high priest was allowed to enter, and even he only once a year. In the city and in the Temple the king's deed caused a great upheaval—and as a result of the prayer of the high priest, Simon, a miracle happened. Ptolemy collapsed inside the Temple and had to be carried out.

The author of *3 Maccabees* adopts this motif of the narrative from another narrative. In 2 Maccabees (3.9-40) another story containing the same motif may be found. Here it is Heliodorus, the chief minister of Seleucus, who dares to venture into the sanctuary of the Temple. As a punishment Heliodorus is paralysed on the spot, and thus the treasury of the Temple is spared.[132] Ptolemy's visit to Jerusalem itself is proven to be a fact according to an inscription found in 1924.[133] Polybius also mentions the fact that after the battle the king spent three months in various cities of Syria and Phoenicia.[134]

In the second part of the narrative (2.25–7.22)—maybe as a result of the setback suffered at the Temple—this same Ptolemy Philopator turns against the Jews of Alexandria. He orders them to offer a sacrifice to Dionysus. Those who do not obey the command are punished. According to the king's plan those Alexandrians who resist are gathered together at the Alexandrian hippodrome, and they are to be trampled to death by elephants. However, the Jews of Alexandria miraculously escape: instead of them the drunken elephants trample to death the soldiers of Ptolemy. To commemorate their deliverance they hold a feast, which the king grants them permission to do. This is a kind of Egyptian 'Purim', which the Egyptian Jews celebrate annually, between 8–14 of the month called *epiphi*. In addition, upon the request of the Jews, the king also grants permission to the hitherto persecuted Jews to revenge themselves on the apostates, on some 300 people (*3 Macc.* 6.39; 7.10-15).

It is a generally accepted view that the book, even though it describes events taking place in the third century BCE, came into being much later, at the end of the first century BCE. Some suppose an even later

132. For an analysis of the legend see Bickerman 1939–44: 5-40.

133. Tcherikover 1961: 5.

134. Polybius 5.86-87.

terminus ante quem (up until 70 BCE). Tcherikover's detailed analysis[135] examines all those historical sources which may have been used by the author of *3 Maccabees*, as well as the literary traditions which may have influenced the formulation of the narrative.

From the point of view of historical sources the two narratives constituting the book are not of equal weight. The text of the part describing the battle of Raphia indicates that the author was very familiar with these events. The battle which took place between Ptolemy IV Philadelphos and Antiochus III is also known from the description of Polybius. The narratives of Polybius[136] and of *3 Maccabees* only differ in a few details. It is clear that the Greek historiographer and the author of *3 Maccabees* used a common source.[137] At the same time, any mention of Ptolemy's visit to Jerusalem is missing from Polybius, and, naturally the description of the miraculous event which happened in the Temple is also absent. Although both authors mention Theodorus's unsuccessful attempt on Ptolemy's life,[138] Polybius is not familiar with the tradition according to which the king's life was saved by the Jewish Dositheus, the son of Drimylas.[139] This element which appears in the narrative of *3 Maccabees* is without doubt mythical, although the name, which the author of *3 Maccabees* attributes to the rescuer, is also known from an Egyptian papyrus.[140] The papyrus may be dated to 222 BCE.

The second half of *3 Maccabees* also contains both mythical elements and elements which are to some extent based on historical documents—the number of the former increases in this section. This part of the narrative informs the reader that upon returning from Jerusalem, Ptolemy issues a decree. The decree is engraved on a stele, and is placed at the palace gate (*3 Macc.* 2.27-30).[141] According to the decree all Jews have to undergo *laographia*: 'all Jews should be required to enrol in the census and be reduced to the condition of slaves' (*pantas de tous Ioudaious eis laographian kai oiketikēn diathesin akhthēnai*) (*3 Macc.* 2.28). Those who resist will be killed and 'those who were enrolled

135. Tcherikover 1961: 1-26.

136. Polybius 5.79-86.

137. Emmet, apud Charles 1973: I, 159; Bickerman and Heinemann 1928: col. 779-805. It is likely that this common source was a certain Ptolemy Megalopolites, who wrote a book about Ptolemy Philopator.

138. Polybius 5.81.3; 3 *Macc.* 1.2-3.

139. *3 Macc.* 1.3.

140. *Dōsitheos tou Drimylou*, cf. Willrich 1907.

141. Cf. Tcherikover 1961: 3.

should be branded by fire on their bodies with an ivy leaf, the emblem of Dionysus' (*dia pōros eis to sēma parasēmó Dionusou kissophullu* (2.29). The text of the decree adds: 'But if any of them prefer to join those who are initiated in the mysteries, thcy would be on the same footing as the citizens of Alexandria' (*toutous isopolitas Aleksandreusin einai*) (2.30). According to *3 Maccabees*, only few Jews gained Alexandrian citizenship this way, through denouncing their religion. Enraged at his lack of success Ptolemy Philopator decides that he is going to have all Egyptian Jews killed and commands that they should be rounded up in Alexandria, so as the punishment should be carried out on them at the hippodrome (3.18). He intends to carry out the punishment by means of elephants, made drunk on wine. However, he is prevented from carrying out his revenge by yet another miracle; two angels descend from heaven: 'two angels, clothed in glory... visible to all except the Jews' (6.17), who inspired fear in both beast and man. In their terror the elephants turn against the soldiers of the king, and trample them to death (6.19).

Like the narrative of the first part, here too, the author of *3 Maccabees* mixes data from diverse eras and also mingles mythical and the historical elements. In his *Contra Apionem* Josephus wrote that when Ptolemy VII Euergetes (Physcon) (145–116 BCE) fought for the throne against Cleopatra, the widow of his brother Ptolemy VI, Onias and Dositheus, two Jewish generals, were at the helm of Cleopatra's army.[142] Ptolemy's anger therefore turned against the Jews and he ordered them to be rounded up and thrown in front of drunken elephants. His plan backfired because the elephants did not harm the Jews but turned against Ptolemy's friends killing many of them.[143] Thus Josephus also links the legend about the elephants to actual events of political struggle. The author of *3 Maccabees* transposed this same legend, for which we find no basis in reality among the documents of the Ptolemaic period, to the third century BCE, the reign of Ptolemy Philopator.

The dating of *3 Maccabees* is a complex question. Willrich considered it to be a *roman à clef*, to which the key is provided by the events of 88 BCE in Egypt: the outbreak of hostilities between Alexandrian Jews and Greeks during the reign of X Ptolemy I Alexandros (101–88 BCE).[144] Emmet, Bickerman and others date it to the first century BCE.[145]

142. *Apion* 2.5.
143. *Apion* 2.5.
144. Willrich 1904: 244-58.
145. See Licht 1971: col. 298.

According to Eissfeldt it may have been created during the first century CE, up until 70 CE.[146] Tcherikover, Hadas and Rost date it to the last third of the first century BCE, more precisely to the beginning of the reign of Augustus.[147] The narrative of *3 Maccabees* contains numerous historical references to the third century BCE. Thus, in addition to what has already been mentioned, the text referring to Ptolemy IV as an adherent of Dionysus seems to be based on fact. That the ruler was a follower of the mysteries of Dionysus is witnessed by papyrii.[148] Despite realistic details which may link the story to the third century BCE it is of much later origin than the age of Ptolemy IV. The text mentions that the Jews have to undergo a census, *laographia*. This term, or rather its possible identification and dating, constituted the key for Tcherikover's determination of the date of the creation of the story. In Egypt this term was only known during the Roman period; the term for tax assessment employed by the Ptolemaids was *syntaxis*. This form of tax assessment was used intermittently.[149] The regular census which was referred to as *laographia*, and which served as a means of collecting a head tax, only appeared during the time of Augustus. This (that is to say the head tax) did indeed serve as a tool for thrusting people into servitude (this is how the narrative of *3 Maccabees* views *laographia* too). That is to say the head tax was not paid by the inhabitants of the Greek city states of Egypt, and although the inhabitants of the metropolises did pay something, they paid but a limited amount. Practically the whole of the tax fell on the inhabitants of the *chore*, that is to say, the countryside. Thus *laographia* was a means of social discrimination.

Laographia as a tool of discrimination against Jews, then, most likely made its way into the text under the influence of the institutions of the Roman period. The reason why the narrative talks of anti-semitism is also to be found in this historical background. However, it was not the authorities who wished to impose institutional discrimination on the Egyptian Jews, but rather it was the anti-semitism of the Alexandrian Greeks, which gave rise to this narrative. The strange religious practices of the Jews often caused consternation among the Greeks.[150] This

146. Eissfeldt 1964: 789.

147. Hadas 1949: 155-62; Tcherikover 1961: 1-26; Rost 1971: 79. For a similar dating see also Parente 1988.

148. Hengel 1969: 480.

149. Tcherikover 1956: 179-207; 1961: 7.

150. Anti-semitism first appears in the Alexandrian Greek literature during the first

atmosphere is also reflected in Josephus's *Contra Apionem* in which the author puts the question into the mouth of Apion, the pagan rhetor: 'But', Apion persists, 'why, then, if they are citizens, do they not worship the same gods as the Alexandrians?'[151] This perspective sprang from the religious practices of the Greek city states, where worshipping the gods of the city and participation in the city's cults were among the most basic duties of the citizens.

The outbreak of Alexandrian anti-semitism has a long pre-history. The works of Egyptian Jewish literature clearly reflect the changing relationship of the Ptolemaic rulers and the Egyptian Jewish communities. The *Letter of Aristeas* (third century BCE)[152] still depicts the relationship as ideal. It was at this time that those Jewish mercenaries who later played an important role in the life of this area settled down on the 'land of Onias' and many Jewish mercenaries and officials served in the court of Ptolemy VI Philometor. Under the reign of Ptolemy VIII Euergetes II (Physcon) their position changed significantly: the new ruler persecuted the Jews, as earlier they had supported his rival in the fight for the throne. Similar events took place in 88 BCE and at the very end of the Ptolemaic era. By the time of the beginning of Roman rule anti-semitism had become general in Alexandria, both at the court and in the army. This is what is reflected in Apion's anti-Jewish pamphlet and also in Josephus's response to it.[153]

3 Maccabees is the product of this atmosphere. The work, however, speaks of the problems of the age metaphorically. The author transposes the extreme animosity to two centuries earlier. He attempts to authenti-

century BCE. Apion's first work (at the end of the first century BCE–beginning of the first century CE) on the history of the Jews bears witness to this. The extremist anti-semitic work did not survive; some of its fragments survived in Josephus's *Contra Apionem*, which constitutes a refutation of the work. Some of the works of Philo of Alexandria, a contemporary of Apion's—*In Flaccum*, *Legatio ad Gaium*—are also apologies written on behalf of Jews, or rather they are pamphlets which reflect the conditions prevailing at Alexandria at the time. In effect, the entire oeuvre of Philo serves apologetic purposes: in his allegories he attempts to reconcile the traditions of the Old Testament with the system of Greek philosophy; see Wolfson 1948.

151. *Apion* 2.66.

152. Pelletier 1962. For the dating of the work see Bickerman 1930. On its propagandistic intent see Tcherikover 1958.

153. The anti-Jewish accusations of Apion and others are based on the false accusations compiled by the court historiographers of Antiochus IV Epiphanes; see Bickerman 1937.

cate the story by infusing it with historical details. For this he had good sources: a historical work about the age of Ptolemy IV, and probably other contemporary documents as well, as demonstrated by casual remarks in the text about the customs of the royal court and familiarity with the names of officials. He links these realistic details and narrative traditions to mythical elements (the legend about the divine punishment of the person violating the holiness of the sanctuary and the tale of vengeance turned against its perpetrator).

The perspective of the narrative of *3 Maccabees*, the method of combining reality and myth, and the structure of the narrative are reminiscent of the perspective, methods and structure of other, earlier, works of Jewish tradition,[154] especially the books of Esther and Judith. The author of *3 Maccabees* obviously sees these works as a model.[155] The narrative structure of *3 Maccabees* shows the greatest similarity to the book of Esther, as well as to the deliverance story of the book of Exodus, which had in part also served as a model for the book of Esther. The royal decree ordering the annihilation of an entire people, the unexpected, miraculous deliverance from a hopeless situation, as well as the feast held to commemorate the event (Pesah, Purim, and the feast held in the month of *epiphi*) are common features to all three stories.

In the book of Esther Mordecai and Esther are saved accidentally (the king's sleeplessness, and as a result his recollection of Mordecai's role in the discovery of the conspiracy, on the one hand; and the unexplained goodwill of the king towards Esther, who enters despite the king's prohibition, on the other). The author of *3 Maccabees*—like the author of the book of Judith—excludes all coincidence; in these works it is the people's faith in their God and the divine providence which follows irrevocably from this faith which determines the turn of events.

Undoubtedly *3 Maccabees*, written in Egypt in Greek, reflects the

154. Hadas (1953: 6-16) points out the similarities between *3 Maccabees* and the 'festal legend' of 2 Maccabees.

155. For example the attempts of the enemy to annihilate the entire Jewish nation, as well as the deliverance motif. Sometimes the similarities are numerical: according to *3 Macc.* 7.14-15 the Jews killed 300 of their fellow Jews who had become apostates. According to the book of Esther (9.15) the Jews killed 300 of their enemies at Susa. Vermes (Schürer 1973–79: III.1, 540) supposes the use of the Greek text of Esther in *3 Maccabees*. Parente (1988) supposes that a first redaction of *3 Maccabees* was modelled on Esther (and this redaction presented the king favourably). The supposition according to which the Greek translator of Esther would have used *3 Maccabees* (Motzo 1924) is not very plausible.

influence of Hasmonean propaganda which began a century earlier. This is evident in the perspective of the book, its view of the cause and effect relationship between faith and divine assistance, and in the motif of merciless revenge against the apostates, as well as in the use of certain motifs originating from Hasmonean propaganda (such as the motif of Heliodorus, the story of the paralysis of the person violating the Temple).

Chapter 6

EVALUATION OF THE HASMONEAN PERIOD IN THE *PESHARIM* OF QUMRAN AND IN THE REVISED VISION OF THE *ASSUMPTION OF MOSES*

The body of Qumran texts which is summarily referred to as *pesharim* shows common features which sets it apart even within the group of other works that were most likely created in the community.[1] These texts are based on biblical texts and present their interpretations in a peculiar manner.[2] Two groups have been differentiated within them: the so-called 'thematic *pesharim*' which interpret biblical excerpts of diverse origin (usually from the texts of the 'earlier prophets' with a messianic meaning),[3] and the 'continuous *pesharim*' which are longer, continuous prophetic texts, sometimes even an entire prophetic book.[4] These works

1. The vast field of studies on the emergence and history of the Qumran community cannot be surveyed here; I will refer only to some classical comprehensive works such as Delcor 1978; Cross 1995; Vermes 1981a. Acquaintance with the texts under publication (especially those of Cave IV) will modify several theses concerning the community and its literary tradition. For an outline of the problems see Charlesworth 1991. For a bibliography of recent research on Qumran see van der Woude 1990.

2. On the special interpretation of biblical texts at Qumran see Patte 1975; Fishbane 1988a: 443-505; 1988b; Vermes 1989. Intertextuality, that is the use of biblical text in later works is a general problem; it has recently raised a growing attention; see Carson and Williamson 1988; Draisma 1989; Samely 1991; Eslinger 1992.

3. Texts which may be placed into this group are the so-called 'Florilegium' (4Q 174 = 4Q Florilegium), the texts of 'Catena' (4Q 177 = Catena[a]; 4Q 182 = Catena[b]), and Tanhumim (4Q 176). See Allegro 1968: 53-57, 60-74, 80-81; Brooke 1985.

4. Texts known as 'continuous *pesharim*' are the commentaries to various prophetic books and to Ps. 37. Publications of the texts: 1Q pHab: Burrows *et al.* 1950: I, plates lv-lxi; recently Nitzan 1986; 1Q 14 = 1Q pMi, 1Q 15 = 1Q pSoph: Barthélemy and Milik 1955: 77-80; 4Q 161 = 4Q pIsa[a]; 4Q 162 = 4Q pIsa[b]; 4Q 163 = 4Q pIsa[c]; 4Q 164 = 4Q pIsa[d]; 4Q 167 = 4Q pIsa[a] in Allegro 1968: 11-30; 4Q 169 = 4Q pNah; 4Q 170 = 4Q pZeph; 4Q 171 = 4Q pPsalms[a]; 4Q 173 = 4Q pPsalms[b] in Allegro 1968: 31-53.

interpret the text in such a way that they relate the events in them to the events of the age of the author of the *pesher*, to events touching upon the community. The time of the creation of the extant *pesharim* found at Qumran must have been during the second half of the first century BCE.[5]

The genre of the *pesher* seems to appear at Qumran without any precedents.[6] There is, however, another work in the canonical literature which, based on several of its characteristics, may be regarded as a precursor to the *pesharim*. This work is ch. 9 of the book of Daniel, which belongs to the second century BCE layer of the Danielic tradition. Some of its characteristic features, however, set it apart from the other pieces of the second part of the Danielic collection. This piece uses a different system than the other narratives created at the same time (Dan. 7, 8, 10–11). Unlike the other prophecies of the book of Daniel it does not contain descriptions of visions, although this text also communicates a prophecy. The visual representation of the idea is missing from Daniel 9. Instead it is strongly attached to the biblical written tradition: it cites an earlier prophetic text, and it is its interpretation, *pesher*, which contains the

5. Judging by the content of the texts, there are some instances which could only be referring to the Roman conquest which took place in 63 BCE; based on these the *terminus post quem* of such texts is 63 BCE. The texts of the *pesharim* were only found in single copies; in view of the number of copies and the careful method of their writing it may be supposed that these are unique works which were created in the community. The general consensus is that the Qumran *pesharim* are the work of a single author. Naturally, the works could not have come into being without some precedent for the genre.

6. Several authors have already pointed out the link between the genre of the *pesharim* and of Dan. 9. Filling the void of the period between the two texts, or rather groups of texts, is not an easy task; according to Davies (1987: 27) 'no continuous tradition can be established as lying behind them' (the *pesharim*). This is indeed so—nevertheless, it may be suggested that a text that may possibly shed light on the method of the *pesharim* and on the origin of the names is the Damascus Document. This text is more recent than Dan. 9 and is older than the *pesharim*. It is familiar with the term *pesher* and essentially also with the method of interpretation, and it may be supposed that the names used in the *pesharim* originate in those biblical texts which also served as the background for the Damascus Document. We may also assume connections between the genre of individual texts found mostly in Qumran Cave IV, which are now being continuously published. Thus for example the so-called Pesher Genesis (4Q 252) and the prophetic *pesharim* will be extremely important in the study of the methods of interpretation and in the unravelling of the precedents of the genre of the Qumran *pesharim*. As I completed this book before these materials became available I will not discuss the above questions here.

prophecy that Daniel 9 wishes to characterize. The text which the author of Daniel 9 interprets is the prophecy of Jeremiah about the seventy-year-long Babylonian exile (Jer. 25.11-12; 29.10); the author of Daniel 9 himself also mentions that he is talking about Jeremiah's prophecy (Dan. 9.2). The angel, Gabriel, communicates the *pesher*, that is to say the interpretation of the text, to Daniel (9.21-22). According to the interpretation, the 70 years mentioned in the prophetic text have to be interpreted as 70 year-weeks (= 490 years) (9.24). The events of the period of 70 year-weeks may be identified with the historical events during and after the Babylonian exile. The period starts with the destruction of the Temple of Jerusalem and the Babylonian exile. The latest event which the prophecy of Daniel 9 mentions is the defiling of the Temple of Jerusalem by Antiochus Epiphanes in 168 BCE (9.27). The time period between the two dates, 586 and 168, is 418 years. The author of the prophecy divides this into two periods. The first period lasts 7 year-weeks. Its beginning is the time of Jeremiah's prophecy, or of the beginning of the exile (586 BCE). The period will last 'till the appearance of one anointed, a prince' (משיח נגיד) (9.25). The second period lasts 62 year-weeks. At the end of the period an anointed one (משיח) 'will be removed (יכרת), and no one will take his part' (9.26). The last period of one year-week is exactly half gone at the time of the author. The author of Daniel 9 mentions the cessation of sacrifices in the Temple of Jerusalem during this era (9.27).

The events with which the allusions of the prophecy may be identified are the following: the 'anointed prince' (משיח נגיד) may be Zerubbabel, who returned to Jerusalem during the Persian rule and was appointed governor, or his contemporary, Joshua, the high priest.[7] The rebuilding of squares and walls unequivocally refers to the rebuilding of Jerusalem under Persian dominion. The identification of the removed 'anointed one' is problematical. It is probable that the text refers to a historical person here as well. If so, here too, the author of Daniel 9 might have had a political leader in mind, or someone bearing the title of high priest. We only know of one 'anointed' one from the Persian and Hellenistic periods who died a violent death: Onias III, the last of the high priests of the Zadokite dynasty. Onias was relieved of his office by Antiochus IV Epiphanes around 175 BCE; he then appointed Jason, the brother of Onias, who promised him a significant sum for the office of high priest.

7. Induction into these two offices involved being anointed with oil. Zerubbabel did not have a royal title, but he was from the house of David.

Not much later he appointed Menelaus, of the generation of Balga, who had promised more than Jason for the position of high priest c. 172 BCE. Soon after this same Menelaus had Onias, who had in the meanwhile escaped to Antiochia, killed (about 170 BCE) (2 Macc. 4.34).[8] Onias, the last Zadokite high priest may have been the person to whom the text of Daniel 9 refers. This identification is doubtful due to the difference between the chronology of the Danielic text and that of the historical tradition: according to the calculations of Daniel 9 the killing of the 'anointed one' would have fallen in the 483rd year after 586 BCE (7 year-weeks + 62 year-weeks = 49 years + 434 years = 483 years), that is 103 BCE; almost 70 years later than the death of the historical Onias. This is a significant difference even if we take into consideration that the chronological calculations of the author of Daniel 9 do not correspond precisely to those of modern chronology. Nonetheless, the most likely answer to the question is that the text of Daniel 9 refers to the historical Onias; the author of Daniel 9 clearly insists on a numerical schema (7 + 62 + 1 = 70), into which, however, he cannot fit all the historical events.

The author of Daniel 9 did not choose this particular prophecy of Jeremiah about the seventy-year-long exile as the subject of his interpretation accidentally. In the *pesher*, which interprets the prophesied time period as 70 year-weeks, he wishes to provide a new interpretation for an earlier view of history, according to which the passing of the period of 70 years, theend of the exile, was signalled by the rebuilding of the Temple of Jerusalem during the Persian reign. In all likelihood this also contributes to the fact that the date of the rebuilding of the Temple does not appear as a line of demarcation (notwithstanding the fact that the Temple plays an emphatic role in this text as well, and especially in the description of the third period). The three periods constituting the 70 year-weeks are defined by the activities of certain individuals and by events relating to the Temple. The author of Daniel 9 characterizes the first period by the rule of an 'anointed one', the second by the death of an 'anointed one' (the last Zadokite high priest), and the third by the truncation and distortion of the cult itself. Overall the 70 year-weeks stand for the period of sins (פשע, עון), which is contrasted with the coming new era, which will be hallmarked by 'eternal truth' (צדק עלמים) and the anointment of the Most Holy Place (ולמשח קדש קדשים) (9.24). This new era will begin a few years (half a year-week, that is to say three-and-a-half years) after the beginning of religious persecution. Most likely

8. 2 Macc. 4.7-34; *Ant.* 12.5.1; *War* 1.1.1; Bickerman 1937: 66-67.

the author of Daniel 9 has the Maccabean revolt and its early successes in mind (the text probably came into being shortly after these events).

The fate of Jerusalem and the Temple is the focus of attention in Daniel 9. The activity of the 'anointed' of the first period is followed by the death of the 'anointed one' of the second period, and this event is followed in the third period by transgressions against the cult.[9]

From the point of view of its genre, the text of Daniel 9 belongs to the tradition of the *pesher*. In his prophecy the author uses the method already familiar from the earliest Danielic tradition. Daniel 9 differs, however, from the earlier *pesharim* in that in this work no visual representation, a traditional element of the genre, appears. For the vision is substituted a prophetic text: the prophecy of Jeremiah about the seventy-year-long Babylonian exile. The *pesher* in Daniel 9 (as in the prophecies of Daniel 7 and 8) comes from divine revelation (here the interpreter is Gabriel 'the man Gabriel, whom I had already seen in the vision', which refers back to the interpreter of the earlier visions, the angel, Gabriel, 9.21-23).

The tradition begun by Daniel 9, in which the basis of a historical overview and the associated prophecy is the 'interpretation' of an earlier prophetic text—that is to say, a reinterpretation, an interpretation diverging from the traditional interpretation—is later continued in the genre of the Qumran commentaries (*pesharim*). Only the *pesharim* of the prophetic texts, the 'continuous pesharim', contain references to historical events, to historical prophecies.[10] No matter how controversial the possibility of the historical identification of the personages and events mentioned in the *pesharim*, it is clear that the structure of the texts and their system of symbols lend themselves to analysis, and that the historical identifications can only be accomplished after an ordered and precise

9. The defiling of the Temple (at the time of Antiochus IV Epiphanes), and its later recovery and cleansing (in the course of the battles of Judas Maccabeus) is the main theme of the Second Book of Maccabees which was most probably written later, during the Hasmonean dynasty, and which praises the dynasty. This work puts the transgression against the cult of the Temple at the apex of a series of injuries (2 Macc. 6–7) and sees it as the cause of armed resistance (2 Macc. 8). Cf. 1 Macc. 1.20-24; *Ant.* 12.5.3; *Apion* 2.7.

10. The evaluation of these varies greatly. Davies (1987: 104) incidentally does not consider the historical identifications very plausible; according to him the *pesharim* are 'a development late in the history of the community and have little to do with the activities of the Teacher' or with history. On the various tendencies in the identification of the figures with historical personalities see below.

analysis of the system of literary characteristics.[11] It seems that a uniform structure and symbolic system may be demonstrated for the texts. We do not know if the author (possibly authors) wrote an interpretation to all the prophetic books, or whether they commented upon the entire length of the longer prophetic books, such as the book of Isaiah. From among the surviving commentaries only one was written on a longer prophetic book: this is the *pesher* of the book of Isaiah (4Q 161 [pIsa^{a}], 162 [pIsa^{b}], 163 [pIsa^{c}], 164 [pIsa^{d}], 165 [pIsa^{e}]).[12] At Qumran, however, in all probability commentary was prepared for only one part of the book. The thematic modifications of the text make it impossible for the author of the commentary to satisfy the main requirement of the genre of *pesher*, that is to draw a parallel between all the events he wishes to deal with in the *pesher* and all the events mentioned in the prophetic text. All the texts which served as a basis for the extant Qumran *pesharim* essentially describe a similar situation: the attack of an external enemy (Assyrian or Babylonian armies) against the kingdoms of Israel or Judea, and the danger of total annihilation. It is likely, then, that the Qumranite author selected the prophetic texts to be commented upon deliberately, so that all the texts describe the conflicts of a group chosen and protected by Yahweh against its enemies.[13]

The *pesher* of the text is not the same as a commentary in the traditional sense of the word,[14] that is to say, it does not constitute an explanation which would shed light upon the background of the text; it is a kind of identification of two events or persons, based on some

11. Recent analyses—such as Brooke 1991—demonstrated that the presentation of various persons and groups in Qumran *pesharim* is determined not so much by the historical reality as by literary stereotypes.

12. See Allegro 1968: 11-30.

13. As has already been remarked by several scholars, in the Qumran commentaries there is a disregard for the original historical context of the biblical prophetic text cited, and the interpretations are really not derived from the biblical texts; see Collins 1987. In addition, the texts cited in the commentaries often differ from the text that we know as the Masoretic text. Some of these deviations may be the result of deliberate alterations, as was demonstrated in Lim 1990; others result from the use of different pre-Masoretic texts; see Vegas Montaner 1989.

14. Brownlee likened it to the rabbinical *midrash*. In his view the *pesher* is a type of *midrash*, and classifying it as a separate group, he called it *midrash pesher*, which is akin to the *halakah* and the *haggadah*, but also differs from them. Brooke (1985) calls the group of the Florilegium 'Qumran midrash'. On the entire question see Kraft and Nickelsburg 1986: 247-53.

common feature of the two. It has retained the peculiarity which also characterized the vision and its *pesher*, in that it is a kind of identification (like the dream or vision interpretations, and the Mesopotamian oneiro-criticisms or the dream interpretations of Dan. 2–6).[15]

In cultures which are familiar with the practice of dream interpretation the interpretation of dreams and other omina is never arbitrary: like other areas of knowledge, this too is a science, a system regulated by uniform and strict rules. There is a consistent correspondence between the signs (omina) and the interpretations: the same motif is always interpreted with the same meaning. The motif itself only provides the basic meaning—the specifics of the meaning are determined by other, complementary characteristics of the motif.[16] As for the Qumran *pesharim*, the system of interpretation of these is much more complex than that of the omina. The author of the *pesharim* uses a dual code: in the text of the Qumran *pesharim* fictive names appear in place of the names of those people to whom the texts of the *pesharim* refer.[17] In all likelihood these personages were very well known to the audience for whom the *pesharim* were written—to the covenanters. Today, however, they can only be identified with great difficulty, and the identification often is equivocal or impossible.

To introduce people and events, however, the prophetic text itself uses poetic images. For example in the book of the prophet Nahum the attacking power, Assyria, is symbolized by a lion setting out for a kill (2.12-14). The *pesher* Nahum, that is to say the appropriate lines of the *pesher* written to accompany the book of Nahum, identifies this denotation with the expression 'furious young lion'[18] (כפיר החרון); this latter name most probably denotes a Hasmonean high priest ruler, Alexandros

15. On the similarity with the interpretation of dreams see Rabinowitz 1973 Fröhlich 1986; Fishbane 1988a: 447-57; Basser 1988; Collins 1987. The *pesher* of Dan. 9 on Jeremiah's prophecy on the Babylonian exile (Jer. 25.12; 29.10) is the first known example of the *pesher*-like method of interpretation of a written text. On the exegetical method of Dan. 9, see Szörényi 1966.

16. In the dream book of Susa (see Oppenheim 1956: 258), for example, we can read about a dream, in which the dreamer walks on calm and on turbulent water. In both cases the dream means illness. In the interpretation, the meaning of the image of 'water' remains unchanged; the variations (mild or serious illness) are provided by the changing attributes of the water.

17. Fröhlich 1986; Jucci 1987.

18. Vermes 1987: 280. This is his translation which is more precise than the widespread 'Lion of the Wrath'.

Jannaios (103–76 BCE).[19] In the two texts, then, the Hasmonean ruler and Assyria correspond to each other; the author of the *pesher* had identified the ruler of his own people with the foreign conqueror of the prophetic text. The author of the text identifies—by a similar method—the Pharisees (דורשי החלקות, 'interpreters of smooth things'), and the events related to them with the fate of two cities, Thebes and No-Amon, mentioned in the text (4QpNah. 1.2, 4 *et passim*).

Beside the fictive names which may be called 'associative' (that is to say, names which are based on the system of signs of the interpreted prophetic text) another naming system may also be demonstrated in the text of the Qumran *pesharim*, which is independent of the prophetic text at hand. These names also have two groups. 1) Names which seemingly are based on specific characteristics of the person denoted by them, so-called 'symbolic' names, such as 'scoffer' (איש הלצון), 'righteous teacher' (מורה הצדק), 'wicked priest' (כהן הרשע), 'men of righteousness' (אנשי אמת), 'interpreters of smooth things' (דורשי החלקות), 'those who lead astray many' (מתעי רדים), 'liar' (איש הכזד). The bearers of these symbolic names always belong to one of two sharply opposed groups.[20] 2) The so-called typological names; they may have been based on the tradition of Genesis, and they may be read not only in the texts of *pesharim*, but in other Qumranite documents as well. Such names are בית אבשלום, פלג בית, מנשה, אפרים, כתיים, ישראל, בית יהודה.

With the help of the comments and characteristics attached to the typological names, as well as with the help of the rare genuine historical names mentioned in the text, we can attempt the identification of persons and events and seek those genuine historical personages and groups who played some kind of central role in the life of the Qumran community. From among the personages mentioned in the *pesharim* the identification of the person of the Wicked Priest is the one for which the

19. Allegro 1956: 92; 1959; Stern 1960; Rowley 1956; Amussin 1971: 220.

20. The origin of the names—the meaning of which probably corresponded to the characteristics of the persons and groups denoted by them—probably can be traced back to an earlier exegetical tradition. The basis for the naming is to be found in the prophetic literature, primarily in expressions found in the book of Isaiah; these originate from those places of the prophetic literature which are also frequently interpreted by the author of the Damascus Document. It may be supposed that the names, of which many are used not just by the prophetic *pesharim*, but also by other Qumran texts, originate from these texts, which for some reason were especially popular and respected in the community. On an exegesis anterior to the commentaries see Dimant 1992.

external sources may provide the most support, and this is where the problem of identification has provoked the most heated debates.[21] At this point there are two sides in the controversy: the followers of the 'Alexandrists' and the 'Jonathanists'. The basis for the argument of the 'Jonathanists' is one point of the *pesher* Habakkuk (9.12), where the text mentions that the beginning of the office of the Wicked Priest was legitimate (more precisely: the author of the *pesher* regarded the tenure of the priest, at its beginning to be legitimate) (נקרא בשם הקודש)[22] and it mentions the death of the high priest, which had been caused by pagans. These latter words may refer to Jonathan (cf. *Ant.* 13.6.1-2), and they cannot easily be fitted into the biography of Alexandros Jannaios. At the same time the 'Jonathanists' leave out of consideration another text, that place in the Nahum commentary which without a doubt refers to the events of the rule of Alexandros Jannaios, as well as the recurring references of the *pesharim* to the conflicts of the Wicked Priest and the Pharisees. These cannot be fitted into the biography of Jonathan. In that part of the Habakkuk *pesher* which is supposed to mention the death of the Wicked Priest, the meaning of the term לענות used is 'so as to humiliate' and not 'so as to kill'.[23] The violent death of the historical Jonathan is not the only event to which the allusion of the *pesher* may be connected.

The key to the identification of the figures appearing in the Qumran *pesharim* is given by the few concrete names occurring in the text, such

21. With regard to the historical background of the *pesharim* essentially six hypotheses have come into being. According to these the persons and events mentioned refer to a) the era of Antiochus Epiphanes (175–163 BCE); b) the era of the first Maccabean rulers (Jonathan, 152–142 BCE, Simon 142–135 BCE); c) the period of Alexandros Jannaios (103–76 BCE) or rather the era of his sons (76–63 BCE); otherwise it has been suggested that we should look for their background in d) the birth of Christianity, e) the Jewish revolt against Rome, or f) some medieval origin. Among these the Christian and the medieval hypotheses did not prove to be tenable. On the various hypotheses, see Vermes 1981b: 22. In the light of the paleographic examination of the Qumran manuscripts (the earliest manuscripts originate from the first half of the second century BCE) today only the b) and c) hypotheses are accepted. On the debates, see Burgmann 1977.

22. Hebrew קרא בשם; cf. the Akkadian expression 'called by his name', which, in connection with Nabuna'id and other Mesopotamian rulers indicates the legitimacy of the person referred to; see Beaulieu 1989: 112-13.

23. Cf. Vermes 1981b: 23; ענה iii. 'be bowed down', 'afflicted', in Gesenius and Robinson 1978.

as the Acco city name in the Isaiah *pesher* (4Q 161 = 4Q pIsa[a]). Most recently these have been convincingly identified by Amussin with the historical events of the beginning of the first century BCE.[24] The author of the commentary describes the events of the battle between Ptolemy Lathyros and Alexandros Jannaios in the 90s BCE. This battle ended with the defeat of Alexandros (cf. *Ant.* 13.12.2-6). Incidentally, these events are the oldest of the events mentioned by the text of the Qumran *pesharim*.

The commentary written to the book of the prophet Habakkuk is the longest *pesher*, the text of which survived almost in its entirety. This text mentions on several occasions the conflicts of the Righteous Teacher (מורה הצדק) and the Wicked Priest (כהן הרשע) (1QpHab. 1.12; 5.10-11; 9.9-12; 11.4-6). Judging by the context, in the place where the text mentions the Wicked Priest for the first time, his figure may be identified with that of Alexandros Jannaios.[25] The Righteous Teacher may have been a leader of the community, not known to us by name. The section that follows is a prophecy (2.5-7); it refers to the Roman attack of 63 BCE. In the following (3.12-5.2) the author of the *pesher* writes about the 'Kittim' (כתיים), that is to say the Romans (4.1-3 refers to their manner of conducting warfare, according to which military campaigns are led by appointed generals). According to the author of the Habakkuk *pesher*, God will not destroy the nation by means of the Kittim (2.12-4.13). The next section of the text contains an eschatological prophecy. It is about the coming of God's chosen one (בחירו) (5.3-6), then the author of the *pesher* returns to the events of the ancient past, to the conflict of the Righteous Teacher with the Wicked Priest (5.9-12). The remainder of the text can be divided into sections analogous to the series mentioned here. These series usually contain three elements: the events of the rule of Alexandros Jannaios; events that took place during the rule of the sons of Alexandros; and events which will take place in the future.[26]

It seems, then, that the Qumran *pesharim* always refer to the same events, to the events of a relatively brief period, from the rule of Alexandros Jannaios to the Roman conquest of 63 BCE. In the Habakkuk *pesher* the references to this historical period and to the future are periodically repeated in chronological order. Mention of historical events is always followed by an eschatological prophecy. The characteristic

24. Amoussin 1974; 1978.
25. Allegro 1956: 92; 1959; Stern 1960; Rowley 1956; Amussin 1971: 220.
26. Fröhlich 1986: 391-92.

motifs in the historical references are: the failures of Alexandros, his cruelty toward the Pharisees, and the attack of the Kittim, that is the Romans. The above-mentioned section of the Habakkuk *pesher* (9.9-12) interprets the Roman conquest as divine punishment, in the course of which the Wicked Priest falls into the hands of his enemies, because of the sin he committed against the Righteous Teacher (בעוון מורה הצדק). This excerpt is the decisive argument of the 'Jonathanists' against the identification of the Wicked Priest with Alexandros Jannaios. The events of the life of Alexandros cannot under any circumstances be linked with these references. It seems that the 'Alexandrist' hypothesis also fails at this point—which is why Amussin also doubts the identification of the Wicked Priest with Alexandros Jannaios.[27] The dilemma can only be resolved if we suppose that the term Wicked Priest does not refer to a specific individual but is a collective name. In the Qumran *pesharim* there are certainly several other names which were used in a collective sense: the term Kittim usually denoting Romans cannot be identified with the army of Pompeius in the fragment of the Isaiah *pesher* (4QpIsa/a = 4Q 161, frag. 8-10, 3-9), as here the context indicates that the term refers to Alexandros Jannaios. According to the text the Kittim set out from Acco. Military campaigns starting from Acco are only known from the time of Alexandros: it was Ptolemy Lathyros who, crossing over from Cyprus, began his attack against Alexandros from Acco, with shocking cruelty (cf. *Ant.* 13.12.2).[28] The rule for the use of the typological name Kittim—and most probably for other terms as well—is that the name has a collective, general meaning (in the case of the Kittim: 'strangers arriving from the sea, from the direction of Cyprus'). The actual meaning of the name in a given instance is always determined by the characteristics of the term, that is, those events which the text mentions as a reference in connection with the name (sometimes, as in the case of Acco in the aforementioned text, one key word is the determining factor).

Keeping this principle in mind the figure of the Wicked Priest in the relevant excerpt (9.9-12) of the Habakkuk *pesher* may also be identified. When reviewing the circle of historical references we determined that the *pesharim* only refer to two sets of historical events: to the events of the rule of Alexandros and to the Roman conquest, or to the events of the period immediately preceding it. The Habakkuk *pesher* considers the

27. Amussin 1967.
28. Amussin 1978.

conquest to be divine punishment for the sin committed against the Righteous Teacher. The next sentence, however, mentions the 'the last/or later priests of Jerusalem' (כהנים האחרונים) (9.4), whose riches are handed over to the generals of the Kittim, 'at the end of thc days' (הימים באחרית). This reference most likely concerns the fight for the throne between the sons of Alexandros Jannaios, in the course of which both pretenders gave handsome sums and gifts to Aemilius Scaurus, the Roman general, and Pompeius, who was the mediator in their dispute (cf. *Ant.* 14.2-3). The contradiction of the two parts of the text can only be resolved if we interpret the term Wicked Priest as a collective name.[29]

Interpreting the term Wicked Priest as a collective name we find that it refers to Alexandros Jannaios and his two sons in the Habakkuk *pesher*. The Roman conquest, which in the eyes of the author is divine punishment, takes place during the rule of the sons, because of the father's sins against the Righteous Teacher. This punishment is followed by judgment (9.3-5).

There is one other argument in favour of interpreting the names of the Habakkuk *pesher* (and most likely of the other *pesharim* as well) in a collective sense: the text of Daniel 10–11, which gives a historical overview of the events of the period from Alexander the Great to the era of Antiochus IV Epiphanes. The overview concludes with a prophecy of the imminent death of Antiochus, which will take place in Jerusalem (11.40-43), and this is followed by the description of the judgment (Dan. 12). Apart from a few geographical names (Persia, 11.1; Egypt, 11.8), which may be regarded as keys to the identification, the part of the text which briefly reviews the historical events uses only fictive names. These fictive names may be classified into two types:

a. typological names, usually from the tradition of Genesis (יון, 11.2; כתיים, 11.30);
b. names which had been created on the basis of a characteristic peculiar to the denoted person (מלך הנגב 'king of the south', and מלך צפון 'king of the north' for the designation of the Ptolemaic and Seleucid kings (11.5 *et passim*); משכילי עם 'wise leaders' for the author and his intellectual circle (11.33, 35); מרשיאי ברית, עזבי ברית 'those who are ready to violate the covenant', for those outside the author's circle (11.32).

29. First Brownlee (1952) and more recently van der Woude (1982) have identified the figure of the Wicked Priest with successive rulers of the Hasmonean dynasty.

In the text of Daniel 10–11 these names appear with collective meanings. Thus מלך הנגב and מלך צפון denote a whole series of Ptolemaic and Seleucid rulers. The identification of the names with actual historical personages—as in the case of the Qumran *pesharim*—must be done with the context in mind, by identifying the events to which the text refers in connection with individual characters.[30]

We find a similar usage of names in the texts of the Enochic tradition from the second century BCE, as in the *Apocalypse of the Weeks* (*1 En.* 93 + 91), where the term for humankind and for the chosen ones of Israel is 'a man'. Another contemporary piece in the same collection, the *Animal Apocalypse* (*1 En.* 85–90) presents to the reader a whole series of characters—the elect—as a 'white bull'.[31] Prior to the Qumran *pesharim*, the use of names or symbols with a collective meaning is only known from the tradition of the Hasidim, from the later collection of the Danielic circle (Dan. 10–11) and from the second-century pieces of the Enochic circle mentioned above. The systematic application of this method can only be found among a special group of works, the prophetic commentaries, called *pesharim*, created by the consistent and radical followers of the Hasidic tradition, the Qumran community. Thus this work which earlier was considered to be without precedents and without connections can be shown to have at least some roots in the tradition of the book of Daniel:[32] on the one hand in the exegetic method of ch. 9, which constitutes an interpretation of the prophetic text in such a way that the

30. In connection with the historical overview of the book of Daniel presented in the form of oracles, the possible influence of the so-called 'Akkadian apocalypses' on Jewish tradition and on Jewish apocalyptic texts should be mentioned. The texts called 'Akkadian apocalypses' always refer to some historical period in the future; instead of genuine names their authors also use symbolic names. This genre—which first occurs in the Neo-Babylonian period, and continues in the Hellenistic period—may have influenced the tradition of Jews living at the time of the exile and during the Persian period in Mesopotamia, and like the tradition of dream interpretation, it may have survived in the Danielic tradition, which could have transmitted it to later periods.

31. The elect is either a white bull, or a white human figure, or the two may alternate: Adam is a white bull (ch. 85), Enoch is a white human figure (ch. 89), the messiah is a white bull (ch. 90).

32. On the question of the connections of the book of Daniel and the Habakkuk commentary see Mertens 1971 (examination of word usage, along with angelology, methods of interpretation and eschatological beliefs). Mertens supposes the existence of relations between the Maccabean period redactor of the book of Daniel and the Qumran community; on this question see Kraft and Nickelsburg 1986: 252.

pronouncements of the prophetic text are made to refer to a later era; on the other hand, in the method of Daniel 10–11, which overviews a historical period through the use of symbolic names used with a collective meaning.[33]

The Assumption of Moses

The *Assumption of Moses* is a work only known in Latin translation. Based on the events narrated in the work and on its perspective it too is clearly a product of the Jewish tradition of the Hellenistic period. Its original language may have been either Hebrew or Aramaic, and several translations had been prepared from this, of which the Latin version survived.[34] The final text of the work, based on the latest event mentioned in it, may be dated to somewhere after 4 BCE.[35] The frame of the narrative—similarly to that of *Jubilees*—is a divine revelation which Moses receives about the future of his people. Thus, the narrative begins with the age of Moses, with the story of the covenant between God and the chosen people (cf. Exod. 19). However, according to the author of the *Assumption of Moses*, the people had been chosen since the beginning of the history of humankind, and God had already made a covenant with them at that time (1.12-15).

From the history of Israel, the *Assumption of Moses* singles out the crossing of the Jordan following the wandering in the wilderness (2.1-2).

33. The use of the book of Daniel at Qumran is evidenced by 4Q 174: 4Q 174, col. ii, the text of line 3: [...אש]ר כתוב בספר דניאל הנבי 'as it is written in the book of Daniel the prophet'—this indicates that the book of Daniel was classified among the prophetic documents, and just as in the case of the prophetic books, they may have paid special attention to it. The apocryphal Danielic tradition at Qumran—Pr Nab and the vision of the trees—proves that the Danielic tradition at Qumran was more encompassing than the Danielic collection of the Masoretic text.

34. The first publisher of the work was Ceriani (1861). Later Charles published the text with an introduction and translation (Charles 1897). Its most recent edition is Laperrousaz 1970. Translations are Charles 1973: II, 407-24; Priest, apud Charlesworth 1983–85: I, 919-34 (entitled *Testament of Moses*). In addition to the above see also Denis 1970: 128-41; Rowley 1963: 106-10, 149-56; Nickelsburg 1973.

35. Charles (1897: xxxvi-xlv; 1973: II, 4), and following him others, have dated the entire work to between 7–30 CE. Nickelsburg (1973), following the conclusions of Licht (1961), formulated the theory according to which most of the text of the *Assumption of Moses* came into being during the time of Antiochus IV Epiphanes and that this text was later amended (chs. 6–7 rewritten after 6 CE). See also Kraft and Nickelsburg 1986: 239-47.

Of the following era, the history of the united and later divided monarchy, the work only gives a cursory summary. The period under discussion is presented according to a peculiar chronological order: 24 'years' pass from the time of settling in Canaan until the end of the united monarchy, then a further 36 'years' elapse from the breaking off of the northern kingdom until the conquest of Jerusalem by Nebuchadnezzar (2.6-9). The period following this is the age of the Babylonian exile which lasts for 77 'years' (3.14). The text describes the circumstances of the exile in great detail—the author regards the exile itself as a punishment for the sins of the people (3–5). The next, fourth, period is the age of 'high priest kings', that is to say the era of Hasmonean rulers (6.1). The author characterizes this age also as an era of sin and godlessness. This view is unusual in the Jewish tradition of the Hellenistic period, since in other respects the *Assumption of Moses* follows the pattern of the early apocalyptic works which had been created during the second century BCE and which still see this age as the fulfilment of messianic expectations.[36]

The 'king' following the Hasmonean dynasty may be identified as Herod the Great (37–4 BCE). According to the text of the *Assumption of Moses*, this character (who is not named) ruled for 34 years, was not of priestly origin, and his sons did not inherit his kingdom. The text also emphasizes his extraordinary cruelty (6.2-9).[37]

The remainder of the text (6.8-9) mentions a 'mighty western king' and the occupation of the country following the death of the previous 'king', that is to say, of Herod. This statement may indeed be linked to events following the death of Herod, when under the commandership of the legate, Varus, troops were dispatched to the area.[38] According to the assessment of the *Assumption of Moses* the Roman occupation is a means of punishment.

The historical overview concludes with a prophecy: Taxo and his seven sons, who are descendants of the tribe of Levi, will rise against the conquerors (9.1). The characters and the circumstances are reminiscent of descriptions of the outbreak of the Maccabean revolt, familiar from the

36. The *Animal Apocalypse* (*1 En.* 85–90) and the *Apocalypse of the Weeks* (*1 En.* 93 and 91).

37. The adjective describing the otherwise nameless character is *acervus*. The description is restricted to generalities, and the character cannot be identified on the basis of the cruel acts known from the tradition of Josephus; see *Ant.* 14.9-17.8.

38. Cf. Josephus, *Ant.* 17.10; *War* 2.3-6.

Jewish tradition, and actually originate from Hasmonean propaganda.[39]

It is a peculiarity of the narrative that following the section criticizing the Hasmonean dynasty (ch. 5), the prophecy concluding the text nonetheless invokes the ancestors of the dynasty, the leaders of the Maccabean revolt. In the figures of Taxo and his seven sons the author commemorates them similarly to the manner of Hasmonean propaganda. In the period following the death of Herod there are no figures with whom Taxo and his seven sons may be identified, neither from the Hasmonean house nor in the form of any other well-known figure. The author of the *Assumption of Moses* most likely awaits the arrival of a transcendental, idealized 'saviour'.

However, originally Taxo and his seven sons were not mere ideals but were based on reality. In its present form the text of the *Assumption of Moses* is the result of revision. The sections dealing with the period from the Hasmonean dynasty to the reign of Herod (chs. 5–6) have most probably been inserted later on.[40] The original text may have been written by a Jewish author living in the Seleucid empire during the reign of Antiochus IV Epiphanes, at the time of the Maccabean revolt. To the author, the revolt led by the Maccabees may have meant the fulfilment of promises about the future of Israel. The narrative of the original version then is contained in chs. 1–5 and in ch. 7. The narrative is based on Deuteronomy 31–34, and contains the following parts:

1. The announcement of the death of Moses
   Deut. 31.1, 14 — *Ass. Mos.* 1.15
2. The appointment of Joshua
   Deut. 31.7, 14, 23 — *Ass. Mos.* 1.7-11
3. The command that he should preserve the books
   Deut. 31.19, 25-26 — *Ass. Mos.* 1.16-18
4. The revelation of the history of Israel
   Deut. 32 (vv. 28-30) — *Ass. Mos.* 2-9
5. The blessing bestowed on Moses
   Deut. 33 — *Ass. Mos.* 10

In the course of the overview of the history of Israel the author presents events—by means of defining their sequence and evaluating them—in

39. Cf. 1 Macc. 2–3 and Josephus, *Ant.* 12.6, which may have served as models for the narrative of the *Assumption of Moses*.

40. This is the theory of Collins, Nickelsburg and Goldstein; see Nickelsburg 1973: 15-52.

such a way that they constitute two cycles of the sin-punishment-turning point-deliverance schema. The deliverance element of the second cycle is represented by the Maccabean revolt (Taxo and his sons). This kind of historical perspective first appears in Deuteronomic historiography which came into being during the seventh century BCE. A similar perspective is also recognizable in the book of Jubilees.[41]

The cycles of *Assumptio Mosis* are as follows:

Cycle I

1. The sins of Judea (*Ass. Mos*. 2.7-9)
2. Punishment: the conquest of Nebuchadnezzar (3.1-3)
3. The people recall the words of Moses in their song (3.10-14)
4. Upon the request of an unnamed intermediary they are allowed to return to their country (4.8)

Cycle II

1. The sins of the Hellenists during the time of Antiochus Epiphanes, the defiling of the Temple (5.23)
2. Divine punishment (the deeds of Antiochus) (8.1-5)
3. Taxo gathers his sons and they die, making reference to the divine vengeance which will follow their death. (ch. 9)
4. God's fury on behalf of the innocent (ch. 10).[42]

This schema of a dual cycle was supplemented by the second author, the final redactor of the text, who lived after the death of Herod. He inserted his own narrative about the age of the Hasmonean dynasty and of Herod into the sequence of the punishments of the second cycle.

Beside the cyclical schema, a numerical schema can be recognized in the work. According to the text from the time of settling down in Canaan until the division of the kingdom (the breaking off of the ten tribes) altogether 24 'years' pass (2.1-3). From this time on until the violation of the 'covenant of the Lord' altogether 40 'years' elapse (2.5-9). The period of Babylonian captivity which follows lasts for 77 'years' (3.14). At the end of the text there is a statement which indicates that the reign of Herod lasts 34 'years' (6.6). With the exception of this last bit of information, in all likelihood the 'years' do not mean calendrical years, but longer periods, year-weeks.[43] Herod's reign, however, is known

41. Licht 1961; Priest 1971.

42. See Nickelsburg 1981: 81-82.

43. In Jewish tradition the year-week means a seven-year period; in the Jewish historical overview literature there is a tradition of measuring time in year-weeks, see the chronology of Dan. 9 and *Jubilees*.

from other sources to have lasted for 34 years. The numerical values of year-weeks are of increasing values, and all the numbers are so-called symbolic numbers. The purpose of the author most likely was not so much to provide precise data to his readers about historical chronology, but rather to inform them of the time of the end of the last period. It is of course impossible to know what kind of chronological knowledge he had. His intention to extend the duration of the last chronological period, of the time elapsed since the Babylonian captivity, is obvious.

According to Jewish tradition, the length of the exile was 70 years (based on Jer. 25.11 and 19.10). From the second century BCE, authors of historical surveys began to calculate these 70 years in year-weeks, thus 'deliverance' was not identified with the return during Persian rule, but compared to their own era, it was projected into the future.[44] The author of *Assumptio Mosis* also does this, but he extends the traditional period by another seven 'years'; that is to say, year-weeks. If we translate the calculations of the author of Assumptio Mosis into our own chronology the end of the Babylonian exile is 47 BCE (77 × 7 = 539; 586-39 = 47). This falls a few decades before the possible time of the revision of the text. Adding 34 years to this time, the length of Herod's reign—this time in actual years—we get 13 BCE. It is following this time that the redactor expects a turning point, and the awaited divine forgiveness. These numbers, even if they do not correspond exactly to our historical chronology, are not very far off the mark. The author of the historical chronology which may be reconstructed from the text may have been the redactor, who inserted his own chronicle into the narrative, and who divided the entire historical overview into periods reckoned in year-weeks. With this calculation he validated, as it were, the expectations of the amended text regarding the future.

Who could have been the author, and who could have been the redactor? The perspective of the original—that is to say pre-revision—work shows certain similarities with the attitude of the author of the *Jubilees*. The cyclical view of history, as well as the structure of the cycles, is similar in both works. The attitude of *Assumptio Mosis* is peaceful, it has no militant ideology.[45] The Temple receives an important place in the work. However, the author does not consider the second sanctuary to be of equal rank to the Solomonic sanctuary. This indicates that most likely the author of *Assumptio Mosis* did not belong to the circle of the

44. Cf. the exegesis of the same prophetic verses in Dan. 9.
45. Collins 1973b: 198-201.

Temple or to circles near it. It is also clear that he approved of the Maccabean revolt, since he presented this event as a precursor to the period of forgiveness.

The redactor, however, may have been hostile to the rule of the Hasmonean dynasty, which descended from the leaders of the revolt, since along with the reign of Herod he classified this reign among the periods of 'punishment' (see the second cycle of the cyclical schema). In this instance, his perspective is similar to that of the author of the Qumranite *pesharim*, who also pronounces the Hasmonean rulers to be sinners—the foreign occupation of the country is divine punishment for their sins.[46] There is one other feature of the text which may point to the identity of the author or the redactor. This is the mysterious name Taxo,[47] which in all probability originally was not a personal name, but a noun denoting the function of the character which came to be used as a name. The word appearing in this place in the Greek translation was *taksōn* 'commander', which is a translation of the Hebrew word מחקק, which has a similar meaning.[48] The Latin text already uses the word as a personal name. Taxo is descended from the tribe of Levi, thus the name denotes a priest.[49] In the perspective of the author of the *Assumption of Moses*, Taxo will become the leader of the events heralding the turning point expected to occur after the death of Herod. Bearing in mind that the meaning of the supposed original word, מחקק, is 'interpreter of [the] law',[50] Taxo probably did not refer to a military but rather to a spiritual

46. In this regard the perspective of the *Assumption of Moses* is reminiscent of the Qumranite prophetic *pesharim*; on the structure and perspective of the latter see the chapter on *pesharim*.

47. The name has been interpreted both as a contaminated form of a genuine historical name, and as a cryptogram; on the various theories see Schürer 1973–79: III.1, 180, n. 16.

48. The word may be originated from the Greek verb *tassō* (*tattō*), meaning 'to order, state, command'; the possible original Hebrew word is מחקק, meaning 'prescriber (of laws), commander' (חקק Po'el Pt.; see Deut. 33.21; Judg. 5.14; Isa. 33.22; Num. 21.18; Ps. 108.9). It is noteworthy that the word and its interpretation with regard to Num. 21.18 constitutes the subject of several exegetical works from Qumran, and the expression may have played a significant role in the tradition of the community. On the above-mentioned etymology of the word 'Taxo' see Schürer 1973–79: III.1, 280. On the use of the word מחקק see Vermes 1961: 49-55.

49. 2 Macc. also refers to Mattathias, the father of Judas Maccabeus and his brothers, as a priest from the tribe of Levi.

50. The word מחקק, appears several times with this meaning in the so-called sectarian works found at Qumran, that is to say, among those documents which were

leader in the text of the *Assumption of Moses*. This and other characteristics of the *Assumption of Moses* indicate that the author's ideas may have been influenced by the world-view of the Qumran community. Earlier a great variety of theories have been put forth regarding the circles of the author of the *Assumption of Moses* and the background of the work.[51] Although most likely the work did not belong to the literature of the Qumran community,[52] the similarities in perspective—the sharp condemnation of Hasmonean rulers, the use of certain key terms known from Qumran—seem to indicate that the author could not have been very far from these circles. The links to the tradition, which in Qumran had developed into a special genre—a historical overview which used nouns and adjectives as names of characters instead of real names—may indicate an even closer connection.

created by a group which most likely considered itself to be separate and which expressed this sense of separateness in its writings.

51. On these see Schürer 1973–79: III.1, 283.

52. Not one fragment of any of the versions (Hebrew, Greek) of the *Assumption of Moses* has come to light from the Qumran caves.

Chapter 7

'REWRITTEN BIBLES' AND VISIONARY LITERATURE AFTER THE JEWISH REVOLT

The work known as *Liber Antiquitatum Biblicarum* is a chronicle-like (but not historiographical) work adapting a biblical tradition which most likely dates from the first century CE. It is much more recent than the other known 'rewritten Bible', the *Book of Jubilees*. At present we know very little about the road which led from *Jubilees*, that special genre of Jewish exegetic tradition which could be termed 'narrative exegesis', to *Liber Antiquitatum Biblicarum*.[1]

The document has only survived in Latin translation. It was transmitted together with the works of Philo of Alexandria,[2] and for a long time Philo was also considered to be its author. In point of fact, *LAB* is the work of an unknown Jewish author, probably from the period following the destruction of the Second Temple (70 CE).[3] The identity of

1. The question of the relationship of the 'rewritten Bibles' and of the biblical interpretation was raised first by Vermes (1961; 1970). Attridge (1976) gives an analysis of the rewriting of biblical history in Josephus. On Pseudo-Philo, see C. Perrot, in Perrot and Bogaert 1976: II, 22-28. In addition to the method of omitting from and enlarging of the biblical text, Pseudo-Philo uses the method of modelling some of his narratives after various biblical narratives. On the various midrashic methods used in *LAB* see Fröhlich 1981; Bauckham 1983.

2. The manuscripts contain it together with the Latin translations of Philo, *Quaestiones et solutiones in Genesim*, and *De essaeis* (a fragment of *De vita contemplativa*).

3. It is difficult to date the work based on its content as there is no reference in it which would unequivocally point to the author's era. Cohn, based on a remark of *LAB* 19.7, suggested that the work was written after 70 CE, that is to say, after the destruction of the Second Temple. This opinion has remained valid to this day; see Cohn 1898: 327; James 1917: 30-33; Strugnell 1973: 408; Harrington *et al.* 1976: II, 78. According to Nickelsburg (1980) the succession of good and bad leaders refers to the period prior to the Jewish revolt. James (1917: 32-33) puts it to the end of the first century CE. More recently Bogaert (Perrot and Bogaert 1976: II, 68-70) has sug-

the author cannot be determined from the work, and the literature refers to him as Pseudo-Philo. The original language of *LAB* may have been Hebrew or Aramaic,[4] and from this text a Greek translation was prepared, which has not survived. The extant Latin text was translated from the Greek.[5] Excerpts of the work may be found in the Medieval Chronicles of Jerahmeel, and the question whether these could have been part of the original text has been raised. However, repeated analyses have proved that Jerahmeel did not use the original text, but rather a text translated back into Hebrew.[6]

LAB is based on the narrative traditions of Genesis and Exodus and on the historical narrative tradition extending from Joshua to the second book of Samuel.[7] The surviving text of the work seems to be incomplete: the text breaks off at the dying Saul's speech. Despite its incompleteness a certain structure may be reconstructed for the text, from which we get a glimpse of the author's overall view of world history, his ideas about the beginning and the end of the process, and about his teleological perspective. He chooses the narrative of the books of Chronicles as his model:[8] he begins the history of the world by enumerating the generations

gested an origin earlier than 70 CE, based on various arguments (sacrificial worship receives an important role in the work, and the text makes no reference whatsoever to the Jewish revolt). On the question see Vermes, in Schürer 1973–79: III.1, 328-29. According to Olyan (1991) the arguments of a narrative passage in the text reflect the ideology of the war itself. For an earlier dating of the work (proto-zelote, Galilee), see Hadot 1985. Wadsworth (1978) first fixed the date of the composition to the end of the first century CE; recently Zeron 1989 fixed a *terminus post quem* in the time of the end of the Bar Kochba revolt (135 CE).

4. Cf. Cohn 1898; James 1917: 28-29; Dietzfelbinger 1975: 92; Harrington and Cazeaux 1970. Feldman and Hata (1971: xxvi-xxvii) consider the question unproven.

5. Based on several manuscripts J. Sichardus published its *Editio princeps* in Basel in 1527. The modern editions of the complete text are Kisch 1949; Harrington and Cazeaux 1976 (with a commentary in Perrot and Bogaert 1976).

6. Gaster (1899: xxx-xxxix) considered Jerahmeel's Hebrew text original; on the contrary, Cohn considered it a retranslation from the Latin; see Cohn 1915. The analysis of the Hebrew fragments of Jerahmeel by Harrington confirmed Cohn's hypothesis; see Harrington and Cazeaux 1974: 2-7.

7. Perrot (Perrot and Bogaert 1976: 24-28) differentiates between 'texte expliqué' and 'texte continué'; in the former the written biblical text is the focus of attention, whereas in the case of the latter, 'le point de référence est le texte même de la Bible'.

8. The literary bond between *LAB* and 1 Chronicles was noted by Cohn (1898: 315). This fact was pointed out also by Riessler (1928: 1315). See also Spiro 1951. By reason of this supposed relationship Delcor (1966), Feldman (Feldman and Hata

of the patriarchs (*LAB* 1–2). The list begins with Adam. The history of the Flood follows the biblical tradition, but God's words to Noah, after Noah's offer of a sacrifice following the Flood, represent an addition to the biblical story. According to the words of the Lord *cum autem completi fuerunt anni seculi...vivificabo mortuos...et erit terra alia... habitaculum sempiternum* ('But when the years appointed for the world have been fulfilled...I will bring the dead to life...and there will be another earth and another heaven, an everlasting dwelling place', 3.10). The text bears witness to the fact that in the eyes of the author the tradition of the Flood and the covenant made in its wake has special significance. (The narrative of *LAB* does not even mention the biblical narrative tradition from creation until the period of the Flood.) The author considers the Flood to be of key significance within the historical tradition. This is made clear by the fact that he attaches a revelation to the story of the covenant made after the Flood, a revelation concerning the end of human history, the completion of the historical tradition.[9] In all likelihood he expected the events predicted at the time of the covenant to be fulfilled in his own era, in the not too distant future, and he attached this revelation to the story of the covenant because he saw an analogy between the sins of the generation preceding the Flood and those of his own era. With regard to his own generation he expected a similar judgment and punishment to what had happened to the generation of the Flood. This element of his perspective constitutes a continuity with the oldest tradition of the Enochic circle (*1 En.* 6–11).[10] In *LAB* the revelation associated with the covenant of the Flood becomes the starting point of an eschatological historiography. The author of *LAB* is writing a chronicle—this chronicle is determined by the same rules and divided by the same milestones as the less detailed, briefer apocalyptic overviews of the

1971: lxxvii), and Perrot (Perrot and Bogaert 1976: 21-22) consider *LAB* a completed work. The work is incomplete according to James 1917: 60-65; Kisch 1949: 29; Dietzfelbinger 1975: 96-97.

9. On the idea of the 'two aeons' in Pseudo-Philo, see Ferch 1977. On the problem of the 'end of the times' in *LAB*, see Gry 1939; Wadsworth 1977. Beside the idea of the 'end of the times' there is no idea of an eschatological 'son of man' in *LAB*; see Jacobson 1983.

10. Similarly, the authors of the later pieces of the Enochic circle, which had been created during the middle of the second century BCE (*Animal Apocalypse* and *Apocalypse of the Weeks*) place the historical tradition within the chronological framework of a judgment taking place at the end of the Flood and of their own age. The visions tell of events symbolically.

Enochic circle. Pseudo-Philo, like the author of *Jubilees*, highlights certain personages of the historical tradition, and compared to the biblical tradition, attributes new characteristics to them and inserts new episodes into the tradition concerning them. These insertions are never accidental, but always spring from the theological and historical perspective of the author.[11] As the insertions of the *Book of Jubilees* have already shown the reason for these haggadic insertions is never the *Flucht vom Unbekannten*, the author's fear that certain details of the tradition will remain obscure. The insertions are almost always provided for theological reasons.

The first highlighted personage in the narrative of *LAB* is Abraham. According to the tradition of the priestly codex of Genesis Abraham lived in Mesopotamia, in the city of Ur (Gen. 11.27, 31). Pseudo-Philo directly connects this tradition with the tradition of Genesis about the building of the tower of Babel (Gen. 11.9), which there appears independently of the story of Abraham. In *LAB* the inhabitants of Babel build a tower to revolt against their future fate, that of being scattered, and that of fighting against each other, which will come at the end of time and which is already known to them: *ecce futura est ut dispergamur unusquisque a fratre suo, et in novissimis diebus alterutrum erimus expugnantes nos. Nunc ergo... edificamus nobis ipsis turrim* ('Behold it will happen that we will be scattered every man from his brother and in the last days we will be fighting one another. Now come, let us build for ourselves a tower...', *LAB* 6.1). Abraham, however, does not join those building the tower, and therefore the Lord makes a covenant with him (*LAB* 6.3-4). The rebels decide to burn Abraham and his companions who oppose the plan of building a tower. They want to throw their victims into a fiery furnace (*LAB* 6.5). Abraham's companions flee to the mountains with the help of the 'leader of the sons of Shem' (*LAB* 6.6-14). Abraham, who firmly believes in God, stays behind. He is cast into the furnace; however, the fire does not harm him, but leaps out of the furnace and destroys the rebels (6.15-18).[12]

11. Strugnell (1973: 408) points out the presence of a large number of Septuagintal, proto-Lucianic and Palestinian readings in Ps.-Philo's text. See also Jacobson 1989.

12. Parallels of the story based on the narrative of Dan. 3 may also be found elsewhere in *LAB*: in the story of Jair (*LAB* 38); in the story about Micah, the son of Samson and Delilah, who suffers death by fire for his idolatry (*LAB* 44.5; 47.12). The motif—most likely following Pseudo-Philo—was widespread in the haggadic tradition; see Ginzberg 1938: I, 202, V, 215; for a thorough analysis of the story of the fiery furnace, see Vermes 1961: 88.

According to Pseudo-Philo Abraham deserved to be chosen, he earned the covenant that the Lord made with him (*LAB* 6.11).[13] The motif of the election of Abraham's twelve companions appears together with the motif of Abraham's election—the number most probably symbolizes the future twelve tribes. Abraham's companions had run away from the revenge of the rebels—the Lord, however, delivers them together with Abraham (*LAB* 6.6). The covenant following the salvation will be graded—just as the earning of it had also been graded. Abraham represents the highest level; the next level is represented by the twelve righteous ones, the companions of Abraham; the third level is Jectan, the commander of the sons of Shem, who had helped the fugitives, but did not join them. Although Pseudo-Philo later only mentions the divine covenant as having been made with Abraham, he does not classify the other two groups with the rebels and does not condemn them.

The significance of Pseudo-Philo's revision of the Abrahamic tradition, on the one hand, is that by means of the revisions he enhances the significance of the covenant established with Abraham as opposed to the one made with Moses. On the other hand, by going into the details of the story he has a chance to express his views on the gradations of election. These views are similar to the ideas associated with election familiar from the circle of the somewhat earlier Qumran community. In the Qumran commentaries the community is symbolized by the name יהודה (Judea), and the entire nation and religious community by the name ישראל (Israel). At Qumran too the criterion for election is action, joining the community and observing its laws.[14]

Following the Abraham episode Pseudo-Philo's work continues as the story of the elect—Abraham and his descendants. The text only mentions briefly the other traditions relating to Abraham known from Genesis. However, the author pays special attention to the birth of Isaac. Partly because the author omits several other episodes from the Abrahamic tradition, and partly because the story of the birth appears immediately after the story of the establishment of the covenant, the promise (covenant) appears to be followed immediately by its fulfilment (the birth of Isaac).

Pseudo-Philo discusses the story of Jacob only briefly—in any case,

13. On the idea of the covenant in *LAB* see Murphy 1988b. The story of Abraham in *LAB* exemplifies the observance of the Law before Moses; for other examples of Pseudo-Philo's understanding of the law as universal and eternal see Reinmuth 1989.

14. Cf. the ideas relating to the various degrees of election of different groups evident both in the book of Judith and at Qumran.

he generally omits or revises all novelistic elements. He only provides the history of the period from Isaac to the Egyptian exile in the form of genealogies (*LAB* 8.4-14). The description of the stay in Egypt and the story of the birth of Moses is more detailed. Like the story of Abraham, the motif of unconditional faith and trust in God appears here also—this time in relation to Moses's father. Amram sires a child despite the fact that he is aware of pharaoh's edict because he unconditionally believes in the covenant made with Abraham, and in the promise of the land given at that time (*LAB* 9.2-6). Thus Amram also earns the second covenant, this time established with Moses. In Pseudo-Philo the motif of the covenant made with Moses is enriched by the motif of mercy shown towards the tribes of Israel: *Sciens autem scio, quoniam corrumpent vias suas et reliquam eos et obliviscentur testamenta quae disposui patribus eorum, et ego tamen non in sempiternum obliviscar eos* ('I know for sure that they will make their ways corrupt and I will abandon them, and they will forget the covenants that I have established with their fathers; but nevertheless I will not forget them forever') says the Lord about his chosen people (*LAB* 13.10).

The material depicting the historical tradition of the period following the exodus is interwoven with motifs symbolizing the theme of election. Divine assistance due to the elect is expressed by motifs representing the charismatic characteristics of the leaders. Such is the motif of the rod of Moses, which represents Moses' God-given power at the crossing of the Red Sea (*LAB* 10.5). The subsequently mentioned *vestimenta sapientiae* and *zona scientiae* ('garments of wisdom' and 'belt of knowledge') transform Joshua, endowing him with special powers (*LAB* 20.2).[15] According to the text the judge Kenaz who followed Joshua *indutus est spiritus virtutio et tranamutatus est in viram alium* ('was clothed with the spirit of power and was changed into another man', *LAB* 27.10). The Lord imparted special power to Gideon with the following words: *vade et cinge limbos tuos et Dominus erit tecum* ('go and gird your loins, and the Lord will be with you'); later Gideon 'put on the spirit of the Lord' and went to battle thus (*LAB* 35.5, 36.2). At the same time the disintegration of the covenant also begins with Gideon. In the case of

15. Cf. the system of *Jubilees* where certain motifs recur in connection with several outstanding characters—these characters are not the same as the ones mentioned in *LAB*; in *Jubilees* these motifs concern knowledge. The emphasis on the shared features of certain characters indicated by the similarity of special motifs associated with them is common to the system of *Jubilees* and of *LAB*.

the later judges the continuity of the charismatic power given to the leader is interrupted from time to time.[16]

The narrative of *LAB* provides three stories illustrating the reasons for this. The first one, a story which is absent from the biblical tradition, tells how Gideon collects the gold bracelets of the Israelite soldiers, casts idols from them and worships them (*LAB* 36.3). The narrative is clearly reminiscent of the story of the golden calf in the Bible (Exod. 32), and had been written with that story as a model. The events described in the story—Gideon's idolatry—disturb the so far harmonious relationship between God and the judges, the relationship through which Israel, or rather their representatives, maintain the covenant through their faith in God. The other event, which has the same consequence, is the story about the kingdom of Abimelech, son of Gideon; this story also appears in the biblical tradition (Judg. 9). This element of the biblical tradition is of nomadic origin, and condemns the institution of monarchy[17] and here Pseudo-Philo also follows suit. According to the third story (38.1-4) the judge Jair[18] builds a sanctuary for Baal, and on pain of death he tries to force everyone to offer sacrifices to Baal. Seven people refuse to do this. Jair wants to cast them into fire;[19] however, through the intervention of the angel Nathaniel, the fire burns the servants of Jair, and those who had refused to offer the sacrifice are free to escape.[20] This story, according

16. See Nickelsburg 1980.

17. Cf. Judg. 9.7-15: before the story of the rule of Saul, the parable of Jotham enumerates those burdens which will fall upon the nation after the introduction of the monarchy.

18. 'Jair, the Gileadite' is mentioned by Judg. 10.3-6, but apart from listing his activities and giving the number of his sons nothing else is said about him.

19. Their names are Defal, Abiesdrel, Getalibal, Selumi, Assur, Iondali, Memihel—due to their corruption in the course of translations the names cannot be interpreted. The story of the refusal to perform pagan sacrifices and the number of the apostates, however, are strongly reminiscent of 2 Maccabees 7, to the refusal of Mattatiah and his seven sons at the time of the decree of Antiochus Epiphanes. The precursor of the motif of the 'refusal to worship a pagan deity' and its punishment—casting into fire—may have been Dan. 3. Moreover, Pseudo-Philo considers idolatry as the primary sin of Israel; see Murphy 1988a.

20. Numerous other elements complement the story: the name of the intervening angel is Nathaniel 'the angel who was in charge of fire'. His name is not known from other documents in this capacity. In order to ensure the escape route of the fugitives, the angel blinds the people; Jair, who arrives on the scene, also dies in the fire, and according to the prophecy of the angel: 'and in the fire in which you will die there you will have a dwelling place' (38.4). Fire is mentioned as the dwelling place of sinners

to the system of *LAB*, is the parallel of the story about the tower of Babel, where the leaders of the land of Babylon want to cast Abraham, who resists the order to build the tower, into fire (6.3-18). The escape motif[21] in the story of Jair also alludes to the story associated with Abraham.

The three stories in Pseudo-Philo—Gideon violates the covenant, the son of Gideon wants to be king, Jair forces the people to worship Baal—together explain the loss of charismatic power. Despite his sin Gideon remains a judge, and according to a divine statement he himself is not punished (*LAB* 36.4). At the same time the turning point which comes about at his time is foreshadowed, as it were, at the beginning of the story: he is the first among the judges who, when called upon, doubts his own suitability, and conducting a long dialogue with the angel communicating the revelation he asks for a sign proving his ability (*LAB* 35.5).[22]

In the case of Jephthah the people entrust him with the power of leadership (*LAB* 39.3). Pseudo-Philo amends the tradition about the sacrifice of the daughter of Jephthah[23] and condemns Jephthah for his deed.[24] With the insertion of the lament of Jephthah's daughter—which incidentally shows a surprising similarity to Antigone's lament in Sophocles, and to the laments on epitaphs of Greek and Hellenistic literature[25]—the author of *LAB* awakens the sympathy of its readers towards the unfortunate girl.

The motif of charismatic power does not appear in relation to the figures of judges who come after Jephthah. Israel has no leader until David—he is the next person to appear as the chosen leader (*LAB* 44.4). In connection with David miraculous portents appear once again. Divine

in *2 Baruch* as well, which had probably been written not long after *LAB*; see *2 Bar.* 44.15; 48.39, 43; 59.2; 64.7, 85.13.

21. Cf. the story of the fleeing of the companions of Abraham to the mountains, *LAB* 6.9.

22. Cf. Judg. 6.36-40, where Gideon plays a much more active role. Throughout the episodes of the narrative of *LAB* Pseudo-Philo tries to enhance God's role, especially regarding the protection of Israel; see Murphy 1988c. On the relation of God and humans in *LAB* see also Murphy 1986.

23. On the literary relationship of the story of Jephthah see Sypherd 1948

24. *LAB* 39.11—cf. Judg. 11.29-40, which regards Jephthah's sacrifice as merely keeping his word.

25. Alexiou and Dronke 1971; Fröhlich 1981. The story of Jephthah's daughter shows a marking similarity with the story of Iphigenia: on this, see Philonenko 1973. On the portraits of the girl and women in Pseudo-Philo, see Horst 1989; Halpern-Amaru 1991; Brown 1992.

assistance is symbolized here by a new motif: David is helped by an angel in the battle against Goliath (*LAB* 61.1).

In connection with Saul, however, Pseudo-Philo suppresses those sections of the biblical tradition which mention his election. He does not mention anywhere that Samuel would have anointed Saul (cf. 1 Sam. 10–11). In the narrative of *LAB* the tragic end of Saul's reign is known in advance; it is told in a divine revelation (*LAB* 66.3). Saul himself is unaware that the 'spirit of the Lord'[26] has left him (60.1). In an ecstatic state he himself prophesies his own downfall; afterwards, however, he has no idea of what he had foretold (*LAB* 62.2). He wishes to have David killed (62.1)—and actually the author of *LAB* does not condemn him for this as, according to him, Saul has merely fulfilled his calling, his fate had been preordained. The 'spirit of the Lord' had left him and its place had been taken by 'an evil spirit' (*LAB* 60.10). This point of view, as well as the juxtaposition of Saul and David, is further highlighted by the two psalms sung by David (59.4; 60.2-3). In the second psalm David appears as a victorious force which triumphs over the forces of chaos, embodied by Saul.[27] This kind of juxtaposition, and the alternation of the 'spirit of the Lord' and the 'evil spirit' in Saul, attributes a dualism to the figures of Saul and David which is not unlike the dualism appearing in the works created in the midst of the Qumran community, and which also appears in some apocryphal works which were also transmitted at Qumran though they had been created elsewhere. A similarity to the perspective of the *Book of Jubilees* is also noticeable here: in *LAB* Saul is 'evil fulfilling its calling'—just as Mastema is in *Jubilees*.[28]

Saul's other characteristics in *LAB* make him similar to the figure of 'Messiah ben Ephraim' (משיח בן אפרים) familiar from the Jewish rabbinical tradition.[29] According to the narrative of *LAB*, he is not from the tribe of Benjamin, but of Ephraim. According to the rabbinical tradition, originating not long after the creation of *LAB*, the messiah from the

26. Spiritus sanctus; in the original text probably רוח קדושה.

27. Philonenko (1959; 1961; 1967a; 1967b) presumes an Essene milieu of Pseudo-Philo. The absence of sectarian bias in Pseudo-Philo does not support this hypothesis; see Perrot, in Perrot and Bogaert 1976: 32. For a survey of the possible relations of the tradition of the exorcistic songs from Qumran and Pseudo-Philo, see Bogaert 1978.

28. In Pseudo-Philo two spirits—'spiritus sanctus' and 'spiritus pessimus'—are juxtaposed. 'Spiritus pessimus' appears among the secondarily created things which had been created after the conclusion of the first act of creation; see *LAB* 42.2.

29. Spiro 1951; Fröhlich 1983: 371-73.

tribe of Ephraim was a kind of precursor to the successful one coming from the house of David. The Davidic messiah is represented by David himself in the narrative of *LAB*. The adjective *christus*,[30] anointed one, only appears in the text of *LAB* in connection with him (59.2).

The juxtaposition of the personages and reigns of Saul and David indicates the eschatological ideas of the author of *LAB*.[31] In the Jewish literature of the first century CE numerous works mention the 'end' of history, the judgment, which is to take place soon. In the usage of the rabbinical literature there is a sharp dividing line between the period of עולם הזה and of עולם הבא ('the present time' and 'the coming time'), and this dividing line is the expected judgment.[32] In the view of Pseudo-Philo too, history is a process which has a beginning and an end; the historical process is determined in advance and its events are directed by divine providence. The outcome of events is predetermined. Man must act with unfailing faith in divine assistance—and in case this is not forthcoming—with acceptance. The author illustrates this view through numerous historical examples: Abraham's speech (6.11), Amram's speech (9.3-6), Moses' speech told before the crossing of the Red Sea (10.4), as well as in the narrative about Balaam (38.1-14). In the latter, Balaam bows before Israel, because he wants to fulfil the wishes of the God of Israel.[33]

We do not know for certain whether there had been a continuation of the story of Saul and David in the narrative of *LAB*, nor to what point, and nor how Pseudo-Philo adapted the Jewish historical tradition. It is likely that the narrative of *LAB* did not extend much further than what has been preserved. The supposition according to which *LAB* was in essence written as a 'supplementary introduction'[34] to the book of Chronicles may well be correct. *LAB* leaves off where the historical narrative of the Chronicles begins (naturally the genealogies introducing the Books of Chronicles have to be disregarded here). Like the *Book of Jubilees*, *LAB* only focuses on a particular phase of the historical tradition and revises it according to its own theological and historical perspective. The analogy between the present 'Saulic' era and the coming

30. Cf. Hebrew משיח.

31. Gry 1939.

32. An excellent collection of the rabbinical ideas relating to the eschatological future is provided by Str-B IV.2, pp. 799-976. On the idea in the pseudepigraphic literature, see Schürer 1973–79: II, 501-13.

33. For an analysis of the story see Vermes 1961: 174-75.

34. Schürer 1973–79: III.1, 326 quoting Riessler 1928: 1315.

'Davidic' era must have been clear to contemporary readers of the story.

The focus placed on the Enochic tradition and on the covenant following the Flood, as well as the analogy between the history of antediluvian humankind and his own age, link Pseudo-Philo's work to the historical perspective of the Enochic circle. The idea of the earned covenant and of its gradations as formulated by the author of *LAB* in the story of Abraham indicates a perspective which sets the author and his group apart even within their own religious community. It is akin to the attitude of earlier works—such as that of the 'covenanters' of the Damascus Document. In any case the dualistic ideas, expressed in several instances about a helping spirit, or about the 'two spirits', which had been based on the biblical traditions (the concept of the charismatic power of the judges and of the spirit tormenting Saul) are noteworthy.[35] The concept of 'evil fulfilling its calling' is based on the same idea in the Saul story, and we find the nearest parallel to it in the *Book of Jubilees*.[36]

LAB was created after 70 CE following the suppression of the Jewish War, and the scattering of the Qumranite and other communities. The work bears none of the characteristics of the so-called sectarian literature; it does not use symbolic names instead of historical ones, it does not obfuscate its message, does not make it ambiguous, or only comprehensible to an isolated group. With regard to its genre, it belongs to the biblical historiographical tradition. With regard to its content, however, its system of emphases, insertions, and omissions—just as the much earlier *Book of Jubilees*—imparts a certain esoteric message. The message of both books bears a resemblance to the literature of Qumran; however *Jubilees* most likely is the intellectual product of a community which had its own tradition but had not yet become institutionalized as an isolated enclave, whereas *LAB* was created much later, in the wake of a devastating military defeat which destroyed the possibility of the existence of any kind of community.

35. The theory of Philonenko about the Essene and gnostic character of the work, based on the second psalm of David over Saul (60.2-3), does not prove the Essene and gnostic origin of the work; see Philonenko 1959; 1961; 1967. The psalms inserted in the narrative of *LAB* reflect different views, and they seem to be either independent compositions used by the author, or later interpolations. On the great variety of views in *LAB* see Schürer 1973–79: III.1, 327-28.

36. According to *Jub*. 10.8-9, following the Flood God intends to bind all the evil spirits, but Mastema, their chief, asks God to leave some of the evil spirits, in order that he might to exercise his function in the world.

The Recreation of the Danielic Apocalyptic Tradition after the Defeat of the Jewish Revolt

After the tradition of the Danielic circle (the final compilation of which happened in the 60s of the second century BCE) the vision literature seemingly ceases to exist.[37] During the second half of the first century CE, however, following the defeat of the Jewish revolt, once again works inspired by the Danielic apocalyptic appear in the Jewish tradition. This is not only the renaissance of the genre itself—vision and its interpretation, or *pesher*. The content of the visions and the problems they tackle show surprising similarities to the Danielic tradition; the world historical overview, and the use of the fourfold historical schema are equally as characteristic of these works as of most of the visions of the Danielic cycle.

Two works—or rather certain details, certain visions, in them—represent this genre in the first century CE; the so-called *Fourth Book of Ezra*,[38] and the *Second Book of Baruch* (*Syriac Baruch*) which survived in a Syriac translation.[39] The two works were probably written in Hebrew.[40] They are not only closely linked regarding the time of their

37. Acquaintance with the material of the pseudepigraphic prophecies from Qumran will certainly change this picture. The Qumran manuscripts are mostly from the Herodian era, and none is later than 70 CE—all of them are earlier than the present text of *4 Ezra*. Beside the similarity of some formal elements, there are sometimes even verbal correspondences between some Qumran texts and *4 Ezra*; see Dimant-Stragnell 1988; García-Martínez 1991.

38. The work has survived in Greek and Latin, and has became part of the Vulgate, annexed to the books of the New Testament. The Latin and Greek church fathers refer to it as to an original prophetic work. The work was written, in all probability, in Hebrew, then translated into Greek; only a Greek fragment (*P. Oxy* 1010) has survived; see Rubinkiewicz 1976. Besides the Latin translation Syriac, Ethiopic, Arabic, Armenian, Georgian, and Coptic (one fragment) translations of the work are known. For a survey see Schürer 1973–79: III.1, 303-305.

The best critical edition of the Latin text and of ancient translations is Violet, 1910. For the Syriac see Ceriani 1868: 45-108; Bidawid 1966–73: I-IV, 1-50. For the Armenian version, see Stone 1989: 39-42; 1971. A fresh commentary of the text is Stone 1990.

39. The first edition of *2 Baruch* is Ceriani 1871: 113-80. Later editions are Kmoskó 1907; Dedering 1973. Translations with commentary in Bogaert 1969; Klijn, apud Charlesworth 1983–85: I, 615-52.

40. Most likely both works were created in Palestine and their original language was Hebrew; on the original of *4 Ezra* see Box 1912: xiii-xix; Kaminka 1932; 1933;

creation[41]—according to current opinion both may have been written not long after the defeat of the revolt, and their authors may have originated in the same, or in closely related, circles.[42]

4 Ezra contains several historicizing overviews in vision form. The first vision (*4 Ezra* 9.26–10.59) is about a woman who mourns for her son. The woman tells Ezra that she had been barren for thirty years, when a son was born to her. The son, however, died young, just as he was standing under the wedding canopy. Not much later Ezra glimpses the woman once more; this time she appears in the form of a city. According to the interpretation of the vision, the woman and the city represent Jerusalem. The thirty years of barrenness mean thirty thousand years, that is to say the period stretching from the creation of the world until the erecting of the Temple of Solomon (*4 Ezra* 8.44-46). The birth of the son symbolizes the beginning of the Temple and the Temple sacrifices (*4 Ezra* 8.46-47). The death of the son means the destruction of the Temple (586 BCE) (4 *Ezra* 10.48). The period of mourning means the period beginning with 586 BCE. At this time, however, after the Most High has seen Ezra's genuine grief for the city he shows him its coming brightness: 'For now the Most High, seeing that you are sincerely grieved and profoundly distressed for her, has shown you the brightness of her glory, and the loveliness of her beauty' (*4 Ezra* 10.51-52). These words tell of the future; however, the revelation does not predict the time of their fulfilment.

The vision and its interpretation about the woman, like certain pieces of the Danielic collection, consists of an image (the vision), the individual elements of which are interpreted as signs, and placed into a new system of meaning, into the circle of Jewish historical tradition. Although the *pesher* of the vision refers to the past (the revelation extends only to the

Gry 1938: xxiii-lxxvi; Torrey 1945: 122; Bloch 1957–58; Zimmermann 1960–61; Stone 1990.

On *2 Baruch* see Charles 1896: xliv-liii; 1973: II, 472-74; Wellhausen 1899: 234-41; Zimmermann 1962; Bogaert 1969: I, 378-80. See also Klijn, apud Charlesworth 1983–85: I, 617.

41. Most scholars date *4 Ezra* to 95 CE: Myers 1974: 129-31; Robinson 1976: 247, 315; Stone 1990. Zimmermann (1985) dates it to 150 CE, after the failure of the Bar Kokhba revolt.

42. Similarities between *4 Ezra* and *2 Baruch* are significant; on the opinions see Schürer 1973–79: III.1, 753, n. 4; Lupieri 1992. There are similarities between *4 Ezra* and *2 Baruch* and Pseudo-Philo; see Violet 1910: lxxvii-lxxxi; Gry 1939; Bogaert, 1969: 242-57; Stone 1984: 409; Berger 1992.

present, and the author only makes a brief reference to the future), the method of 'vision and its interpretation' show familiarity with that of the prophecies of the Danielic book, or the Qumran tradition of the *pesharim* of the prophetic texts.

The basis, the literary raw material of the vision, is once again completely different from either the images born of the experiences of the authors of the Danielic book, or the prophetic texts constituting the raw material of the Qumran *pesharim*. The fourth vision of *4 Ezra* represents visually one of the traditions of the prophetic literature, the female figure symbolizing cities or nations. It may be said that the fourth vision of *4 Ezra* represents the amalgamation of the literary traditions of the Danielic and the Qumran *pesharim*, and the unification of the traditions of the 'interpretations' associated with the prophetic text tradition. The image of the woman representing a nation or a city is a recurring motif of the prophetic literary tradition from the eighth century BCE. Amos talks of 'the virgin Israel' (5.1), in Micah 'Zion...like a woman in childbirth' represents Jerusalem (4.10-13). In Hosea the female figure representing Ephraim or Israel appears in several instances (8.9-10; 9.1; 13.2). The dual motif of the woman and her child which stands for the nation may also be found in Hosea (13.2). Hosea's symbolic acts, his marriages, also represent the Yahweh–Israel relationship, and the children born of these unions represent the further fate of Israel (see the meaning of the names of his children, the later generations, Hos. 1.2-8). The symbols, 'daughter of Zion', 'daughter of Tarshish', are continued in Isaiah, and the birth of a child, Immanuel, represents the future (6.10; 9.1-6) there as well. Jeremiah continues the same symbolism, when he represents Israel as a prostitute or a maiden fallen victim to rape (Jer. 2–4; 13.22).

The woman in the first vision of *4 Ezra*, then, represents Jerusalem as the centre of the nation and of the religious community which is a continuation of the poetic images of the prophetic tradition. The long awaited son who dies in his prime symbolizes the Temple, which Jewish tradition has always identified with the continuity of the national and religious tradition.

The vision and its interpretation about the woman—just as the *pesher* interpreting the prophetic text of Daniel 9—singles out the history of the Temple of Jerusalem, its building and its destruction. The reason for this may be the author's shocking experience of witnessing the Jewish revolt and the destruction of the Temple (66–70 CE).[43] The text makes no

43. Mendels notes that the apocrypha of the second half of the first century CE

mention of the destruction of the Second Temple: the author most probably regards the two events as analogous. The 'age of revelations' which will follow the period of mourning will take place after the laying bare of the Second Temple, and this is when the Lord will deliver the nation.

The Temple plays an especially significant role in the first vision of *4 Ezra*. For the author of the vision the Temple may have been the only symbol which could stand for the nation and the religious community, as there no longer was another community, body or institution which could have fulfilled this role. This is how a building, the Temple which is invoked here with the help of the imagery of the prophetic literature, becomes the symbol of the fate and hoped for future of the community.

The second vision of *4 Ezra* may be found in chs. 11.1–12.51. In this Ezra sees an eagle which rises from the sea. The text provides a detailed description of the animal, which has twelve pairs of wings and three heads, the middle of the heads being larger than the two others. 'And out of the wings grows eight secondary wings.' The eagle spreads its wings above the whole world (*4 Ezra* 11.1-7). And the twelve wings rule one after the other (the second for more than twice as long as any of the others, 11.17) and then disappear; likewise also two of the winglets until only six small wings and three heads remain (*4 Ezra* 9.23). Two of the small wings detach and go over to the head on the right. One by one the remaining four wings lift off, to bring war, then they alight. The head on the left side rises up and 'makes a covenant' with the other two heads (*4 Ezra* 9.24-30). It acquires power over the entire world (*4 Ezra* 9.32). The large head is suddenly annihilated, and the remaining two heads rule the world, then the head on the right devours the one on the left (*4 Ezra* 11.35). At this point a lion bursts forth from the forest, and informs the eagle that he is the last of the four beasts whom the Most High had assigned to rule the world. The end of the reign of the fourth beast, however, means the 'end of times', which had also been determined by the Most High (*4 Ezra* 11.39). While the lion is making his speech the last two wings of the eagle rise up to rule, but their reign is brief and turbulent (12.2). After their downfall, the body of the eagle is consumed by fire.

According to the interpretation of the vision, the eagle symbolizes the 'fourth empire'. The text of *4 Ezra* does not mention—most likely

'reveal an indifference about the Land'—despite the fact that the Roman occupation led to further segmentation; these apocrypha do not mention the tradition of settlement either; see Mendels 1992: 242-75.

because the author considers it to be self-evident—that the concept of the four kingdoms goes back to the tradition of the book of Daniel (chs. 2 and 7). The vision of *4 Ezra* also continues the visual tradition of the vision of Daniel 7. The protagonist of the vision, the eagle, is one of the beasts of the vision of Daniel 7. The author of *4 Ezra* most likely chose this animal as a symbol, because—after the eagle emblem of the legions—the eagle aptly and recognizably symbolized, the Roman empire. Despite the similarities—the use of the fourfold schema and the method of the *pesher*—there also are characteristic differences between Daniel 2, 7 and *4 Ezra* 11–12. Daniel 2 analyses the fourfold schema diachronically, whereas the author of Daniel 7 most probably uses a synchronic system. The author of *4 Ezra*, however, only uses the fourfold schema as a matter of form, as an allusion to the book of Daniel, since after mentioning the 'four empires' only one empire appears, and the interpretation only deals with the fate of this one empire. Incidentally, *4 Ezra* follows the vision of Daniel 7 in the motif of the beast appearing from the sea, and in using the attributes of the beast to refer to certain events in the history of the empire represented by it. The figure of the beast, and thus the interpretation—*pesher*—as well, is much more complex than in the case of the vision of Daniel 7. In the interpretation of the author of *4 Ezra* 11–12 the wings of the eagle refer to rulers, and so do the heads. The size of the wings and heads demonstrates the greatness of the rulers. The 'rising up' and 'descent' of the wings represent the beginning and the end of a reign. Particular elements of the imagery of the vision may be identified with particular events of Roman history.[44] The twelve wings represent Roman rulers from Caesar to Piso.[45] The eight small wings may represent local rulers (vassal princes or governors) of Judea until Vespasianus.[46] The three heads symbolise the Flavian emperors, Vespasianus, Titus and Domitianus. The lion is the symbol of the messiah. It is the only figure of the vision which cannot be identified with incidents of the past; rather, the animal representing the tribe of Judah expresses the expectations of the author. The author of the second vision of *4 Ezra* expects a triumphant messiah from the tribe of Judah, from the house of David (משיח בן דויד). In the aftermath of the downfall of the Jewish revolt his expectations have no realistic basis, and the messiah becomes a transcendental figure.

44. This is the generally accepted interpretation of the vision about the eagle. For a survey of modern interpretations see Myers 1974: 299-302.

45. Knibb 1979: 240-42.

46. Oesterley 1933: 147.

For the author of the second vision of *4 Ezra* the perspective of historical time and space has vanished—this is indicated by the fourfold schema becoming a mere formal element in the vision. At the same time the element symbolizing the future—the lion—has been amplified. The lion is not only the symbol of the tribe of Judah, but in the prophetic literature it also symbolizes battle, fighting power. Thus it is the lion who will mete out justice after the hated 'fourth rule', which here truly means empire just as in the later tradition of the Danielic book (second century BCE).

In the third vision of *4 Ezra* (ch. 13) the image of a man appears, who also rises from the sea, and with his fiery breath annihilates the army sent against him by the four countries of the earth. Following this he summons his own army. According to the interpretation (*4 Ezra* 13.25) the man symbolizes the messiah. The enemy armies mean the nations of the world who fight against the messiah. Although the text does not refer to actual historical events, the author nevertheless follows the tradition of the visions containing historical prophecies. For him, however, historical events in which signs and regularities may be discovered are no longer important—the only important thing is the long-awaited, but in truth unrealistic, coming of the messiah.[47]

The other collection of the reinterpretation of the Danielic apocalyptic is the *Syriac Apocalypse of Baruch*, also known as the *Second Book of Baruch*. This work, like *4 Ezra*, came into being at the end of the first century CE, some time after 70 CE.[48] Its text was preserved in a Syriac translation, which is why it is called the *Syriac Apocalypse of Baruch* (and also to differentiate it from another work which survived in a Greek translation and which also bears the name of Baruch in its title, although its content is different). There is only one vision in *2 Baruch* which may be regarded as a continuation of the Danielic oracles. In a night vision Baruch sees an enormous forest, which is surrounded by mountains (35–46). Opposite the forest there is a vinestock, and a spring issues forth

47. The visions 1–3 are characterized by a spirit of scepticism while the following visions reflect confidence in the future; see Hallbäck 1992. The redactor of the seven visions of *4 Ezra* used pre-existent material; however, the visions bear an overall meaning and form a literary unity; see Stone 1990: 23; Myers 1974: 120-21; Knibb 1979: 109-110.

48. Judging by some references of the text it was created some time after 70 CE, around 100 CE, although most probably the author also used earlier materials; Bogaert 1969: I, 294-95. On this dating see Schürer 1973–79: III.1, 752-53; Klijn, apud Charlesworth 1983–85: I, 617. For a dating after the Bar Kokhba revolt, see Bietenhard 1948.

from under it. The spring flows towards the forest, becomes a mighty river, and engulfs the forest and the surrounding mountains. Only one cedar remains of the forest. Presently the cedar also falls to the ground, and the vinestock prophesies the imminent destruction of the tree. The cedar bursts into flames and is destroyed, and the vinestock surrounded by flowers begins to grow new shoots. According to Baruch's interpretation the forest means the four empires and the cedar is the symbol of the fourth empire. The vinestock and the spring mean the reign of Israel and the messiah, which begins after the conclusion of the reign of the fourth empire.

The author of *2 Baruch*, like the author of *4 Ezra*, identifies the fourth empire of his vision with the Roman empire. Its symbols, however, differ from those of the other work. The symbols of *2 Baruch* originate in the parables and prophecies of the Old Testament. In the Bible the cedar is the symbol of power and dignity, it is the king of plants.[49] In a later oracle coming from an exilic milieu—Ezekiel's cedar vision (Ezek. 31)—it is the symbol of a kingdom, that of Egypt. The vinestock as the symbol of Israel appears both in the psalms[50] and in the poetic imagery of prophetic literature.[51]

The author's view of history lacks perspective just as that of the writer of the visions of *4 Ezra*. Only one aspect of the entire historical prophecy interests him: the downfall of the fourth empire and the coming of the messianistic age.

The naming of the fictive authors of the two works is not meaningless, and in fact clearly constitutes a historical reference. Both are historical personages: Ezra and Baruch lived and worked in the sixth–fifth centuries BCE. Of the two Baruch was the earlier. He was Jeremiah's scribe, and most probably he was the transmitter of Jeremiah's works as well.[52] Ezra was a legendary rebuilder after the resettlement of the Persian era.[53] There is a similarity between the burning questions and

49. See the parable of 2 Kgs 14.19.

50. Ps. 80.9-12, etc.

51. E.g. Isa. 5.1-4.

52. Baruch was Jeremiah's scribe, aide, and the recorder and transmitter of his works during the time of the prophet's persecution, and after his death; see Jer. 32.12-16; 36.4-32; 43.6; 45.1.

53. According to *4 Ezra* 3.1, Ezra sees his first vision 'thirteen years after the destruction of our city [i.e. Jerusalem]' in Babylon. This statement about the destruction of the city probably refers to 70 CE, which Jewish tradition considered to be the counterpart of the catastrophe of 586 BCE. Based on this reference and other characteristics

circumstances of the age in which the fictive authors lived, and the age in which the authors whose names have been borrowed lived and worked. Thus the fictive names of the authors constitute historical references and at the same time they also express the hope that, just as the works of Jeremiah have survived thanks to Baruch, and a new life could begin after the resettlement thanks to Ezra, life will also return to normal after the downfall of the Jewish revolt.

There is one other section of the *2 Baruch* which may be regarded as the continuation of the Danielic apocalyptic (53–76). Regarding its form this too is a revelation given to Baruch. A small cloud appears in front of Baruch's eyes, from which alternately and several times light-coloured then dark water falls. The waters represent historical eras, and their colour characterizes the era: white means 'good', black means 'evil'. The evaluation of an era, that is to say, what makes an era 'good' or 'evil', is always determined by the relationship between the nation and God; those eras whose people observe the Law are 'good', those in which people violate the Law are considered 'evil'.

In the *2 Baruch* history is divided into thirteen periods. The first period lasts from the beginnings to the Flood. In this period Adam violates God's prohibition and the angels sin with the daughters of men—thus the period is characterized by the story of two revolts. In comparison with earlier stories the historical perspective of Baruch's vision is new in as much as the story of the Garden of Eden constitutes part of the historical tradition for him. This narrative which appears in the so-called Yahwistic source of Genesis (Gen. 2.4b–3.24) is absent from either the Enochic tradition, or from the related Danielic apocalyptic. As already mentioned above the suppression of this tradition in the Enochic circle may be conscious: the authors of the Enochic circle associated the origin of evil with another tradition, the story of the fallen angels and the daughters of men (cf. Gen. 6.1-4). Although the reference to the tradition of the Garden of Eden in the vision of *2 Baruch* only reinforces, but does not of itself signify the 'evil' nature of the period, nevertheless the inclusion of the tradition in Baruch, which purported to be a conscious continuation of the second-century apocalyptic work, illustrates the dissolution of the Enochic theology.

The first period ends with the Flood which is the punishment of the angels and the people for their sins. The author of the vision does not

the text has been dated to the end of the first century CE, see Metzger, apud Charlesworth, I: 1983–85: 520.

mention the covenant, following the Flood, with Noah—this omission is most likely due to the fact that the author accounts it to the next period, which reflects the author's wish to emphasize the 'evil' nature of the first era.

The next period is the era of Abraham. The story of the ancestors of Israel begins with him. This is a 'good' period. Baruch's vision—similarly to the point of view of the *Book of Jubilees*—projects the knowledge of the Mosaic Law to the age of Abraham. According to the text it is Abraham alone who observes the Law (57.2). The vision also mentions here the judgment which will come in the future. In the light of the fact that the author expects the coming of the messiah in the thirteenth, concluding period (71–75), the eschatological concepts which link the age of Abraham and the thirteenth period constitute a time frame which encapsulates the history of Israel. Thus in the overview of *2 Baruch* 'world history' and the tradition of the Enochic circle (which had a more encompassing perspective) is lost.

The author of the vision does not follow the tradition systematically in his overview of the history of Israel, but only refers to those events which he himself considers to be of symbolic importance. From the period following the age of Abraham he mentions the Egyptian captivity. Due to the transgressions of the people,[54] he deems this era to be an 'evil' one (*2 Bar*. 58.1-2). A 'good' period begins, however, with the appearance of Moses, Aaron and Miriam, and this is continued during the time of Joshua ben Naveh and Kaleb (*2 Bar*. 59.1-12) as well.[55]

Dark water symbolizes the age of judges, when, according to the author of the vision Israel defiled itself by the sins of the Amorites—that is, the Canaanites (*2 Bar*. 60.1-2). Light-coloured waters characterize the period of David (however, the author of the vision does not even mention the reign of Saul—most likely because it does not fit into his system) and of Solomon, the period of the building of the Temple (*2 Bar*. 61.1-3). The period of the northern kingdom of Israel is an 'evil' period, at the end of which punishment—captivity—is meted out to the inhabitants of Israel (reference to the deportation of 721 BCE) (*2 Bar*. 62.1-8). The period of the southern kingdom at the time of Hezekiah is a 'good'

54. Exod. 1–12, the source describing the Egyptian exile, does not mention any transgressions.

55. Here, however, the author of the vision does not acknowledge the sins and rebellions mentioned in the tradition of Exodus–Deuteronomy which justify the forty-year wandering.

period, at the end of which Sanherib—who according to the author is the same monarch who had taken the people of the northern kingdom into captivity[56]—is unable to destroy the southern kingdom (*2 Bar*. 63.9). The reign of Manasse, the next ruler of Judea, brings another 'evil' period (*2 Bar*. 65.1-2). The rule of his successor, Josiah is once again a 'good' one, due to the religious reforms of the king (*2 Bar*. 66.1-8). Dark water symbolizes the historical events of the year 586 BCE, the time of the destruction of the Temple (*2 Bar*. 67.1-7). This is followed by another good period, represented by light coloured water: the period of the rebuilding of the Temple (516 BCE) (*2 Bar*. 68.1-8). The following long period lasting from the rebuilding of the Temple until the age of the author is again characterized by dark water, and it will be followed by a 'good' period, the era of the coming of the messiah.

The concept that alternating 'good' and 'evil' periods constitute the history of humankind and Israel may also be found in the pre-exilic biblical tradition, and in fact it plays an increasingly significant role from the Persian period onwards. Chronicles[57] which had been compiled at that time always evaluates the periods of individual rules in a summary way, with the following words: 'did what was wrong in the eyes of the Lord' (2 Chron. 22.4) or 'did that which was right in the sight of the Lord'. The vantage point of the evaluation is always the relationship to the cult of the officially condoned Yahweh sanctuary of Jerusalem. The attempt to present—whenever possible—the rulers of the southern, Judean kingdom, as 'good', and the northern, Israelite kings as 'evil' is obvious. The authors of the Chronicles cannot, however, completely ignore the facts, and therefore their assessment does not yield a consistent system. In the final analysis, then, the facts, rather than the abstract concept of alternating 'good' and 'evil' periods, determine the evaluation of the periods.

It is not impossible that the point of view of the clerics compiling the Chronicles was influenced by certain Mesopotamian traditions as well. The so called 'Akkadian Apocalypses' known from the Neo-Babylonian period may also have influenced the clerical tradition. Recently several

56. Cf. the tradition of the book of Tobit, where the ruler deporting the people of the northern kingdom is also Sanherib—the historical Sîn-ahhē-eriba; see Tobit, ch. 1.

57. The *terminus post quem* is the period around 400 BCE, which is the period following events recounted in 2 Chronicles. *Terminus ante quem* can be derived from the fact that the book of Ben Sira written around 200 BCE already mentions the Chronicles (Ben Sira 47.2-11).

scholars have stressed this possibility.[58] The Akkadian Apocalypses are oracles which talk of historical periods, and thus they are narratives pertaining to the future. They evaluate individual periods—usually the reign of kings—as either 'good' or 'evil'. Incidentally, such assessments have a long tradition in ancient Mesopotamian literature.[59] It is not impossible that the Mesopotamian historical traditions and the Akkadian Apocalypses influenced Jewish tradition during and following the exile through several channels. Although the main goal of the priestly circles of the Second Temple in the Chronicles may have been to demonstrate the primacy of the Temple and to re-evaluate the earlier tradition from the point of view of the cult, nevertheless, the tradition about 'good' and 'evil' periods may also have some roots in the Mesopotamian literature.

The author of the vision of *2 Baruch* continues and further develops this system of classification (*2 Bar.* 53–76). He, however, is much less influenced by the earlier historical tradition than the compilers of the Chronicles. It is clear that the primary goal of his overview is to create a system of alternating 'good' and 'evil' periods—if necessary even at the price of suppressing or reassessing certain aspects of the earlier tradition.

The circle, however, in which *2 Baruch* had been created is not the priestly circle of the traditions of the Chronicles. This vision, according to the intention of its author, is to serve as the continuation of the historical overviews of the apocalypses of the Enochic circle—the *Animal Apocalypse*, the *Apocalypse of the Weeks*—and of Daniel 9. This is reflected not only in the work's textual contextualization (Baruch's earlier vision makes conscious references to the Danielic apocalyptic) but also in its emphatically visionary form (the introductory words) and in the symbolism employed ('waters' representing individual epochs, and the interpretations following the monotonous symbolism). Hardly anything remains of the features of the original model: the palpable elements of the visions fade away, the rich symbolism of the Danielic and Enochic circle is simplified into black and white 'waters', where the symbol only

58. See the discussion of this question in the previous section. On the 'Akkadian Apocalypses' see Lambert 1978.

59. The dream-interpreting tradition using water as an omen may be found in the dream book of Susa (Oppenheim 1956: 258). The omen of water predicts illness—of a more or less serious nature—thus it has a completely different meaning than the water motif appearing in the *Baruch* apocalypse. In Jewish tradition it is only in *2 Baruch* that water appears as an omen, or rather as an interpretable sign—it is impossible to determine on what kind of precedents and tradition it is based.

has one characteristic left (its colour). The perspective of the historical tradition also changes: it is no longer the analogy of the chosen ones of the antediluvian era and the 'righteous ones'[60] of the present that matters to the author, but the mechanical alternation of 'good' and 'evil', and some kind of stubborn hope which expects the passing of current 'evil'.

The same single-minded concentration and lack of perspective characterize both the author of the visions of *4 Ezra* and of *2 Baruch*. These authors attempt stubbornly to bring back the apocalyptic which flourished in the second century BCE, but neither the old forms nor the hopeful atmosphere of the era of the Maccabean revolt can be recaptured after the devastation of the Jewish war. In effect, the authors of *4 Ezra* and *2 Baruch* are not interested in the historical tradition; lonely and without perspective, but nonetheless hopeful, they look to the future.

60. The author of *2 Baruch* does not make any reference to a community, or separate group, which would stand behind him.

CONCLUSION

The whirl of the events of the sixth century BCE—the capture of Jerusalem followed by the Babylonian exile, and a few decades later the sudden break of the world-power of Babylon and the change-over of their rule by the Persians, resulting in the liberation of the Jews from their exile—were determining historical experience for the Jews. The theme of the changing of rules may have appeared in the Jewish tradition simultaneously with the events, in the form of the idea of the four successive reigns. The Aramaic oracles of Daniel 2–6, shaped in their first form probably during the Persian period are the expressions of the idea of the succession of four 'kingdoms' and the fifth reign following them. On the turn of the Babylonian and Persian eras a similar approach of the Persian takeover is given in Deutero-Isaiah, where Cyrus is taken as a liberator and called 'anointed' (*mashiah*). The idea of retributive justice is present in further oracles of the older part of the Danielic collection (chs. 4, 5).

The tradition on the origin of the evil (*1 En.* 6–11), an alternative tradition to the tradition of the Fall (Gen. 2) may have taken shape from Mesopotamian elements—possibly stemming from the Babylonian exile—during later centuries of the Persian period. This tradition may have served as a basis both for the sophisticated demonology and the idea of the judgment of the evil which appear in the later Enochic tradition, and in *Jubilees*.

As to the Danielic tradition, in Daniel 7—written probably at the beginning of the revolt by the Maccabees—a re-formulation of the four kingdoms scheme of an older prophecy of Daniel 2 appears with a new meaning. Later pieces of the Danielic collection—the prophecies of chs. 8–12, written in Hebrew—adopt elements of the earlier prophecies. The apex of the second-century Danielic prophecies is the fall of Antiochus Epiphanes which had by then become the symbol of the 'fourth reign' (Dan. 8–12).

The Hasmonean dynasty, gaining power after the revolt, initiated works praising the revolt led by their ancestors. The 'official' chronicles of the battles are the legendary works of *1* and *2 Maccabees*. Besides these chronicles, propagandistic pseudo-historical works (Esther, Judith) were written, based on the Exodus-pattern, using motifs of the popular literature (e.g. the Ahiqar-story). The stories are aetiological legends of feasts admitted or initiated in the Hasmonean era—simultaneous reminders of the battles of the revolt (Exodus pattern). They had an effect on the literature of the Diaspora (*3 Maccabees*).

Likewise during the rule of the Hasmonean dynasty, a special genre—the genre of the *pesharim* of Qumran—came into being. Among its literary sources are certain traditions of the book of Daniel. The highlight of the genre is represented by the *pesharim* rendered into certain prophetic books; they speak, in an esoteric language of the history of the author's community, of a future retribution of their enemy.

The LAB (a special example of 'rewritten Bibles') and two works of the visionary literature (Syriac Baruch, *4 Ezra*) were probably written after the fall of the Jewish War (70 CE). Their authors consider the situation analogous to that of the era following 586 BCE. Contrary to the era of the Babylonian exile, there is no liberation following the tragedy. The historical past and its recurrences no longer play a part in the visions; they are centred around the future, while using motifs and techniques of the Danielic tradition.

BIBLIOGRAPHY

Abel, F.-M.

1933–38 *Géographie de la Palestine* (2 vols.; Paris: Gabalda).

1949 *Les Livres des Maccabées* (EBib; Paris: Gabalda).

1952 *Histoire de la Palestine depuis la conquête d'Alexandre jusqu'à l'invasion arabe* (Paris: Gabalda).

Abel, F.-M. and J. Starcky

1961 *Les Livres des Maccabées* (trans. F.-M. Abel; Paris: Cerf, 3rd edn).

Ackroyd, P.R.

1968 *Exile and Restoration: A Study of Hebrew Thought of the Sixth Century BC* (London: SCM Press).

1991 *The Chronicler in his Age* (JSOTSup, 101; Sheffield: JSOT Press).

Ackroyd, P.R. and C.F. Evans (eds.)

1970 *The Cambridge History of the Bible: From the Beginnings to Jerome*, I (London: Cambridge University Press).

Adler, J.J.

1990–91 'The Book of Esther—Some Questions and Responses', *JBQ* 19: 186-90.

Aistleitner, J.

1959 *Die Mythologischen und Kultischen Texte aus Ras Schamra* (BOH, 8; Budapest: Akadémiai Kiadr).

Alexiou, M. and P. Dronke

1971 'The Lament of Jephthah's Daughter: Themes, Traditions, Originality', *Studi Medievali* 12: 819-63.

Allegro, J.M.

1956 'Further Light on the History of the Qumran Sect', *JBL* 75: 89-95.

1959 'THRAKIDAN, the "Lion of Wrath" and Alexander', *PEQ* 91: 47-51.

1968 *Discoveries in the Judaean Desert*, V (Oxford: Clarendon Press).

Alonso-Schökel, L.

1975 'Narrative Structures in the Book of Judith', in *Colloquies of the Center for Hermeneutical Studies in Hellenistic and Modern Culture* (Colloquy 11; Berkeley: Center for Hermeneutical Studies in Hellenistic and Modern Culture): 1-20.

Alt, A.

1954 'Zur Menetekel-Inschrift', *VT* 4: 303-305.

Altheim, F. and R. Stiehl

1963 *Die aramäische Sprache unter den Achämeniden*. I. *Geschichtliche Untersuchungen* (Frankfurt am Main: Klostermann).

Amussin, I.D.

1956 'Ad Pap.Lond. 1912', *JJP* 9-10: 169-209.

1958 'Kumranskij fragment "molitvi" vavilonskogo tsaria Nabonida', *Vestnik Drevnei Istorii* 4.66: 104-117.

1963 'Ephraim et Manassé dans le Pésher de Nahum (4QpNahum)', *RevQ* 15: 389-96.

1967 'The Qumran Commentaries, and Their Significance for the History of the Qumran Community' (XXVII International Congress of Orientalists, papers presented by the USSR Delegation, Moscow).

1971 *Teksti Kumrana* (Moscow: Nauka).

1974 'A propos de l'interprétation de 4Q 161 (fragments 5–6 et 8)', *RevQ* 31: 381-92.

1978 'The Reflection of Historical Events of the First Century BC in Qumran Commentaries (4Q 161; 4Q 169; 4Q 166)', *HUCA* 48: 123-52.

1983 *Kumranskaja obshtchina* (Moscow: Nauka).

Attridge, H.W.

1976 *The Introduction of Biblical History in the Antiquitates Judaicae of Flavius Josephus* (HDR, 7; Missoula, MT: Scholars Press).

Avi-Yonah, M.

1971 'Bethulia', *EncJud* 4: col. 749.

Avishur, Y.

1986–87 'Toward the Historical Background of the Scroll of Esther', *Beth Mikra* 32: 290-91 [Hebrew].

Baillet, R. *et al.*

1956 'Le travail d'édition des fragments manuscrits de Qumrân', *RB* 63: 49-67.

Baltzer, D.

1971 *Ezechiel und Deuterojesaja* (BZAW, 121; Berlin: de Gruyter).

Bardtke, H.

1963 *Das Buch Esther* (KAT, 17.5; Gütersloh: Gerd Mohn): 239-408.

Barstad, H.M.

1987 'On the So-Called Babylonian Literary Influence in Second Isaiah', *SJOT* 2: 99-110.

Barthélemy, D. and J.T. Milik

1955 *Discoveries in the Judaean Desert*. I. *Qumran Cave I* (Oxford: Clarendon Press).

Bartholomae, C.

1904 *Altiranisches Wörterbuch* (2 vols.; Strasbourg: K.J. Trübner).

Basser, H.W.

1988 'Pesher Hadavar: The Truth of the Matter', *RevQ* 13: 389-405.

Bauckham, R.

1983 'The LAB of Pseudo-Philo and the Gospels as "Midrash"', in R.T. France and D. Wenham (eds.) *Gospel Perspectives: Studies in Midrash and Historiography*, III (Sheffield: JSOT Press): 33-76.

Baudry, G.-H.

1992 'Le Péché originel dans les Pseudépigraphes de l'Ancien Testament', *Mélanges de Science Religieuse* 49: 163-92.

Bauer, W.

1925 'Menetekel, Vierter Deutscher Münzforschungstag zu Halle', *Halle*: 27-30.

Baumgarten, J.M.
1958 'The Beginning of the Day in the Calendar of Jubilees', *JBL* 77: 355-60.
1982 'Some Problems of the Jubilees Calendar in Current Research', *VT* 32: 485-89.
1987 'The Calendars of the Book of Jubilees and the Temple Scroll', *VT* 37: 71-78.

Baumgartner, W.
1926 'Susanna. Die Geschichte einer Legende', *ARW* 24: 259-80.
1927 'Zum Traumerraten in Daniel 2', *AfO* 4: 17-19.
1945 'Zu den vier Reichen von Daniel 2', *TZ*: 17-22.

Bea, A.
1940 'De Origine Vocis *pwr*', *Bib* 21: 198.

Beaulieu, P.-A.
1989 *The Reign of Nabonidus King of Babylon 556–539 BC* (Yale Near Eastern Researches, 10; New Haven, CT: Yale University Press).

Beckwith, R.T.
1991 'The Essene Calendar and the Moon: A Reconsideration', *RevQ* 15: 457-66.

Beek, M.A.
1935 *Das Danielbuch. Sein historischer Hintergrund und seine literarische Entwicklung. Versuch eines Beitrags zur Lösung des Problems* (Leiden: Ginsberg).

Beer, B.
1856 *Das Buch der Jubiläen und sein Verhältnis zu den Midraschim* (Leipzig: W. Gerhard).

Bellet, P.M.
1963 'Libros de los Macabeos', in *Enciclopedia de la Biblia*, IV (Barcelona: Garriga): 1137-42.

Bentzen, A.
1950 'Der Hedammu-Mythos, das Judithbuch und ähnliches', *ArOr* 18: 1-2.
1952 *Daniel* (HAT 1.19; Tübingen: Mohr [Paul Siebeck], 2nd edn).

Berg, S.B.
1979 *The Book of Esther: Motifs, Themes and Structure* (SBLDS, 44; Missoula, MT: Scholars Press).

Berger, K.
1981 *Das Buch der Jubiläen* (JSHRZ 2.3; Gütersloh: Gütersloher Verlagshaus).
1992 *Synopse des Vierten Buches Esra und der Syrischen Baruch-Apokalypse* (Texte und Arbeiten zum Neutestamentlichen Zeitalter, 8; Tübingen: Francke).

Bergey, R.
1984 'Late Linguistic Features in Esther', *JQR* 74: 66-78.
1988 'Post-Exilic Hebrew Linguistic Development in Esther: A Diachronic Approach', *JETS* 31: 161-68.

Betz, O.
1960 *Offenbarung und Schriftforschung in der Qumransekte* (WUNT, 6; Tübingen: Mohr [Paul Siebeck]).

Beyer, K.
1984 *Die aramäischen Texte vom Toten Meer samt den Inschriften aus Palästina, dem Testament Levis aus der Kairoer Genisa, der Fastenrolle und den alten talmudischen Zitaten, aramaistische Einleitung, Text, Ubersetzung, Deutung, GrammatikWorterbuch, deutsch-aramaische Wortliste* (Göttingen: Vandenhoeck & Ruprecht).
1994 *Der Aramaïschen Texte vom Toten Meer: Ergänzungsband* (Göttingen: Vandenhoeck & Ruprecht).

Bezold, C.
1883 *Ma'arrath Gazze: Die Schatzhöhle* (2 vols.; Leipzig: Hinrichs).

Bic, M.
1968 *Trois prophètes dans un temps de ténèbres. Sophonie–Nahum–Habaquq* (LD, 48; Paris: Cerf).

Bickerman, E.
1930 'Zur Datierung des Pseudo-Aristeas', *ZNW* 29: 280-98.
1933 'Ein jüdischer Festbrief vom Jahre 124 v.Chr. (2 Makk. 1,1-9)', *ZNW* 32: 233-53.
1935 'La charte séleucide de Jérusalem', *REJ*: 44-85.
1937 *Der Gott der Makkabäer: Untersuchungen über Sinn und Ursprung der Makkabäischen Erhebung* (Berlin: Schocken Books).
1938 *Institutions des Séleucides* (Bibliothèque archéologique et historique, 26; Paris: P. Geuthner).
1939–44 'Héliodore au temple de Jérusalem', *Annuaire de l'Institut de Philologie et d'Histoire Orientales et Slaves* 7: 5-40.
1944 'The Colophon of the Greek Book of Esther', *JBL* 63: 339-62.
1955 'Une question d'authenticité: les privilèges juifs (parmi les Séleucids)', in *idem*, *Studies in Jewish and Christian History* (AGJU, 9.2; repr.; Leiden: Brill, 1980): 24-43.
1967 *Four Strange Books of the Bible. Jonah, Daniel, Koheleth, Esther* (New York: Schocken Books).
1970 *From Ezra to the Last of the Maccabees: Foundations of Post-Biblical Judaism* (New York: Schocken Books).
1980 'La Charte séleucide de Jérusalem', in *idem*, *Studies in Jewish and Christian History* (AGJU, 9.2; repr.; Leiden: Brill, 1980): 44-85.

Bickerman, E. and I. Heinemann
1928 Makkabäerbücher (I–II; III), RE XIV.1: 779-805.

Bidawid, R.J.
1966–73 *4 Ezra. The Old Testament in Syriac, according to the Peshitta Version—Sample edition: Song of Songs, Tobit, 4 Ezra* (Leiden: Brill).

Bietenhard, H.
1948 'Die Freiheitskriege der Juden unter den Kaisern Trajan und Hadrian und der messianische Tempelbau', *Judaica* 4: 164-66.

Biggs, R.D.
1967 'More Babylonian "Prophecies"', *Iraq* 29: 117-32.

Black, M. (ed.)
1970 *Apocalypsis Henochi Graece* (PVTG, 3; Leiden: Brill).

Black, M.
1974 'The Fragments of the Aramaic Enoch from Qumran', in W.C. van

Unnik (ed.), *La Littérature juive entre Tenach et Mischna* (Leiden: Brill): 15-28.

1976 'The Throne-Theophany Prophetic Commission and the "Son of Man". A Study in Tradition-History', in R. Hammerton-Kelly and R. Scroggs (eds.), *Jews, Greeks and Christians: Religious Cultures in Late Antiquity. Essays in Honor of William David Davies* (Leiden: Brill): 53-73.

1987 'The Strange Visions of Enoch', *RB* 3.2: 20-33, 38-42.

Bloch, J.

1957–58 'The Ezra Apocalypse: Was it Written in Hebrew, Greek, or Aramaic?', *JQR* 48: 279-94.

Bogaert, P.-M.

1969 *Apocalypse de Baruch: introduction, traduction du Syriaque et commentaire* (Sources Chrétiennes, 144-45; 2 vols.; Paris: Cerf).

1978 'Les Antiquités Bibliques du Pseudo-Philon à la lumière des découvertes de Qumrân. Observations sur l'hymnologie et particulièrement sur le ch.60', in Delcor 1978: 313-31.

Borger, R.

1974 'Die Beschwörungsserie FBIT MESERI und die Himmelfahrt Henochs', *JNES* 33: 183-96.

Bousset, W. and H. Gressmann

1926 *Die Religion des Judentums im späthellenistischen Zeitalter* (HNT, 21; Tübingen: Mohr).

Bousset, W.

1903 *Die jüdische Apokalyptik, ihre religionswissenschaftliche Herkunft und ihre Bedeutung für das Neue Testament* (Berlin: Reuter & Reichard).

Box, G.H.

1912 *The Apocalypse of Ezra* (Translation of Early Documents, Series 1: Palestinian Jewish Texts; London: SPCK).

Braun, H.

1957 *Spätjüdisch-häretischer und frühchristlicher Radikalismus: Jesus von Nazareth und die essenische Qumransekte* (BHT, 24; 2 vols.; Tübingen: Mohr [Paul Siebeck]).

Braverman, J.

1978 *Jerome's Commentary on Daniel. A Study of Comparative Jewish and Christian Interpretation of the Hebrew Bible* (CBQMS, 7; Washington, DC: Catholic Biblical Association of America).

Bréhier, E.

1925 *Les Idées philosophiques et religieuses de Philon d'Alexandrie* (Etudes de philosophie médiévale, 8; Paris: J. Vrin, 2nd edn).

Bright, J.

1972 *A History of Israel* (OTL: London: SCM Press [1960]).

Bringmann, K.

1983 *Hellenistische Reform und Religionsverfolgung in Judäa. Eine Untersuchung zur jüdisch-hellenistischen Geschichte* (Abhandlungen der Akademie der Wissenschaften zu Göttingen, philologisch-historische Klasse, 3.132; Göttingen: Vandenhoeck & Ruprecht).

Brockington, L.H. (ed.)
1969 *Ezra, Nehemiah and Esther* (New Century Bible; London: Nelson).

Brooke, G.J.
1985 *Exegesis at Qumran. 4Q Florilegium in its Jewish Context* (JSOTSup, 29; Sheffield: JSOT Press).
1991 'The Kittim in the Qumran Pesharim', in L.C.A. Alexander (ed.), *Images of Empire* (JSOTSup, 122; Sheffield: JSOT Press): 135-59.

Brown, C.A.
1992 *No Longer Silent: First Century Jewish Portraits of Biblical Women. Studies in Pseudo-Philo's Biblical Antiuities and Josephus's Jewish Antiquities. Gender and the Biblical Tradition* (Louisville: Westminster Press).

Brownlee, W.H.
1951 'Biblical Interpretation among the Sectaries of the Dead Sea Scrolls', *BA* 14: 54-76.
1952 'The Historical Allusions of the Dead Sea Habakkuk Midrash', *BASOR* 126: 10-20.

Brunner, G.
1940 *Der Nabuchodonosor des Buches Judith* (Berlin: Rudolph Pfau).

Bruns, E.J.
1954 'Judith or Jael?', *CBQ* 16: 12-14.
1956 'The Genealogy of Judith', *CBQ* 18: 19-22.

Bunge, J.G.
1971 Untersuchungen zum 2.Makkabäerbuch. Quellenkritische literarische, chronologische, und historische Untersuchungen zum 2.Makkabäerbuch als Quelle syrisch-palästinensischer Geschichte im 2.Jh. v.Chr (Bonn: Rheinische Friedrich-Willhelms Universität): 184-90.

Burgmann, H.
1977 'Gerichtsherr und Generalankläger: Jonathan und Simon', *RevQ* 33: 3-72.

Burn, A.R.
1968 *Persia and the Greeks: The Defence of the West* (London: Edward Arnold).

Burrows, M.
1966 'Ancient Israel', in R.C. Dentan (ed.), *The Idea of History in the Ancient Near East* (AOS, 38; New Haven, CT: Yale University Press): 101-31.

Burrows, M. *et al.* (eds.)
1950 *The Dead Sea Scrolls of St Mark's Monastery: The Isaiah Manuscript and the Habakkuk Commentary*, I (New Haven, CT: The American Schools of Oriental Research).

Burstein, S.M.
1978 *The Babyloniaca of Berossus* (Sources and Monographs from the Ancient Near East; Malibu: Undena).

Cadbury, H.J.
1955 'The Grandson of Ben Sira', *HTR* 48: 219-25.

Callaway, P.
1988 'The History of the Qumran Community. An Investigation', *FO* 25: 143-50.
Caquot, A.
1955 'Sur les quatre bêtes de Daniel VII', *Sem* 5: 5-13.
1962 'L'Alliance avec Abram (Genèse 15)', *Sem* 12: 51-66.
1967 'Les Quatre Bêtes et le "Fils de l'homme" (Daniel 7)', *Sem* 17: 37-71.
Carmignac, J.
1979 'Qu'est-ce que l'Apocalyptique? Son emploi à Qumrân', *RevQ* 10: 1-33.
1961–62 'Notes sur les Peshârim', *RevQ* 3: 505-538.
Carson, D.A. and H.G.M. Williamson (eds.)
1988 *It is Written: Scripture Citing Scripture, Essays in Honour of Barnabas Lindars* (Cambridge: Cambridge University Press).
Cassuto, U.
1943 'The Episode of the Sons of God and the Daughters of Man (Genesis vi.1-4)', in *Essays presented to J.H. Hertz, Chief Rabbi London*, I (Biblical and Oriental Studies; Jerusalem: Magnes Press): 17-28.
Cazelles, H.
1961 'Note sur la composition du rouleau d'Esther', in H. Gross and F. Müssner (eds.), *Textua Veritas Festschrift für Hubert Junker* (Trier: Paulinus Verlag): 17-29.
1962 'Sur les origines du calendrier des Jubilées', *Bib* 43: 202-216.
Ceriani, A.M. (ed.)
1861 *Monumenta sacra et profana ex codicibus praesertim Bibliothecae Ambrosianae* (Milan: Bibliotheco Ambrosiana).
1868 *Monumenta sacra et profana V* (Milan: Bibliotheca Ambrosiana).
1871 *Apocalypsis Baruch, Syriace, Monumenta Sacra et Profana V* (Milan: Bibliotheca Ambrosiana).
Charles, R.H.
1897 *The Assumption of Moses* (London: A. & C. Black).
Charles, R.H. (ed.)
1893 *The Book of Enoch* (Oxford: Clarendon Press).
1895 *The Ethiopic Version of the Hebrew Book of Jubilees* (Oxford: Clarendon Press).
1896 *The Apocalypse of Baruch Translated from the Syriac* (London: A. & C. Black).
1902 *The Book of Jubilees or the Little Genesis* (London: A. & C. Black).
1906 *The Ethiopic Version of the Book of Enoch in Anecdota Oxonensia* (Oxford: Clarendon Press).
1973 *The Apocrypha and Pseudepigrapha of the Old Testament* (2 vols.; Oxford: Clarendon Press [1913]).
Charlesworth, J.H.
1991 'Qumran in Relation to the Apocrypha, Rabbinic Judaism, and Nascent Christianity: Impacts of University Teaching of Jewish Civilization in the Hellenistic-Roman Period', in Talmon 1991: 168-80.

Charlesworth, J.H. (ed.)
1983–85 *The Old Testament Pseudepigrapha* (2 vols.; London: Darton, Longman and Todd).
Clermont-Ganneau, Ch.
1886 'Mané, Thecel, Pharès et la festion de Balthasar', *JA sér* 8.8: 36-67.
Clines, D.J.A.
1984 *The Esther Scroll: The Story of the Story* (JSOTSup, 30; Sheffield: JSOT Press).
1991 'In Quest of the Historical Mordecai', *VT* 41: 129-36.
Cohn, L. and P. Wendland (eds.)
1896–1915 *Philonis Alexandrini Opera quae supersunt* (6 vols.; Berlin: Reimer).
Cohn, L.
1898 'An Apocryphal Work Ascribed to Philo of Alexandria', *JQR* OS 10: 277-332.
1915 'Pseudo-Philo und Jerachmeel', in *Festschrift zum 70. Geburtstage Jakob Guttmanns* (Leipzig: Fock): 173-85.
Collins, J.J.
1973/a 'The Date and Provenance of the Testament of Moses', in Nickelsburg (ed.) 1973: 15-32.
1973/b 'Some Remaining Traditio-Historical Problems in the Testament of Moses', in Nickelsburg (ed.) 1973: 38-43.
1974 'The Son of Man and the Saints of the Most High in the Book of Daniel', *JBL* 93: 50-66.
1975 'The Court-Tales in Daniel and the Development of Apocalyptic', *JBL* 94: 218-34.
1976 'Composition and Redaction of the Testament of Moses 10', *HTR* 69: 179-86.
1977 *The Apocalyptic Vision of the Book of Daniel* (HSM, 16; Missoula, MT: Scholars Press for Harvard Semitic Museum).
1982 'The Apocalyptic Technique: Setting and Function in the Book of Watchers', *CBQ* 44: 91-111.
1987 'Prophecy and Fulfillment in the Qumran Scrolls', *JETS* 30: 267-78.
Colunga, A.
1948 'El género literario de Judit: La Ciencia Tomista', *Salamanca 74*: 98-126.
Conybeare, I.C. *et al.* (eds.)
1913 *The Story of Ahiqar* (Cambridge: Cambridge University Press).
Cowley, A.
1923 *Aramaic Papyri of the Fifth Century BC* (Oxford: Clarendon Press).
Coxon, P.W.
1986 'The Great Tree of Daniel 4', in J.D. Martin and P.R. Davies (eds.), *A Word in Season. Essays in Honour of William McKane* (JSOTSup, 42; Sheffield: JSOT Press): 91-112.
Craghan, J.F.
1986 'Esther: A Fully Liberated Woman', *TBT* 24: 6-11.
Craven, T.
1983 *Artistry and Faith in the Book of Judith* (SBLDS, 70; Chico, CA: Scholars Press).

Cross, F.M.

1969 'New Directions in the Study of Apocalyptic', *JTC* 6: 157-65.

1995 *The Ancient Library of Qumran and Modern Biblical Studies* (Sheffield: Sheffield Academic Press, 3rd edn).

Cumont, F.

1909 'La plus ancienne géographie astrologique', *Klio* 9: 263-73.

Dalman, G.

1935 *Sacred Sites and Ways: Studies in the Topography of the Gospels* (New York: Macmillan).

Dancy, J.C.

1972 'Judith', in *The Shorter Books of the Apocrypha* (The Cambridge Bible Commentary; Cambridge: Cambridge University Press): 67-131.

Davenport, G.L.

1971 *The Eschatology of the Book of the Jubilees* (SPB, 20; Leiden: Brill).

Davies, G.I.

1978 'Apocalyptic and Historiography', *JSOT* 5: 15-28.

Davies, P.R.

1977 'Hasidism in the Maccabean Period', *JJS* 28: 127-40.

1985a *Daniel* (OTG; Sheffield: JSOT Press).

1985b 'Eschatology at Qumran', *JBL* 104: 39-55.

1987 *Behind the Essenes. History and Ideology in the Dead Sea Scrolls* (Brown Judaic Studies, 94; Atlanta, GA: Scholars Press).

de Jonge, M. and A.S. van der Woude

1966 '11Q Melchizedek and the New Testament', *NTS* 12: 301-326.

de Vaux, R.

1960 *Das Alte Testament und seine Lebensordnungen* (2 vols.; Freiburg: Herder).

Dedering, S.

1973 *Apocalypse of Baruch* (Leiden: Brill).

Delauney, J.A.

1976 'Remarques sur quelques noms de personne des archives élamites de Persépolis', *Studia Iranica* 5: 9-31.

Delcor, M.

1966 'Pseudo-Philon', *DBSup* 7: col. 1373.

1971 *Le Livre de Daniel* (Sources Bibliques; Paris: Gabalda).

1976 'Le Livre de Judith et l'époque grecque', in *idem* (ed.), *Religion d'Israël et Proche Orient Ancien: Des Phéniciens aux Esséniens* (Leiden: Brill): 251-80.

1979 'Le Mythe de la chute des anges et de l'origine des géants comme explication du mal dans le monde dans l'apocalyptique juive', in *idem*, *Etudes bibliques et orientales de religions comparées* (Leiden: Brill): 263-313.

Delcor, M. *et al.* (eds.)

1978 *Qumrân. Sa piété, sa théologie et son milieu* (BETL, 46; Leuven: Leuven University Press).

Denis, A.M.

1970 *Introduction aux pseudépigraphes grecs d'Ancien Testament* (Leiden: Brill).

1988 'Les Genres littéraires des Pseudépigraphes d'Ancien Testament: Essai de classification', *Folia Orientalia* 25: 99-112.

Dentan, R.C. (ed.)

1966 *The Idea of History in the Ancient Near East* (OS, 38; New Haven, CT: Yale University Press).

Dexinger, F.

1969 *Das Buch Daniel und seine Probleme* (Stuttgart: Vlg. Katholisches Bibelwerk).

1977 *Henochs Zehnwochenapokelype und offene Probleme der Apokalyptikforschung* (Leiden: Brill).

Diakonov, I.M.

1956 *Istoria Midii ot drevnejshih vremen do kontsa iv veka do n.e.* (Moscow-Leningrad: Akademia Nauk).

Dietzfelbinger, C.

1975 *Pseudo-Philo: Antiquitates Biblicae* (Liber Antiquitatum Biblicarum; Gütersloh: Gerd Mohn).

Dimant, D.

1974 'The "Fallen Angels" in the Dead Sea Scrolls and in the Apocryphal and Pseudepigraphic Books Related to Them' (unpublished PhD dissertation, Hebrew University, Jerusalem [Hebrew]).

1991 'Literary Typologies and Biblical Interpretation in the Hellenistic-Roman Period', in Talmon 1991: 73-80.

1992 'Pesharim, Qumran', in *ABD*, V: 244-51.

Dimant, D. and J. Strugnell

1988 'The Merkabah Vision in Second Ezekiel (4Q 385 4)', *RevQ* 14: 331-48.

Dommershausen, W.

1964 *Nabonid im Buche Daniel* (Mainz: Grunewald).

Doran, R.

1981 *Temple Propaganda. The Purpose and Character of 2 Maccabees* (CBQMS, 12; Washington, DC: Catholic Biblical Association of America).

1989 'The Non-Dating of Jubilees: Jub. 34–38p; 23.14-32 in a Narrative Context', *JSJ* 20: 1-11.

Dougherty, R.P.

1929 *Nabonidus and Belshazzar: A Study of the Closing Events of the Neo-Babylonian Empire* (YOR, 15; New Haven, CT: Yale University Press).

Draisma, S. (ed.)

1989 *Intertextuality in Biblical Writings: Essays in Honour of Bas van Iersel* (Kampen: Kok).

Driver, G.R.

1957 *Aramaic Documents from the Fifth Century BC* (Oxford: Clarendon Press).

Driver, S.R.

1900 *The Book of Daniel* (Cambridge Bible for Schools and Colleges; Cambridge: Cambridge University Press).

1912 *The Book of Daniel* (CBC; Cambridge: Cambridge University Press).

1913 *An Introduction to the Literature of the Old Testament* (International Theological Library; Edinburgh: T. & T. Clark, 9th edn).

Dubarle, A.-M.

1959 'La Mention de Judith dans la littérature ancienne juive et chrétienne', *RB* 66: 514-49.

1966 *Judith. Formes et sens des diverses traditions* (2 vols.; Rome: Biblical Pontifical Institute).

1969 'La mention de Judith dans la littérature ancienne juive et chrétienne', *RB* 66: 514-49.

Duchesne-Guillemin, J.

1953a *Les Noms d'eunuques d'Assuérus* (Le Muséon, 66; Opera Minora III; repr.; Teheran: Universite de Téhéran, 1974).

1953b *Ormazd et Ahriman. L'Aventure dualiste dans l'antiquité* (Mythes et religions, 31; Paris: Presse Universitaire de France).

1962 *La Religion de l'Iran ancien* (Les anciennes religions orientales, 3; Paris: Presse Universitaire de France).

Dupont-Sommer, A.

1963 'Le Commentaire de Nahum', *Sem* 13: 55-88.

Eerdmans, B.D.

1932 'Origin and Meaning of the Aramaic Part of Daniel', in *Actes du XVIIIe congrès international des orientalistes* (Leiden: Brill): 198-202.

1947 *The Religion of Israel* (Leiden: Leiden University Press).

Efron, J.

1987 'Daniel and His Three Friends in Exile', in *idem*, *Studies on the Hasmonean Period* (SJLA, 39; Leiden: Brill):

Ehrlich, E.L.

1953 *Das Traum im Alten Testament* (Zeitschrift fur die alttestamentliche Wissenschaft, 73; Berlin: Töpelmann).

Eilers, W.

1971 'Der Keilschrifttext des Kyros-Zyliners', in W. Eilers *et al.* (eds.), *Festgabe deutscher Iranisten zur 2500 Jahrfeier Irans* (Stuttgart: Hochwacht Druck): 156-66.

Eissfeldt, O.

1932 *Baal Zaphon, Zeus Kasion und der Durchzug der Israeliten durchs Meer* (Halle: Niemeyer).

1951 'Die Menetekel-Inschrift und ihre Bedeutung', *ZAW* 63: 105-14.

1955 'Zur Kompositionstechnik des Pseudo-Philonischen Liber Antiquitatum Biblicarum', *NTS* 56: 53-71.

1964 *Einleitung in das Alte Testament unter Einschluss der Apokryphen und Pseudepigraphen* (Tübingen: Mohr, 3rd edn)

Eliade, M.

1985 *Forgerons et alchimistes* (Idées et recherches, 12; Paris: Flammarion).

Endres, J.C.

1987 *Biblical Interpretation in the Book of Jubilees* (CBQMS, 18; Washington, DC: Catholic Biblical Association of America).

Engel, H.

1992 'Der Herr ist ein Gott, der Kriege zerschlägt. Zur Frage der griechischen Originalsprache und der Struktur des Buches Judith', in Schunck *et al.* 1992: 155-68.

Enslin, M. and S. Zeitlin
1972 *The Book of Judith* (Jewish Apocryphal Literature, 7; Leiden: Brill).

Eskenazi, T.C.
1992 'Out from the Shadows: Biblical Women in the Post-Exilic Era', *JSOT* 54: 25-43.

Eslinger, L.
1992 'Inner-biblical Exegesis and Inner-biblical Allusion: The Question of Category', *VT* 42: 47-58.

Feldman, L.H. and G. Hata (eds.)
1971 *The Biblical Antiquities of Philo* (Prolegomenon L.H. Feldman; New York: Ktav [1917]).
1989 *Josephus, the Bible and History* (Leiden: Brill)

Ferch, A.J.
1977 'The Two Aeons and the Messiah in Ps.-Philo, 4 Ezra and 2 Baruch', *AUSS* 15.2: 135-51.
1980 'Daniel 7 and Ugarit: A Reconsideration', *JBL* 99: 75-86.

Finkel, A.
1963 'The Pesher of Dreams and Scriptures', *RevQ* 15: 357-70.

Finkelstein, L.
1943 'The Date of the Book of Jubilees', *HTR* 36: 19-24.

Fischer, B. (ed.)
1983 *Biblia Sacra iuxta Vulgatam Versionem* (Stuttgart: Deutsche Bibelgesellschaft).

Fischer, T.
1991 'Heliodor im Tempel zu Jerusalem—ein "hellenistischer" Aspekt der "frommen Legende"', in R. Liwak and S. Wagner (eds.), *Prophetie und Geschichtliche Wirklichkeit im alten Israel* (Stuttgart: Kohlhammer): 122-33.
1980 *Seleukiden und Makkabäer* (Bochum: In Kommission beim Studienverlag N. Brockmeyer).

Fishbane, M.
1985 *Biblical Interpretation in Ancient Israel* (Oxford: Clarendon Press).
1988 'Scripture at Qumran', in M.J. Mulder (ed.), *Mikra: Text, Translation, Reading and Interpretation of the Hebrew Bible in Ancient Judaism and Early Christianity* (CRINT, 1.2; Assen: Van Gorcum): 339-77.

Fitzmyer, J.A.
1970 'The Language of Palestine in the First Century AD', *CBQ* 32: 501-31.
1971 *The Genesis Apocryphon from Qumran Cave I. A Commentary* (Biblica et Orientalia 18.A; Rome: Biblical Institute Press).
1977 *The Dead Sea Scrolls: Major Publications and Tools for Study* (SBLBS, 8; Missoula, MT: Scholars Press, rev. edn).
1979 *A Wandering Aramean. Collected Aramaic Essays* (SBLMS; Missoula, MT: Scholars Press).

Flemming, J.
1902 *Das Buch Henoch: Äthiopischer Text* (Leipzig: Hinrichs).

Flemming, J. and L. Radermacher
1901 *Das Buch Henoch* (GCS; Leipzig: Hinrichs).

Flusser, D.
1972 'The Four Empires in the Fourth Sibyl and in the Book of Daniel', *Israel Oriental Studies* 2: 148-75.

Fohrer, G.
1969 *Geschichte der israelitischen Religion* (De Gruyter Lehrbuch; Berlin: de Gruyter).

Fox, N.S.
1989–90 'The Hidden Hand of God', *DD* 18: 183-87.

Fox, M.V.
1991 *Character and Ideology in the Book of Esther* (Studies on Personalities of the Old Testament; Columbia: University of South Carolina Press).

Frankel, Z.
1856 'Das Buch der Jubiläen', *MGWJ*.

Free, J.P.
1962 'Dothan', *RB* 69: 266-70.

Freedman, D.N.
1957 'The Prayer of Nabonidus', *BASOR* 145: 31-34.

Fröhlich, I.
1979 'Le Manuscrit latin de Budapest d'une oeuvre historique hellénistique', *Acta Antiqua Academiae Scientiarum Hungaricae* 27: 149-86.
1981 'Historiographie et aggada dans le Liber Antiquitatum Biblicarum du Pseudo-Philon', *Acta Antiqua Academiae Scientiarum Hungaricae* 28: 353-409.
1986 'Le Genre littéraire des "pesharim" de Qumrân', *RevQ* 47: 383-98.
1988 'L'Enseignements des Veilleurs dans la tradition de Qumrân', *RevQ* 49-52: 177-87.
1990 'The Symbolical Language of the Animal Apocalypse of Enoch (1 Enoch 85–90)', *RevQ* 56: 629-36.

Frost, S.B.
1962 'Daniel', *IDB* I: 764-67.

Fuks, A. and V.A. Tcherikover (eds.)
1957 *Corpus Papyrorum Judaicarum*, I (Cambridge, MA: Harvard University Press).

Gadd, C.J.
1958 'The Harran Inscriptions of Nabonidus', *Anatolian Studies* 8: 35-92.

Gall, A. von
1895 *Die Einheitlichkeit des Buches Daniel* (Giessen: Ricker).

Galling, K.
1954 'Die 62 Jahre des Meders Darius in Dan. 6.1', *ZAW* 66: 152.

Gammie, J.G.
1976 'The Classification, Stages of Growth and Changing Intentions in the Book of Daniel', *JBL* 95: 191-94.
1981 'On the Intention and Sources of Daniel 1–6', *VT* 31: 282-92.

García-Martínez, F.
1991 'Traditions communes dans le IVe Esdras et dans les MSS de Qumrân', *RevQ* 15: 287-301.

1992 *Qumran and Apocalyptic: Studies on the Aramaic Texts from Qumran* (Studies on the Texts of the Desert of Judah, 9; Leiden: Brill).

Gaster, M.

1892 'An Unknown Hebrew Version of the History of Judith', *PSBA* 25: 156-63.

1899 *The Hebrew Chronicles of Jerahmeel or The Hebrew Bible Historiale* (London: Royal Asiatic Society).

Gaster, T.H.

1950 *Purim and Hanukkah in Custom and Tradition* (New York: Schuman)

Gehman, H.S.

1924 'Notes on the Persian Words in the Book of Esther', *JBL* 43: 321-28.

Gerardi, P.

1986 'Declaring War in Mesopotamia', *AfO* 33: 30-38.

Gerleman, G.

1966 *Studien zu Esther. Stoff–Struktur–Stil–Sinn* (BSt, 48; Neukirchen–Vluyn: Neukirchener Verlag, 2nd edn).

Gesenius, W. and E. Robinson

1978 *A Hebrew and English Lexicon of the Old Testament* (Oxford: Clarendon Press).

Ginsberg, H.L.

1948 *Studies in Daniel* (Texts and Studies of the Jewish Theological Seminary of America, 14; New York).

1954a 'Daniel', in *Encyclopaedia Biblica*, II (Jerusalem): 686-97. (Hebrew)

1954b 'The Composition of the Book of Daniel', *VT* 4: 246-75.

Ginsberg, L.

1938 *The Legends of the Jews* (6 vols.; Philadelphia: Jewish Publication Society).

Glessmer, U.

1993 *Antike und moderne Auslegungen des Sintflutberichtes Gen. 6-8 und der Qumranpesher 4Q 252. Mitteilungen und Beiträge, Theologische Fakultät* (Leipzig, Forschungsstelle Judentum; Leipzig: Thomas-Verlag).

Goez, W.

1958 *Translatio imperii. Ein Beitrag zur Geschichte des Geschichtsdenkens und der politischen Theorien im Mittelalter und in der Neuzeit* (Tübingen: Mohr).

Goldingay, J.

1987 'The Stories of Daniel: A Narrative Politics', *JSOT* 37: 99-116.

Goldman, S.

1990 'Narrative and Ethical Ironies in Esther', *JSOT* 47: 15-31.

Goldstein, J.A.

1976 *I Maccabees* (AB, 41; Garden City, NY: Doubleday).

1983a *II Maccabees* (AB, 41A; Garden City, NY: Doubleday).

1983b 'The Date of the Book of Jubilees', *PAAJR* 50: 63-86.

Gooding, D.W.

1981 The Literary Structure of the Book of Daniel and its Implications', *TynBul* 32: 43-79.

Gordis, R.

1976 'Studies in the Esther Narrative', *JBL* 95: 43-58.

1981 'Religion, Wisdom and History in the Book of Esther', *JBL* 100: 359-88.

Grabbe, L.L.

1987 'The Jewish Theocracy from Cyrus to Titus: A Programmatic Essay', *JSOT* 37: 117-24.

1988 'Another Look at the Gestalt of "Darius the Mede"', *CBQ* 50: 198-213.

1992 *Judaism from Cyrus to Hadrian* (2 vols.; Minneapolis, MN: Fortress Press).

Grayson, A.K.

1975 *Babylonian Historical-Literary Texts* (Toronto Semitic Texts and Studies, 3; Toronto: University of Toronto Press).

1983 'Literary Letters from Deities and Diviners: More Fragments', *JAOS* 103: 143-48.

Grayson, A.K. and W.G. Lambert

1964 'Akkadian Prophecies', *JCS* 18: 7-30.

Greenfield, J.C. and M.E. Stone

1977 'The Enochic Pentateuch and the Date of the Similitudes', *HTR* 70: 51-65.

1979 'The Book of Enoch and the Traditions of Enoch', *Numen* 26: 89-103.

Grelot, P.

1958a 'La Géographie mythique d'Hénoch et ses sources', *RB* 65: 33-69.

1958b 'La Légende d'Hénoch dans les Apocryphes et dans la Bible', *RSR* 46: 5-26, 181-210.

1958–59 'L'Eschatologie des Esséniens et le livre d'Hénoch', *RevQ* 1: 113-31.

1975a 'Observations sur les targums I et II d'Esther', *Bib* 56: 53-73.

1975b 'Hénoch et ses écritures', *RB* 82: 481-500.

1981 'Le Livre des Jubilées et le Testament de Lévi', in P. Casetti *et al.* (eds.), *Mélanges Dominique Barthélemy: Etudes bibliques otteres à l'occasion de son 60e anniversaire* (Fribourg–Göttingen: Editions universitaires–Vandenhoeck & Ruprecht): 110-33.

1985 'L'écriture sur le mur (Daniel 5)', in A. Caquot, S. Légasse, M. Tardieu (eds.), *Mélanges bibliques et orientaux en l'honneur de M. Mathias Delcor* (Neukirchen–Vluyn: Neukirchener Verlag): 199-207.

Grintz, Y.M.

1957 *Sefer Yehudith—The Book of Judith. A Reconstruction of the Original Hebrew Text with Introduction, Commentary, Appendices and Indices* (Jerusalem: Morad Bialik).

Gruenwald, I.

1980 *Apocalyptic and Merkavah Mysticism* (AGJU, 14; Leiden: Brill).

Gry, L.

1938 *Les Dires prophétiques d'Esdras-IV Esdras* (2 vols.; Paris: P. Geuthner).

1939 'La Date de la fin des temps selon les révélations ou les calculs du Pseudo-Philon et de Baruch (Apocalypse syriaque)', *RB* 48: 337-56.

Gunkel, H.
1895 *Schöpfung und Chaos in Urzeit und Endzeit* (Göttingen: Vandenhoeck & Ruprecht).
1958 *Esther* (RV, 2.19-20; Tübingen: Mohr [1916]).
Haag, E.
1962 'Die besondere Art des Buches Judith und seine theologische Bedeutung', *Trierer TZ* 71: 288-301.
1963 *Studien zum Buche Judith: Seine theologische Bedeutung und literarische Eigenart* (Trierer Theologische Studien, 16; Trier: Paulinus Verlag).
Habicht, C.
1976 'Royal Documents in Maccabees II', *Harvard Studies in Classical Philology* 80: 1-18.
Hadas, M.
1949 'III. Maccabees and Greek Romance', *Review of Religion* 13: 155-62.
1953 *The Third and Fourth Book of Maccabees* (Jewish Apocryphal Literature; New York: Harper & Bros): 6-16.
Hadot, J.
1985 'Le Milieu d'origine du LAB', in *La Littérature intertestamentaire, Colloque de Strasbourg, 17-19 ocobre 1983* (Paris: Presse Universitaires de France): 153-71.
Hafemann, S.J.
1990 'Moses in the Apocrypha and Pseudepigrapha. A Survey', *JSP* 7: 79-104.
Hall, R.G.
1991 *Revealed Histories: Techniques for Ancient Jewish and Christian Historiography* (JSPSup, 6; Sheffield: JSOT Press).
Hallbäck, G.
1992 'The Fall of Zion and the Revelation of the Law: An Interpretation of 4 Ezra', *SJOT* 6: 263-92.
Haller, M.
1925 'Das Judentum. Geschichtsschreibung, Prophetie und Gesetzgebung nach dem Exil', *Die Schriften des Alten Testaments* (2.3; Göttingen: Vandenhoeck & Ruprecht, 2nd edn): 271-310.
Hallo, J.J.
1966 'Accadian Apocalypses', *IEJ* 16: 231-42.
Halpern-Amarn, B.
1991 'Portraits of Women in Pseudo-Philo's Biblical Antiquities', in A.-J. Levine (ed.), *Women Like This: New Perspectives on Jewish Women in the Graeco-Roman World* (Early Judaism and its Literature, 1; Atlanta, GA: Scholars Press): 83-106.
Hanhart, K.
1981 'The Four Beasts of Daniel's Vision in the Light of Rev. 13.2', *NTS* 27: 576-83.
Hanhart, R.
1978 *Text und Textgeschichte des Buches Judit* (Mitteilungen des Septuaginta-Unternehmens, 14; Göttingen: Vandenhoeck & Ruprecht).
1979a *Text und Textgeschichte des Buches Judit* (Abhandlungen der

Akademie der Wissenschaften in Göttingen, philologisch-historische Klasse, 3, 109; Göttingen: Vandenhoeck & Ruprecht).

Hanhart, R. (ed.)
1979b *Iudith* (SVTP, 8.4; Göttingen: Vandenhoeck & Ruprecht).

Hanson, P.D.
1971 'Jewish Apocalyptic against its Near Eastern Environment', *RB* 78: 31-58.
1975 *The Dawn of Apocalyptic* (Philadelphia: Fortress Press).
1977 'Rebellion in Heaven, Azazel and Euhemeristic Heroes in 1 Enoch 6–11', *JBL* 96: 197-233.

Harmatta, J.
1971 'The Literary Patterns of the Babylonian Edict of Cyrus', *Acta Antiqua Academiae Scientiarum Hungaricae* 19: 217-31.

Harrington, D.J. and J. Cazeaux
1970 'The Original Language of Pseudo-Philo's LAB', *HTR* 63: 503-14).
1974 *The Hebrew Fragments of Pseudo-Philo's Liber Antiquitatum Biblicarum Preserved in the Chronicles of Jerahmeel* (SBLTT, 3; Missoula, MT: Scholars Press).
1976 *Les Antiquités Bibliques: Pseudo-Philon* (SC, 229.1; Paris: Cerf).

Hartman, L.
1966 *Prophecy Interpreted: The Formation of Some Jewish Apocalyptic Texts and the Eschatological Discourse of Mark 13* (ConBNT, 1; Lund: Gleerup).
1979 *Asking for a Meaning: A Study of 1 Enoch 1–5* (ConBNT, 12; Lund: Gleerup).

Hartman, L.F. and A.A. di Lella
1985 *The Book of Daniel. A New Translation with Notes and Commentary* (AB, 23; Garden City, NY: Doubleday).

Hasel, G.F.
1979 'The Four World Empires of Daniel against its Near Eastern Environment', *JSOT* 12: 17-30.

Hastings, J. (ed.)
1908–19 *Encyclopaedia of Religion and Ethics* (12 vols.; repr.; Edinburgh: T. & T. Clark [1980]).

Haupt, P.
1906 *Purim* (Beitrige zur Assyriologie und Seueitischen sprach Wissenschaft, 6.2; Baltimore: Johns Hopkins University Press).

Heard, W.J.
1986 'The "Maccabean Martyrs" Contribution to the Holy War', *EvQ* 58: 291-318.

Heller, B.
1925 'Das Traumerraten im Buche Daniel', *ZAW* 43: 243-46.
1936 'Die Susannaerzählung: ein Märchen', *ZAW* 54: 281-87.

Hellholm, D. (ed.)
1979 *Apocalypticism in the Mediterranean World and the Near East: Proceedings of the International Colloquium on Apocalypticism* (Uppsala, International Colloquium on Apocalypticism, 12–17 August, 1974; Tubingen: Mohr).

Heltzer, M.
1980 'Eine neue Quelle zur Bestimmung der Abfassungszeit des Judith-Buches', *ZAW* 92: 437.
1992 'The Book of Esther—Where Does Fiction Start and History End?', *Bible Review* 8.1: 24-30, 41.
Hempel, J.
1930 'Die althebräische Literatur und ihr hellenistisch-jüdisches Nachleben', in O. Walzel (ed.), *Handbuch der Literaturwissenschaft* (Wildpark-Potsdam: Athenaion).
Hengel, M.
1969 *Judentum und Hellenismus: Studien zu ihrer Begegnung unter besonderer Berücksichtigung Palästinas bis zur Mitte des 2.Jh. v.Chr.* (WUNT, 10; Tübingen: Mohr).
1980 *Jews, Greeks and Barbarians: Aspects of the Hellenization of Judaism in the Pre-Christian Period* (trans. J. Bowden; London: SCM [1976]).
1989 *The 'Hellenization' of Judaea in the First Century after Christ* (London: SCM Press).
Herdner, H.
1963 *Corps des tablettes en cunéiformes* (Paris: P. Geuthner).
Herrmann, S.
1979 *Geschichte Israels in alttestamentlicher Zeit* (Munich: Kaiser).
Herzfeld , E.
1947 *Zoroaster and his World* (Princeton: Princeton University Press).
Hilgenfeld, A.
1966 *Die jüdische Apokalyptik in ihrer geschichtlichen Entwicklung* (Amsterdam: Rodopi [1857]).
Hintze, A.
1994 'The Greek and Hebrew Versions of the Book of Esther and its Iranian Background', in Sh. Shaked and A. Netzer (eds.), *Irano-Judaica III: Studies Relating to Jewish Contacts with Persian Culture Throughout the Ages* (Jerusalem: Hebrew University): 34-39.
Hoenig, S.B.
1979 'The Jubilees Calendar and the "Days of Assembly"', in A.I. Katsch and L. Nemoy (eds.), *Essays on the Occasion of the 70th Anniversary of the Dropsie University, 1909-1979* (Philadelphia: Dropsie University): 189-207.
Hölscher, G.
1919 'Die Entstehung des Buches Daniel', *TSK* 92: 113-38.
1922 *Geschichte der israelitischen und jüdischen Religion* (Sammlung Töpelmann, I.7; Giessen: A. Töpelmann).
Horbury, W.
1991 'The Name Mardochaeus in a Ptolemaic Inscription', *VT* 41: 220-26.
Horgan, M.P.
1979 *Pesharim: Qumran Interpretations of Biblical Books* (CBQMS, 8; Washington, DC: Catholic Biblical Association of America).
How, W.W. and J. Wells
1928 *A Commentary on Herodotus 1–29* (Oxford: Clarendon Press).

Huey, F.B. Jr.
1990 'Irony as the Key to Understanding the Book of Esther', *SwJT* 32.3: 36-39.

Humphreys, W.L.
1973 'A Life-style for Diaspora: A Study of the Tales of Esther and Daniel', *JBL* 92: 211-23.

Hunger, H.
1976 *Spätbabylonische Texte aus Uruk*, I (Ausgrabungen der Deutschen Forschungsgemeinschaft in Uruk-Warka, 9; Berlin: Gebr. Mann).

Hunger, H. and S.A. Kaufmann
1975 'A New Accadian Prophecy Text', *JAOS* 95: 371-75.

Hutter, M.
1988 'Iranische Neujahrsfestmythologie und der Traum des Mordechai', *BN* 44: 39-45.

Hyldahl, N.
1990 'The Maccabean Rebellion and the Question of "Hellenization"', in P. Bilde and T. Engberg-Pedersen *et al.* (eds.), *Religion and Religious Practice in the Seleucid Kingdom* (Studies in Hellenistic Civilization, 1; Aarhus: Aarhus University Press): 188-203.

Hyman, R.T.
1991–92 'Who is the Villain?', *JBQ* 20: 155-58.

Jacobson, H.
1983 'The Son of Man in Ps.-Philo's LAB', *JTS* 34.2: 531-33.
1989 'Biblical Quotation and Editorial Function in Pseudo-Philo's LAB', *JSP* 5: 47-64.

James, M.R.
1917 *The Biblical Antiquities of Philo* (Translation of Early Documents, 1; London: SPCK)

Jansen, H.L.
1939 *Die Henochgestalt: Eine vergleichende religionsgeschichtliche Untersuchung* (Skrifter utgitt av det Norske Videnskaps-Akademi i Oslo, 1; Oslo: Dybwad).

Janssen, E.
1971 *Das Gottesvolk und seine Geschichte* (Neukirchen–Vluyn: Neukirchener Verlag).

Janssen, J.M.A.
1955–56 'Egyptological Remarks on the Story of Joseph in Genesis', *JEOL* 14: 63-72.

Japhet, S.
1989 *The Ideology of the Book of Chronicles and its Place in Biblical Thought* (Frankfurt: Peter Lang).

Jaubert, A.
1953 'Le Calendrier des Jubilés de la Secta de Qumran', *VT* 3: 250-64.
1957 'Le Calendrier des Jubilés et les jours liturgiques de la semaine', *VT* 7: 35-61.

Jellinek, A.
1853–57 *Beth ha-Midrasch: Sammlung kleiner Midraschim* (4 vols.; Leipzig: F. Nies).

Jensen, P.
1892 'Elamitische Eigennamen: Ein Beitrag zur Erklärung der elamitisoban Inschriften', *WZKM* 6: 47-70, 209-26.

Jeremias, J.
1958 *Jerusalem zur Zeit Jesu* (Göttingen: Vandenhoeck & Ruprecht).
1963 *Der Lehrer der Gerechtigkeit. Studien zur Umwelt der Neuen Testaments*, II (Göttingen: Vandenhoeck & Ruprecht).

Jongeling, B.
1970 'Publication provisoire d'un fragment de la Grotte 11 de Qumrân (11Q Jér.nouv.ar)', *JSJ* 1: 58-64.

Jongeling, B., C.J. Labuschagne and A.S. van der Woude
1976 *Aramaic Texts from Qumran* (SSS, 4; Leiden: Brill): 121-31.

Jucci, E.
1987 'Interpretazione e storia nei "pesharim" qumranici', *BeO* 29: 163-70.

Kabisch, R.
1889 *Das vierte Buch Esra auf seine Quellen untersucht* (Göttingen: Vandenhoeck & Ruprecht).

Kaminka, A.
1932 'Beiträge zur Erklärung der Esra-Apokalypse und zur Rekonstruktion ihres hebräisches Urtextes', *MGWJ* 76: 121-38, 206-12, 494-511, 604-607.
1933 'Beiträge zur Erklärung der Esra-Apokalypse und zur Rekonstruktion ihres hebräisches Urtextes', *MGWJ* 77: 339-55.

Kautzsch, E. (ed.)
1900 *Die Apokryphen und Pseudepigraphen des Alten Testaments* (2 vols.; Tubingen: Mohr [Paul Siebeck]).
1923 *Die Heilige Schrift des Alten Testaments* (2 vols.; Tübingen: Mohr [Paul Siebeck]).

Kippenberg, H.G.
1978 *Religion und Klassenbildung im Antiken Judäa* (SUNT, 14; Göttingen: Vandenhoeck & Ruprecht).

Kisch, G.
1949 *Pseudo-Philo's Liber Antiquitatum Biblicarum* (Publications in Medieval Studies, 10; Notre Dame, IN: The University of Notre Dame).

Kister, M.
1986–87 'Towards the History of the Essene Sect—Studies in the Animal Apocalypse, the Book of Jubilees, and the Damascus Document', *Tarbiz* 56: 1-18 [Hebrew].
1987 'Newly Identified Fragments of the Book of Jubilees: Jub. 23.21-23', *RevQ* 12: 529-36.

Kitchen, K.A.
1965 'The Aramaic of Daniel', in Wiseman *et al.* 1965: 31-79.

Klijn, A.F.J.
1976 *Die Syrische Baruchapokalypse* (JSHRZ 5.2; Gütersloh: Gütersloher Verlagshaus).

Kmoskó, M.
1907 *Epistola Baruch filii Neriae* (Patrologia Syriaca; 1.2; accurante R. Graffin, Paris: Fromin–Didot): cols. 1215-36.

Knibb, M.A. and E. Ullendorf
1977 'Review of Milik, *The Books of Enoch*', *BSOAS* 40: 601-602.

Knibb, M.A.
1979 *The Second Book of Esdras* (The Cambridge Bible Commentary; Cambridge: Cambridge University Press).
1982 *The Ethiopic Book of Enoch: A New Edition in the Light of the Aramaic Dead Sea Fragments* (Oxford: Clarendon Press, rev. edn).
1989 *Jubilees and the Origins of the Qumran Community*.

Koch, K.
1960a 'Die vier Weltreiche im Danielbuch', *TLZ* 85: 829-32.
1960b *Ratlos vor der Apokalyptik* (Gütersloh: Gütersloher Verlagshaus).
1961 'Spätisraelitisches Geschichtsdenken am Beispiel des Buches Daniel', *HZ* 193: 1-32.
1972 'Die Stellung des Kyros im Geschichtsbild Deuterojesajas und ihre überlieferungsgeschichtliche Verankerung', *ZAW* 84: 352-56.
1978 'Die mysteriösen Zahlen der judäischen Könige und die apokalyptischen Jahrwochen', *VT* 28: 433-41.
1980 *Das Buch Daniel* (Erträge der Forschung, 144; Darmstadt: Wissenschaftliche Buchgesellschaft)
1983 'Sabbatstruktur der Geschichte. Die sogenannte Zehn-Wochen-Apokalypse (1Hen 93,1-10 91,11-17) und das Ringen um die alttestamentlichen Chronologien im späten Israelitentum', *ZAW* 95: 403-30.
1986 'Dareios, der Meder', in C.L. Meyers and M. O'Connor (eds.), *The Word of the Lord Shall Go Forth: Essays in Honor of D.N. Freedman* (Winona Lake, IN: Eisenbrauns): 287-99.
1991 'Weltgeschichte und Gottesreich im Danielbuch und die iranischen Parallelen', in R. Liwak and S. Wagner (eds.), *Prophetie und geschichtliche Wirklichkeit im alten Israel* (Stuttgart: Kohlhammer): 189-205

Koch, K. and J.M. Schmidt (eds.)
1982 *Apokalyptik* (Wege der Forschung, 365; Darmstadt: Wissenschaftliche Buchgesellschaft).

Komoróczy, G.
1977 'Umman-manda', *Acta Antiqua Academiae Scientiarum Hungaricae* 25: 43-57.

Kraeling, E.G.H.
1944 'The Handwriting on the Wall', *JBL* 63: 11-18.

Kraft, R. and G.W.E. Nickelsburg (eds.)
1986 *Early Judaism and its Modern Interpreters* (The Bible and its Modern Interpreters, 2; Atlanta, GA: Scholars Press).

Kratz, R.G.
1991 *Translatio imperii. Untersuchungen zu den aramäischen Danielerzählungen und ihrem theologiegeschichtlichen Umfeld* (WMANT, 63; Neukirchen–Vluyn: Neukirchener Verlag).

Kuhrt, A.
1983 'The Cyrus Cylinder and Achaimenid Imperial Policy', *JSOT* 25: 83-97.

Kutsch, E.
1961 'Der Kalendar der Jubiläenbuches und das Alte und Neue Testament', *VT* 11: 31-41.

Lacocque, A.
1976 *Le Livre de Daniel* (Paris: Delachaux & Niestlé).
1983 *Daniel et son temps. Recherches sur le mouvement apocalyptique juif au IIe siècle avant Jésus-Christ* (Le monde de la Bible; Geneva: Labor et fides).
1987 'Haman in the Book of Esther', *HAR* 11: 207-22.

Lagarde
1861 *Libri Veteris Testamenti, Apocryphi syriace* (Leipzig: F.A. Brockhaus).

Lambert, J.-P.
1992 'Esther et le monothéisme', in O. Abel and F. Smyth (eds.), *Le Livre de traverse: de l'exégèse biblique a l'anthropologie* (Paris: Cerf).

Lambert, W.G.
1971 'History and the Gods: A Review Article', *Orientalia* 39: 31-58.
1978 'The Background of Jewish Apocalyptic' (The Ethel Wood Lecture; London: Athlone Press).

Landsberger, B. and P. Bauer
1926-27 'Zu neuveröffentichten Geschichtsquellen der Zeit von Asarhaddon bis Nabonid', *ZA* 37: 61-98.

Langdon, S.
1912 *Die neubabylonischen Königsinschriften: VAB IV* (Leipzig: Hinrichs).

Laperrousaz, E.M.
1970 *Le Testament de Moïse (généralement appelé 'Assomption de Moise'). Traduction avec introduction et notes* (Semitica, 19; Paris: Librairie d'Amérique et d'Orient).
1976 *Qumrân. L'Etablissement essénien des bords de la Mer Morte. Histoire et archéologie du site* (Paris: Picard)

Lebram, J C.H.
1964 'Die Weltreiche in der jüdischen Apokalyptik. Bemerkungen zu Tobit 14.4-7', *ZAW* 76: 328-31.
1972 'Purimfest und Estherbuch', *VT* 22: 208-22.
1974 'Perspektiven der gegenwärtigen Danielforschung', *JSJ* 5: 1-34.
1975 'König Antiochus im Buche Daniel', *VT* 20: 737-72.

Lefèvre, A.
1949 'Le Livre de Judith', *DBSup* 4: cols 1315-21.
1954 'Judith', in A. Robert and A. Feuillet (eds.), *Introduction à la Bible*, I (Tournai: Desclée): 746-52.
1957 'Maccabés: livres I et II', *DBSup* 5: cols 597-612.

Lehman, M.
1992 'The Literary Study of Esther', *Biblical Viewpoint* 26.2: 85-95.

Leslau, W.
1989 *Concise Dictionary of Ge'ez* (Classical Ethiopic) (Wiesbaden: Otto Harrassowitz).

Leszynsky, R.
1912 *Die Sadduzäer* (Berlin: Mayer & Müller).

Lévy, I.
1949 *La Répudiation de Vasti, Actes du XXI Congrès International des orientelistes Paris, 23-31 juillet 1948* (Paris: Société Asiatique): 114-16.

Lewis, J.P.
1968 *A Study on the Interpretation of Noah and the Flood in Jewish and Christian Literature* (Leiden: Brill).

Lewy, J.
1927 'Enthält Judith I–IV Trümmer einer Chronik zur Geschichte Nebukadnezars und seiner Feldzüge von 597 und 591?', *ZDMG* 81: 52-54.
1939 'The Feast of the 14th Day of Adar', *HUCA* 14: 127-51.

Licht, J.
1961 ' "Taxo" or the Apocalyptic Doctrine of Vengeance', *JJS* 12: 95-103.
1971 'Judit', *EncJud*, V: col. 299.
1983 'Biblical Historicism', in H. Tadmor and H. Weinfeld (eds.), *History, Historiography and Interpretation: Studies in Biblical and Cuneiform Literatures* (Jerusalem: Magnes Press): 107-20.

Lignée, H.
1988 'La Place du livre des Jubilées et du Rouleau du Temple dans l'histoire du mouvement essénien. Ces deux ouvrages ont-ils été écrits par le Maître de Justice?', *RevQ* 13: 331-45.

Lightstone, J.N.
1983 'Judaism of the Second Commonwealth: Toward a Reform of the Scholarly Tradition', in H. Josep, J.N. Lightstone and M.D. Oppenheim (eds.), *Truth and Compassion. Essays on Judaism and Religion in Memory of Rabbi Dr Solomon Frank* (Waterloo, Ontario: Wilfred Laurier University Press): 31-40.

Lim, T.H.
1990 'Eschatological Orientation and the Alteration of Scripture in the Habakkuk Pesher', *JNES* 49: 185-94.

Littmann, R.J.
1974–75 'The Religious Policy of Xerxes and the Book of Esther', *JQR* 65: 145-55.

Lods, A.
1950 *Histoire de la littérature hébraïque et juive, depuis des origines jusqu'à la ruine de l'état juif (135 après J.C.)* (Bibliotheque Historique; Paris: Payot).

Löwinger, D.S.
1948 'Nebuchadnezzar's Dream in the Book of Daniel', in D.S. Löwinger and J. Somogyi (eds.), *Ignace Goldzieher Memorial*, I (Budapest: Globus): 336-52.

Lupieri, E.
1992 'The Seventh Night: Visions of History in the Revelation of John and the Contemporary Apocalyptic', *Henoch* 14: 113-32.

Marti, K.
1901 *Das Buch Daniel* (Kurzer Hand-Commentar zum Alten Testament; Tübingen: Mohr).

Martin, F.
1906 *Le Livre d'Hénoch* (Paris: Letouzey et Ané).

Martin, W.J.
1965 'The Hebrew of the Book of Daniel', in Wiseman, *et al.* 1965: 28-30.

McAlpine, T.H.
1987 *Sleep, Divine and Human in the Old Testament* (JSOTSup, 38; Sheffield: JSOT Press).

McNamara, M.
1970 'Nabonidus and the Book of Daniel', *ITQ* 37: 131-49.

Mendels, D.
1987 *The Land of Israel as a Political Concept in Hasmonean Literature: Recourse to History in Second Century* BC. *Claims to the Holy Land* (Texts und Studien zum antiken Judentum, 15; Tübingen: Mohr).
1992 'From the Territorial to the A-Territorial', in *idem*, *The Rise and Fall of Jewish Nationalism* (New York: Doubleday): ch. 9.

Mertens, A.
1971 *Das Buch Daniel im Lichte der Texte vom Toten Meer* (Stuttgart: Katholisches Bibelwerk).

Metzger, B.M.
1978 *An Introduction to the Apocrypha* (Oxford: Oxford University Press).

Meyer, E.
1923–25 *Ursprung und Anfänge des Christentums* (3 vols.; Stuttgart: J.G. Cotta).

Meyer, R.
1938 'Levitische Emanzipationsbestrebungen in nachexilischen Zeit', *OLZ* 41: 721-28.
1960 'Das Qumranfragment "Gebet des Nabonid"', *TLZ* 85: 831-34.
1962 *Das Gebet des Nabonid: Eine in den Qumran-Handschriften Wiederentdeckte Weisheitserzählung* (SSAW.PH 107/3; Berlin).

Michel, A.
1954 *Le Maître de Justice* (Avignon: Maison Aubanel Pere).

Milik, J.T.
1956 '"Prière de Nabonide" et autres écrits d'un cycle de Daniel. Fragments araméens de Qumrân 4', *RB* 63: 407-15.
1958 'Hénoch au pays des aromates. Fragments araméens de la grotte 4 de Qumrân', *RB* 65: 70-77.
1959 *Ten Years of Discovery in the Wilderness of Judaea* (SBT, 26; London: SCM Press).
1976 *The Books of Enoch. Aramaic Fragments of Qumrân Cave 4* (Oxford: Clarendon Press).
1991 'Les Modèles araméens du livre d'Esther dans la Grotte 4 de Qumrân', *RevQ* 15: 321-406.

Millard, A.R.
1977 'The Persian Names in Esther and the Reliability of the Hebrew Text', *JBL* 96: 481-88.
1985 'Daniel and Belshazzar in History', *BARev* 11: 72-78.

Miller, J.E.
1991 'The Redaction of Daniel', *JSOT* 52: 115-24.

Mitchell, T.R. and R. Joyce

1965 'The Musical Instruments in Nebuchadnezzar's Orchestra', in Wiseman *et al.* 1965: 19-27.

Moda, A.

1991 'Libri dei Maccabei', *BeO* 33: 15-30.

Moehring, H.R.

1984 'Joseph ben Matthia and Flavius Josephus: The Jewish Prophet and Roman Historian', *ANRW* II.21: 2864-944.

Momigliano, A.

1966 *Studies in Historiography* (London: Weidenfeld & Nicolson).

1975a 'The Second Book of Maccabees', *Classical Philology* 70: 81-88.

1975b *Alien Wisdom. The Limits of Hellenization* (Cambridge: Cambridge University Press).

1977 *Essays in Ancient and Modern Historiography* (Blackwell's Classical Studies; Oxford: Basil Blackwell).

Montet, P.

1959 *L'Egypte et la Bible* (Cahiers d'Archéologie Biblique, 11; Neuchâtel: Delachaux & Niestlé).

Montgomery, J.A.

1927 *A Critical and Exegetical Commentary on the Book of Daniel* (ICC, 23; Edinburgh: T. & T. Clark).

Montgomery, J.

1990 'Notes on the Aramaic Part of Daniel', *Transactions of the Connecticut Academy of Arts and Sciences* 15: 280-82.

Moore, C.A.

1967 'A Greek Witness to a Different Hebrew Text of Esther', *ZAW* 79: 351-80.

1971 *Esther* (AB, 7B; Garden City, NY: Doubleday).

1973 'On the Origins of the LXX Additions to the Book of Esther', *JBL* 92: 382-93.

1975 'Archaeology and the Book of Esther', *BA* 38.3-4: 62-79.

1977 *Daniel, Esther and Jeremiah: The Additions* (AB, 44; Garden City, NY: Doubleday).

1983 'Esther Revisited Again: A Further Examination of Certain Esther Studies of the Past Ten Years', *HAR* 7: 169-86.

1985a *Judith: A New Translation with Introduction and Commentary* (AB, 40; Garden City, NY: Doubleday).

1985b 'Esther Revisited: An Examination of Esther Studies over the Past Decade', in A. Kort and S. Morschaner (eds.), *Biblical and Related Studies Presented to Samuel Iwry* (Winona Lake, IN: Eisenbrauns): 163-72.

1987 'Eight Questions Most Frequently Asked about the Book of Esther', *BARev* 3.1: 16-31.

Morgenstern, J.

1955 'The Calendar of the Book of Jubilees: Its Origin and Character', *VT* 5: 34-76.

Mörkholm, O.
1963 *Studies in the Coinage of Antiochus IV of Syria* (Copenhagen: Luuds Bogtrykheri).
1966 *Antiochus IV of Syria* (Classica et Medievalia. Dissertationes, 8; Copenhagen: Gyldendahl).
Motzo, B.
1924 'Il Rifacimento di Ester e il III Mac.', in *idem*, *Saggi di Storia e Litteratura Giudeo-Ellenistica* (Firente: F. Le Monnier): 272-90.
Mras, K.
1954–56 *Eusebius, Werke: Die Praeparatio Evangelica*, I-II (8 vols.; GCS, 43.1-2; Berlin: Akademie Verlag).
Müller, H.-P.
1972 'Mantische Weisheit und Apokalyptik', in *Leiden* (VTSup, 22; Leiden: Brill): 268-93.
1976 'Märchen, Legende und Enderwartung. Zum Vertändnis des Buches Daniel', *VT* 26: 338-50.
Murphy, F.J.
1986 'Divine Plan, Human Plan: A Structure Theme in Pseudo-Philo', *JQR* 77.1: 5-14.
1988a 'Retelling the Bible: Idolatry in Pseudo-Philo', *JBL* 107: 275-87.
1988b 'The Eternal Covenant in Pseudo-Philo', *JSP* 3: 43-57.
1988c 'God in Pseudo-Philo', *JSJ* 19: 1-18.
Myers, J.M.
1974 *I and II Esdras: Introduction, Translation and Commentary* (AB, 42; Garden City, NY: Doubleday).
Nestle, W.
1936 'Legenden vom Tod der Gottesverächter', *ARW* 33: 246-69.
Newsom, C.A.
1980 'The Development of Henoch 6–19: Cosmology and Judgment', *CBQ* 40: 310-29.
1985 *Songs of the Sabbath Sacrifice: A Critical Edition* (HSS, 27; Atlanta, GA: Scholars Press).
Nickelsburg, G.W.E.
1971 '1 and 2 Maccabees—Same Story, Different Meaning', *CTM* 42: 515-26.
1977 'Apocalyptic and Myth in 1 Enoch 6–11', *JBL* 96: 383-405.
1980 'Good and Bad Leaders in Pseudo-Philo's Liber Antiquitatum Biblicarum', in J.J. Collins and G.W.E. Nickelsburg (eds.), *Ideal Figures in Ancient Judaism, Profiles and Paradigms* (Septuagint and Cognate Studies, 12; Missoula, MT: Scholars Press for SBL).
1981a *Jewish Literature between the Bible and the Mishnah* (Philadelphia: Fortress Press).
1981b 'Enoch, Levi and Peter, Recipients of Revelation in Upper Galilee', *JBL* 100: 575-600.
1991 'The Qumran Fragments of Enoch and Other Apocryphal Works: Implications for the Understanding of Early Judaism and Christian Origins', in Talmon 1991: 181-95.

Nickelsburg, G.W.E. (ed.)

1973 *Studies on the Testament of Moses* (SBLSCS, 4; Missoula, MT: Scholars Press).

Niditch, S. and R. Doran

1977 'The Success Story of the Wise Courtier: A Formal Approach', *JBL* 96: 179-97.

Nitzan, B.

1986 *Pesher Habakkuk: A Scroll from the Wilderness of Judaea (1Q p Hab). Text, Introduction and Commentary* (Jerusalem: Bialik Institute [Hebrew]).

Noack, B.

1957–58 'Qumran and the Book of Jubilees', *SEA* 22.3: 191-207.

Noth, M.

1926 'Zur Komposition des Buches Daniel', *ThStKr* 98-99: 143-163.

1951 'Noah, Daniel und Hiob in Ezechiel XIV', *VT* 1: 251-60.

1954 'Das Geschichtsverständnis der alttestamentlichen Apokalyptik, Arbeitsgemeinschaft für Forschung des Landes Nordrhein-Westfalen', in *idem*, *Gesammelte Studien zum Alten Testament* (München: Chr. Kaiser Verlag [1960]): 248-273.

1960 'Das Geschichtsverständnis der alttestamentlichen Apokalyptik', in *idem*, *Gesammelte Studien zum Alten Testament* (TBü, 39; Munich: Kaiser): 248-73.

1969 'Zur Komposition des Buches Daniel', in *idem*, *Gesammelte Studien zum Alten Testament* (TBü, 39; Munich: Kaiser, 2nd edn): 11-28.

1987 *The Chronicler's History* (trans. H.G.M. Williamson; JSOTSup, 50; Sheffield: JSOT Press).

Loretz, O.

1967 'Götter und Frauen (Gen. 6.1-4): Ein Paradigma zu AT-Ugarite', *BibLeb* 8: 120-27.

Oesterley, W.O.E.

1933 Oesterley, *II Esdras* (London: Methuen).

Olmstead, A.T.E.

1948 *History of the Persian Empire* (Chicago: University of Chicago Press).

Olyan, S.M.

1991 'The Israelites Debate Their Options at the Sea of Reeds: LAB 10.3, Its Parallels, and Pseudo-Philo's Ideology and Background', *JBL* 110: 75-91.

Oppenheim, A.L.

1956 *The Interpretation of Dreams in the Ancient Near East* (Transactions of the American Philosophical Society, New Series, 46.3; Philadelphia: Fortress Press).

1977 *Ancient Mesopotamia*: *Portrait of a Dead Civilization* (Chicago: University of Chicago Press, rev. edn).

Orr, A.

1956 'The Seventy Years of Babylon', *VT* 6: 304-306.

Osswald, E.

1963 'Zum Problem der vaticinium ex eventu', *ZAW* 75: 27-44.

Parente, F.
1988 'The Third Book of Maccabees as Ideological Document and Historical Source', *Henoch* 10: 143-82.

Paton, L.B.
1908 *A Critical and Exegetical Commentary on the Book of Esther* (ICC, 13; Edinburgh: T. & T. Clark).

Patte, D.
1975 *Early Jewish Hermeneutic in Palestine* (SBLDS, 22; Missoula, MT: Scholars Press).

Pelletier, A.
1962 *Lettre d'Aristée à Philocrate: Introduction, Texte Critique, Traduction et Notes* (SC, 89; Paris: Cerf).

Perrot, C. and P.-M. Bogaert
1976 *Pseudo-Philon. Les Antiquités Bibliques.* II. *Introduction littéraire, commentaire et index* (SC, 230; Paris: Cerf).

Perrot, J.
1989 'Shoshan ha-birah', in A. Ben-Tor, J.C. Greenfield and A. Malamat (eds.), *Yigael Yadin Memorial Volume* (Eretz Israel, 20; Jerusalem: Israel Exploration Society): 155-60.

Pfeiffer, R.H.
1957 *The Books of the Old Testament* (New York: Harper & Bros).

Philonenko, M.
1959 'Origine essénienne des psaumes de David', *Sem* 9: 35-48.
1961 'Remarques sur un hymne essénien de caractère gnostique', *Sem* 11: 43-54.
1967 'Essénisme et gnose chez le Pseudo-Philon. Le symbolisme de la lumière dans le Liber Antiquitatum Biblicarum', in U. Bianchi (ed.), *Le origine dello gnosticismo* (Studies in the History of Religions, 12;. Leiden: Brill): 401-12.
1973 'Iphigénie et Sheila', in *Les Syncrétismes dans les religions grecque et romaine: Colloque de Strasbourg, 2-11 juin 1971* (Paris: Presse Universitaire de France): 135-77.

Porter, P.A.
1983 *Metaphors and Monsters: A Literary-critical Study of Daniel 7 and 8* (ConBOT, 20; Lund: Gleerup).

Porteous, N.W.
1962 *Das Danielbuch* (ATD; Göttingen: Vandenhoeck & Ruprecht).

Portnoy, M.A.
1989–90 'Ahasuerus is the Villain', *DD* 18: 187-89.

Prat, F.
1903 'Judith', *DB* 3: cols. 1824-33.

Priebatsch, H.Y.
1974 'Das Buch Judith und seine Quellen', *ZDPV* 90: 50-61.

Priest, J.
1977 'Some Reflections on the Assumption of Moses', *Perspectives in Religious Studies* 4: 92-111.

Pritchard, J.B. (ed.)
1969 *Ancient Near Eastern Texts relating to the Old Testament* (Princeton, NJ: Princeton University Press, 3rd edn).

Rabinowitz, I.
1973 '*Pesher/Pittaron*: Its Biblical Meaning and its Significance in the Qumran Literature', *RevQ* 8: 219-32.

Rajak, T.
1983 *Josephus: The Historian and his Society* (Classical Life and Letters; London: Duckworth)
1990 'The Hasmoneans and the Uses of Hellenism', in P.R. Davies and R.T. White (eds.), *A Tribute to Geza Vermes: Essays on Jewish and Christian Literature* (JSOTSup, 100; Sheffield: JSOT Press): 261-80.

Redford, D.
1970 *A Study of the Biblical Story of Joseph* (VTSup, 20; Leiden: Brill).

Reinmuth, E.
1989 'Beobachtungen zum Verständnis des Gesetzes im LAB (Pseudo-Philo)', *JSJ* 20: 151-70.

Riessler, P.
1928 *Altjüdisches Schrifttum ausserhalb der Bibel* (Augsburg: Benno Filser Verlag).

Ringgren, H.
1957 'Apokalyptik', *RGG*, 1.3: 465.

Robert, A. and A. Feuillet
1959 *Introduction à la Bible*, I (Tournai: Desclée).

Robinson, J.A.T.
1976 *Redating the New Testament* (Philadelphia: Westminster Press).

Rook, J.
1990 'The Names of the Wives from Adam to Abraham in the Book of Jubilees', *JSP* 7: 105-17.

Rost, L.
1971 *Einleitung in die alttentamentlichen Apokryphen und Pseudepigraphen, einschliesslich der grossen Qumran-Handschriften* (Heidelberg: Quelle & Meyer).

Rowley, H.H.
1924 'The Belshazzar of Daniel and History', *ExpTim* 9.2: 182-95, 255-72.
1929 *The Aramaic of the Old Testament. A Grammatical and Lexical Study of its Relations with other Early Aramaic Dialects* (London: Oxford University Press).
1930–31 'The Historicity of the Fifth Chapter of Daniel', *JTS* 32: 12-31.
1932 'The Bilingual Problem of the Book of Daniel', *ZAW* 50: 256-68.
1935 *Darius the Mede and the Four World Empires in the Book of Daniel* (Cardiff: University of Wales Press Board).
1950–51 'The Unity of the Book of Daniel', *HUCA* 23: 233-73.
1952 'The Unity of the Book of Daniel', in *The Servant of the Lord and Other Essays* (London: Lutterworth Press): 235-68.
1955 'The Composition of the Book of Daniel', *VT* 5: 272-76.
1956 '4QpNah and the Teacher of Righteousness', *JBL* 75: 192-93.
1963 *The Relevance of Apocalyptic. A Study of Jewish and Christian*

Apocalypses from Daniel to the Revelation (London: Lutterworth Press, rev. edn)

Rubinkiewicz, R.

1976 'Un fragment grec du IVe livre d'Esdras', *Le Muséon* 89: 75-87.

1988 'The Book of Noah (1 Enoch 6–11) and Ezra's Reform', *FO* 25: 151-55.

Russell, D.S.

1964 *The Method and Message of Jewish Apocalyptic 200 BC–AD 100* (OTL; London: SCM Press).

Russell, J.

1990 'Zoroastrian Elements in the Book of Esther', in Sh. Shaked and A. Netzer (eds.), *Irano-Judaica II* (Jerusalem: Hebrew University): 33-40.

Sabna, R.B.

1992 'The Hidden Hand of God', *Bible Review* 8.1: 31-33.

Sacchi, P.

1990 *L'apocalittica judaica e la sua storia* (Biblioteca di Cultura Religiosa, 55; Brescia: Paideia).

Sahlin, H.

1969 'Antiochus Epiphanes und Judas Makkabäus', *ST* 23: 41-68.

Samely, A.

1991 'Between Scripture and its Rewording: Towards a Classification of Rabbinical Exegesis', *JJS* 42: 39-67.

Sasson, J.M.

1983 'Mari Dreams', *JAOS* 103: 283-93.

Saunders, E.W.

1962 'Bethulia', *IDB*, I: 403.

Schedl, C.

1965 'Nabuchodonosor, Arpaksad und Darius: Untersuchungen zum Buch Judit', *ZDMG* 115: 242-54.

Schmidt, J.M.

1969 *Die jüdische Apokalyptik* (Neukirchen–Vluyn: Neukirchener Verlag).

Schmidt, W.H.

1967 'Mythos im AT, Kap. II a) Gen. 6.1-4', *EvT* 27: 237-54.

1983 *Exodus, Sinai und Mose, Erwagungen zu Ex 1–19 und 24* (Erträge der Forschung, 191; Darmstadt: Wissenschaftliche Buchgesellschaft).

Scholz, A.

1885 *Das Buch Judith eine Prophetie* (Leipzig).

1896 *Commentar über das Buch Judith* (Würtzburg: Leo Woerl).

Schreiner, J.

1969 *Alttestamentlich-jüdische Apokalyptik. Eine Einführung* (Biblische Handbibliothek, 6; Munich: Kosel).

Schunck, K.D.

1954 *Die Quellen des I. und II.Makkabäerbuches* (Halle: Niemeyer).

Schunck, K.D. *et al.* (eds.)

1992 *Goldene Äpfel in silbernen Schalen. Collected Communications of the XIIIth Congress of the IOSOT, Leuven 1989* (Beiträge zur Erforschung des Alten Testament; Frankfurt: Peter Lang).

Schürer, E.

1973–87 *The History of the Jewish People in the Age of Jesus Christ, 175 BC–AD 135* (ed. G. Vermes and F. Millar; trans. T.A. Burkill, *et al.*; 3 vols.; Edinburgh: T. & T. Clark, rev. English edn).

Schwartz, J.

1946 'Un fragment grec du livre de Judith', *RB* 53: 534-37 and plate 7.

Schwarz, E.

1982 *Identität durch Abgrenzung: Abgrenzungsprozesse in Israel im 2. vorchristlichen Jahrhundert und ihre religionsgeschichtlichen Voraussetzungen. Zugleich ein Beitrag zur Erforschung des Jubiläenbuches* (Europäische Hochschulschriften 162; Frankfurt: Peter Lang).

Schwarz, S.

1991 'Israel and the Nations Roundabout: 1 Maccabees and the Hasmonean Expansion', *JJS* 42: 16-38.

Segal, E.

1989 'Human Anger and Divine Intervention in Esther', *Proof* 9: 247-56.

Sellin, E.

1933 *Einleitung in das Alte Testament* (Leipzig: Quelle & Meyer, 6th edn).

Seyberlich, R.M.

1964 'Esther in der Septuaginta und bei Flavius Josephus', in E.C. Welskopf (ed.), *Neue Beiträge zur Geschichte der Alten Welt*, I (Berlin: Akademie-Verlag): 363-66.

Shaked, S.

1982 'Two Judaeo-Iranian Contributions: I. Iranian Functions in the Book of Esther', in *idem* (ed.), *Irano-Judaica I* (Jerusalem: Hebrew University): 292-303.

Shea, W.H.

1976 'Esther and History', *AUSS* 14.

1985a 'Sennacherib's Second Palestinian Campaign', *JBL* 104: 401-18.

1985b 'Further Literary Structures in Dan. 2–7', *AUSS* 23: 193-202, 277-95.

Singer, W.

1898 *Das Buch der Jubiläen oder die leptogenesis* (Stuhlweissenburg: Singer).

Skehan, P.W.

1962 'Why leave out Judith?', *CBQ* 24 : 147-54.

1963 'The Hand of Judith', *CBQ* 25: 94-109.

1966 'Review of A.M. Dubarle's, *Judith: Formes et sens des diverses traditions*', *CBQ* 28: 347-49.

1975 'Jubilees and the Qumran Psalter', *CBQ* 37: 343-47.

Skinner, J.

1930 *Genesis* (ICC, 1; Edinburgh: T. & T. Clark, 2nd edn).

Smend, R.

1885 'Uber jüdische Apokalyptik', *ZAW* 5: 222-51.

1984 *Die Entstehung des Alten Testaments* (Stuttgart: Kohlhammer, 3rd edn).

Smith, M.

1963 'II Isaiah and the Persians', *JAOS* 83: 415-21.

1971 *Palestinian Parties and Politics That Shaped the Old Testament* (New York: Columbia University Press).

Smith, S.
1924 *Babylonian Historical Texts Relating to the Capture and Downfall of Babylon* (London: Methuen).

Spiro, A.
1951 'Samaritans, Tobiads and Judahites in Pseudo-Philo', *PAAJR* 20: 279-335.
1952 'Pseudo-Philo's Saul and the Rabbis' Messiah ben Ephraim', *PAAJR* 21: 119-37.
1953 'The Ascension of Phinehas', *PAAJR* 22: 91-114.

Stählin, O.
1920 'Das hellenistisch-jüdische Literatur', in W. von Christ (ed.), *Geschichte der griechischen Literatur*, II.1 (Handbuch der Klassischen Altestumswissenschaft, 6.2; Munich: Beck).

Starcky, J. *et al.*
1956 'Le Travail d'édition des fragments manuscript de Qumrân', *RB* 63: 49-67.

Staub, U.
1978 'Das Tier mit den Hörnern', *Freiburger Zeitschrift für Philosophie und Theologie* 25: 351-97.

Stefanovic, Z.
1992 *The Aramaic of Daniel in the Light of Old Aramaic* (JSOTSup, 129; Sheffield: JSOT Press).

Steinmetzer, F.X.
1907 *Neue Untersuchungen über die Geschichtlichkeit der Judith-Erzählung* (Leipzig: Rudolf Haupt).

Stemberger, G.
1991 'Narrative Theologie im Midrash', *Judaica* 47: 155-67.

Stern, M.
1960 'Thracides—Surname of Alexander Yannai in Josephus and Synkellus', *Tarbiz* 29: 207-209.

Steuernagel, C.
1943 'Bethulia', *ZDPV* 66: 342-45.

Stiehl, R.
1956 'Das Buch Esther', *WZKM* 53: 4-22.
1960 'Esther, Judith und Daniel', in F. Altheim and R. Stiehl (eds.), *Die aramäische Sprache unter den Achämeniden*, II (Frankfurt/Main: Klostermann): 195-213.
1963 'Esther, Judith und Daniel', in Altheim and Stiehl 1963: 195-213.

Stokholm, N.
1968 'Zur Überlieferung von Heliodor (2 Makk.3), Kuturnahhunte, und anderen missglückten Tempelräubern', *ST* 22: 1-28.

Stone, M.E. (ed.)
1984 *Jewish Writings of the Second Temple Period. Apocrypha, Pseudepigrapha, Qumran Sectarian Writings, Philo, Josephus* (The Literature of the Jewish People in the Period of the Second Temple and the Talmud, 2; Assen: Van Gorcum).

Stone, M.E.

1968 'The Concept of Messiah in IV. Ezra', in J. Neusner (ed.), *Religions in Antiquity: Essays in Memory of Erwin Ramsdell Goodenough* (Studies in the History of Religions, 14; Leiden: Brill): 295-312.

1971 *Concordance and Texts of Armenian IV Ezra* (Oriental Notes and Studies, 11; Jerusalem: Israel Oriental Society).

1978 'The Book of Enoch and Judaism in the Third Century BCE', *CBQ* 40: 479-92.

1988 'Aramaic Levi and Sectarian Origins', *JSJ* 19: 159-70.

1989 *Features of the Eschatology of IV Ezra* (HSS, 35; Atlanta, GA: Scholars Press).

1990 *Fourth Ezra: A Commentary on the Book of Fourth Ezra* (Hermeneia; Minneapolis, MN: Fortress Press)

Striedl, H.

1937 'Untersuchungen zur Syntax und Stylistik des hebräischen Buches Esther', *ZAW* 55: 73-108.

Strugnell, J.

1960 'The Angelic Liturgy at Qumran', in *Congress Volume, Oxford 1959* (VTSup, 7; Leiden: Brill): 318-45.

1973 'Philo (Pseudo-) or Liber Antiquitatum Biblicarum', *EncJud*, XIII: 408-409.

Strugnell, J. and D. Dimant

1988 '4Q Second Ezekiel', *RevQ* 13: 45-58.

Stummer, F.

1947 *Geographie des Buches Judith* (Bibelwissenschaftliche Reihe, 3; Stuttgart: Katholisches Bibelwerk).

Suter, D.W.

1979 'Fallen Angel, Fallen Priest: The Problem of Family Purity in 1 Enoch 6–16', *HUCA* 50: 115-35.

1981 'Māšāl in the Similitudes of Enoch', *JBL* 100: 193-212.

Swain, J.W.

1940 'The Theory of Four Monarchies, Opposition History Under the Roman Empire', *Classical Philology* 25: 1-21.

Sypherd, W.O.

1948 *Jephthah and his Daughter: A Study in Comparative Literature* (Newark: University of Delaware)

Szörényi, A.

1966 'Das Buch Daniel, ein kanonisierter Pescher?', in *Leiden* (VTSup, 16; Brill): 278-94.

Tadmor, H. and M. Weinfeld (eds.)

1983 *History, Historiography and Interpretation. Studies in Biblical and Cuneiform Literatures* (Jerusalem: Magnes Press, Hebrew University): 107-20.

Talmon, S.

1958 'The Calendar of the Judean Covenanters', in C. Rabin and Y. Yadin (eds.), *Aspects of the Dead Sea Scrolls* (Scripta Hierosolymitana, 4; Jerusalem, Magnes Press, Hebrew University): 162-99.

1963 'Wisdom in the Book of Esther', *VT* 13: 419-55.

1986 'The Emergence of Jewish Sectarianism in the Early Second Temple Period', in *King, Cult and Calendar in Ancient Israel: Collected Studies* (Jerusalem: Magnes Press, Hebrew University): 165-201.

Talmon, S. (ed.)
1991 *Jewish Civilization in the Hellenistic-Roman Period* (JSPSup, 10; Sheffield: JSOT Press).

Tarn, W.W. and G.T. Griffith
1952 *Hellenistic Civilization* (London: Edward Arnold, rev. edn).

Tcherikover, V.A.
1950 'Syntaxis and Laographia', *JJP* 4: 179-207.
1956 'Jewish Apologetic Reconsidered', *Eos* 48: 169-93.
1958 'The Ideology of the Letter of Aristeas', *HTR* 51: 59-86.
1961 'The Third Book of Maccabees is a Historical Source of Augustus' Time', *ScrHier* 7: 1-26.

Testuz, M.
1960 *Les Idées religieuses du livre des Jubilées* (Geneva: Droz)

Thompson, S.
1955–58 *Motif-Index of Folk Literature* (6 vols.; Copenhagen: Rosenkilde & Bagger, rev. edn).

Thorndike, M.
1961–62 'The Apocalypse of Weeks and the Qumran Sect', *RevQ* 3: 163-84.

Torrey, C.C.
1899 'The Site of "Bethulia"', *JAOS* 20: 160-72.
1944 'The Older Book of Esther', *HTR* 37: 1-40.
1945 *The Apocryphal Literature. A Brief Introduction* (New Haven, CT: Yale University Press)
1946 'Medes and Persians', *JAOS* 66: 1-15.
1947 'The Messiah Son of Ephraim', *JBL* 66: 253-77.

Tromp, J.
1993 *The Assumption of Moses. A Critical Edition with Commentary* (SVTP, 10; Leiden: Brill).

Tyloch, W.J.
1988 'Quelques remarques sur la provenance essénienne du livre des Jubilées', *RevQ* 13: 437-52.

van der Horst, P.
1989 'Portraits of Biblical Women in Pseudo-Philo's LAB', *JSP* 5: 29-46.

van der Woude, A.S.
1982 'Wicked Priest or Wicked Priests? Reflections on the Identification of the Wicked Priest in the Habakkuk Commentary', *JJS* 33: 349-59.
1990 'Fünfzehn Jahre Qumranforschung: 1974–1988', *TRu* 55: 245-307.

van Dijk, J.
1962 in H.J. Lenzen *et al.* (eds.), *Vorläufiger Bericht XVIII über die von dem Deutschen Archäologischen Institut und der Deutschen Orient-Gesellschaft unternommenen Ausgrabungen in Uruk* (Abhandlungen der Deutschen Orientgesellchaft, 7; Berlin: Verlag Gebr. Mann).
1963 'Ausgrabungen von Warka. Die Tontafelfunde der Kampagne 1959/60', *AfO* 20.

VanderKam, J.C.

1977 *Textual and Historical Studies on the Book of Jubilees* (HSS, 14; Missoula, MT: Scholars Press).

1978 'Enoch Traditions in Jubilees and other Second-Century Sources', in P.J. Achtemeier (ed.), *SBL 1978 Seminar Papers* (Missoula, MT: Scholars Press), I: 229-51.

1979 'The Origin, Character and Early History of the 364-Day Calendar: A Reassessment of Jaubert's Hypothesis', *CBQ* 41: 390-411.

1981 'The Putative Author of the Book of Jubilees', *JSS* 26: 209-17.

1982 'A Twenty-Eight-Day Month Tradition in the Book of Jubilees', *VT* 32: 504-506.

1984a *Enoch and the Growth of an Apocalyptic Tradition* (CBQMS, 16; Washington, DC: Catholic Biblical Association of America).

1984b 'Studies in the Apocalypse of the Weeks (1 Enoch 93.1-10; 91.11-17)', *CBQ* 46: 511-23.

1988 'Jubilees and the Priestly Messiah of Qumran', *RevQ* 13: 353-65.

VanderKam, J.C. (ed.)

1992 *'No One Spoke Ill of Her': Essays on Judith* (Early Judaism and its Literature, 2; Atlanta, GA: Scholars Press).

VanderKam, J.C. and J.T. Milik

1991 'The First Jubilees Manuscript from Qumran Cave 4: A Preliminary Publication', *JBL* 110: 243-70.

1992 'A Preliminary Publication of a Jubilees Manuscript from Qumran Cave 4: 4Q Jub/d (4Q 219)', *Bib* 73: 62-83.

Veerkamp, T.

1991 'Die Weltordnung der Autonomie—Daniels letzte Visions', *TK* 14.4: 20-37.

Vegas Montaner, L.

1989 'Computer-Assisted Study of the Relation between 1QpHab and the Ancient (Mainly Greek) Biblical Versions', *RevQ* 14: 307-23.

Vergote, J.

1959 *Joseph en Egypte: Génèse chap. 37–50 à la lumière des études égyptologiques récentes* (Orientalia et biblica Lovaniensia, 3; Louvain: Publications Universitaires).

Vermes, G.

1961 *Scripture and Tradition in Judaism. Haggadic Studies* (Studia post-biblica, 4; Leiden: Brill).

1970 'Bible and Midrash: Early Old Testament Exegesis', in P.R. Ackroyd and C.F. Evans (eds.), *The Cambridge History of the Bible*, I (London: Cambridge University Press): 199-232.

1975 *Post-Biblical Jewish Studies* (SJLA, 8; Leiden: Brill).

1981a *The Dead Sea Scrolls. Qumran in Perspective* (Philadelphia: Fortress Press, rev. edn).

1981b 'The Essenes and History', *JJS* 32: 18-31

1987 *The Dead Sea Scrolls in English* (Sheffield: JSOT Press, 3rd edn).

1989 'Bible Interpretation in Qumran', in A. Ben-Tor, J.C. Greenfield and A. Malamat (eds.), *Yigael Yadin Memorial Volume* (Eretz Israel, 20; Jerusalem: Hebrew University): 184-91.

Violet, B.

1910 *Die Ezra-Apokalypse (IV. Esre)* (GCS, 18; Leipzig: Hinrichs).

Vogt, E.

1956 'Precatio regis Nabonaid in Pia Narratione Iudaica', *Bib* 37: 532-34.

Volz, P.

1934 *Die Eschatologie der Jüdischen Gemeinde im Neutestamentlichen Zeitalter* (Tübingen: Mohr).

von der Osten-Sacken, P.

1969 *Die Apokalyptik in ihrem Verhältniss zu Prophetie und Weisheit* (Theologïsche Existenz heute, 157; Munich: Chr. Kaiser Verlag).

von Soden, W.

1935 'Eine babylonische Volksüberlieferung von Nabonid in den Danielerzählungen', *ZAW* 53: 81-89.

Wadsworth, M.

1977 'The Death of Moses and the Riddle of End of Time in Pseudo-Philo', *JJS* 28.1: 12-19.

1978 'A New Pseudo-Philo', *JJS* 29: 189-91.

Waterman, L.

1940 'A Gloss on Darius the Mede in Daniel 7.5', *JBL* 65: 53-61.

Weidner, E.F.

1941–44 'Die astrologische Serie Enuma Anu Enlil', *AfO* 14: 172-95, 308-318.

1954–56 'Die astrologische Serie Enuma Anu Enlil', *AfO* 17: 71-89.

1968–69 'Die astrologische Serie Enuma Anu Enlil', *AfO* 22: 65-75.

Weimar, P.

1973 'Formen frühjüdischer Literatur. Eine Skizze', in J. Maier and J. Schreiner (eds.), *Literatur und Religion des Frühjudentums* (Würzburg: Echter Verlag): 123-62.

Weissbach, F.H.

1911 *Die Keilinschriften der Achämeniden* (VAB, 3; Leipzig: Hinrichs).

Westermann, C.

1985 *Genesis 1–11* (2 vols.; Berlin).

Wiebe, J.M.

1991 'Esther 4.14: "Will Relief and Deliverance Arise for the Jews from Another Place?"', *CBQ* 53: 409-15.

Will, E.

1966–67 *Histoire politique du monde hellénistique, 323-30 av. J.-C.* (2 vols.; Annales de l'Est, 30 and 32; Nancy: Université de nancy).

Will, E. *et al.*

1972–75 *Le monde Grec et l'Orient* (2 vols.; Peuples et civilisations, Histoire genérale, 2; Paris: Presses universitaires de France).

Willi-Plein, I.

1991 'Daniel 6 und die persische Diaspora', *Judaica* 47: 12-21.

Willrich, H.

1900a 'Der historische Hintergrund des Buches Esther und die Bedeutung des Purimfestes', in *idem*, *Judaica: Forschungen zur hellenistisch-judischen Geschichte und Literatur* (Gottingen: Vandenhoeck & Ruprecht).

1900b 'Das Buch Judith eine Quelle zur Geschichte des Demetrios I von Syrien', in *idem*, *Judaica: Forschungen zur hellenistisch-judischen Geschichte und Literatur* (Gottingen: Vandenhoeck & Ruprecht): 28-35.

1904 'Der Historische Kern des III Makkabäerbuches', *Hermes* 39: 244-58.

1907 'Dositheos, Drimylos' Sohn', *Klio* 7: 293-94.

Wills, L.M.

1990 *The Jew in the Court of the Foreign King: Ancient Jewish Court Legends* (HDR, 26; Minneapolis, MN: Fortress Press).

Wiseman, D.J.

1965 'Some Historical Problems in the Book of Daniel', in Wiseman *et al.* 1965: 9-18.

Wiseman, D.J. *et al.*

1965 *Notes on Some Problems in the Book of Daniel* (London: Tyndale Press).

Wolfson, H.A.

1948 *Philo. Foundations of Religious Philosophy in Judaism, Christianity and Islam* (2 vols.; Structure and growth of philosophic systems from Plato to Spinoza, 2; Cambridge, MA: Harvard University Press).

Wright, A.G.

1966 'The Literary Genre Midrash', *CBQ* 28: 133.

Wright, J.S.

1970 'The Historicity of the Book of Esther', in J. Barton Payne (ed.), *New Perspectives on the Old Testament* (Waco, TX: Word Books): 40-41.

Yahuda, A.S.

1946 'The Meaning of the Name Esther', *JRAS* : 174-78.

Yamauchi, E.M.

1990 *Persia and the Bible* (Grand Rapids, MI: Eerdmans)

1992 'Mordecai, the Persepolis Tablets, and the Susa Excavations', *VT* 42: 272-75.

Yelisarowa, M.M.

1966 'Problema kalendarija terapevtov', *Palestinskij Sbornik* 15.78: 107-16.

1972 *Obshtchina terapevtov* (Moscow: Nauka).

Zadok, R.

1979 *The Jews in Babylonia during the Chaldean and Achaemenian Periods according to the Babylonian Sources* (Haifa: University of Haifa).

1986 'Notes on Esther', *ZAW* 98: 105-10.

Zeitlin, S.

1939–40 'The Book of Jubilees, its Character and its significance', *JQR* 30: 8-16.

1945–46 'Criteria for the Dating of Jubilees', *JQR* 36: 187-89.

1957–58 'The Book of Jubilees and the Pentateuch', *JQR* 48: 218-32.

1959 'The Beginning of the Day in the Calendar of Jubilees', *JBL* 78: 153-56.

1975 'Dreams and their Interpretation from the Biblical Period to the Tannaitic Time: A Historical Study', *JQR* 66: 1-18.

Zenger, E.

1974 'Der Judithroman als Traditionsmodell des Jahweglaubens', *TZ* 83: 65-80.

1981 *Das Buch Judith* (JSHRZ, 1.6; Gütersloh: Gerd Mohn).

Zeron, A.

1980 'Erwägungen zu Pseudo-Philos Quellen und Zeit', *JSJ* 11.1: 38-52.

Zevit, Z.

1968 'The Structure and Individual Elements of Daniel 7', *ZAW* 80: 385-96.

Zimmerli, W.

1979 *Ezechiel* (2 vols.; Biblischer Kommentar: Altes Testament, XIII/1-2; Neukirchen–Vluyn: Neukirchener Verlag).

Zimmermann, F.

1938 'Aids for the Recovery of the Hebrew Original of Judith', *JBL* 57: 67-74.

1939 'Textual Observations on the Apocalypse of Baruch', *JTS* 40: 151-56.

1958 'Bel and the Dragon', *VT* 8: 438-40.

1960–61 'Underlying Documents of IV Ezra', *JQR* 51: 107-34.

1962 'Translation and Mistranslation in the Apocalypse of Baruch', in M. Ben-Horin *et al.* (eds.), *Studies and Essays in Honour of Abraham A. Neuman* (Leiden: Brill): 580-87.

1985 'The Language, the Date, and the Portrayal of the Messiah in IV Ezra', *HS* 26: 203-18.

INDEXES

INDEX OF REFERENCES

OLD TESTAMENT

QUMRAN

JOSEPHUS

CHRISTIAN AUTHORS

CLASSICAL

INDEX OF AUTHORS

JOURNAL FOR THE STUDY OF THE PSEUDEPIGRAPHA
SUPPLEMENT SERIES

1 J.R. Levison, *Portraits of Adam in Early Judaism: From Sirach to 2 Baruch*

2 P. Bilde, *Flavius Josephus between Jerusalem and Rome: His Life, his Works, and their Importance*

3 P.R. Callaway, *The History of the Qumran Community: An Investigation*

4 T.W. Willet, *Eschatology in the Theodicies of 2 Baruch and 4 Ezra*

5 J.R. Mueller, *The Five Fragments of the Apocryphon of Ezekiel: A Critical Study*

6 R.G. Hall, *Revealed Histories: Techniques for Ancient Jewish and Christian Historiography*

7 G.J. Brooke (ed.), *Temple Scroll Studies: Papers Presented at the International Symposium on the Temple Scroll (Manchester, 1987)*

8 L.H. Schiffman (ed.), *Archaeology and History in the Dead Sea Scrolls: The New York University Conference in Memory of Yigael Yadin*

9 J.J. Collins & J.H. Charlesworth (eds.), *Mysteries and Revelations: Apocalyptic Studies since the Uppsala Colloquium*

10 S. Talmon (ed.), *Jewish Civilization in the Hellenistic-Roman Period*

11 M.J. Davidson, *Angels at Qumran: A Comparative Study of 1 Enoch 1–36, 72–108 and Sectarian Writings from Qumran*

12 D. Bryan, *Cosmos, Chaos and the Kosher Mentality*

13 G.M. Zerbe, *Non-Retaliation in Early Jewish and New Testament Texts: Ethical Themes in Social Contexts*

14 J.H. Charlesworth & C.A. Evans (eds.), *The Pseudepigrapha and Early Biblical Interpretation*

15 M. Wise, *Thunder in Gemini, and Other Essays on the History, Language and Literature of Second Temple Palestine*

16 R.D. Chesnutt, *From Death to Life: Conversion in Joseph and Aseneth*

17 E.M. Humphrey, *The Ladies and the Cities: Transformation and Apocalyptic Identity in Joseph and Aseneth, 4 Ezra, the Apocalypse and The Shepherd of Hermas*

18 J. Knight, *Disciples of the Beloved One: The Christology, Social Setting and Theological Context of the Ascension of Isaiah*

